No Strangers Here

No Strangers Here

Christian Hospitality and Refugee Ministry
in Twenty-First-Century Hong Kong

JUDY CHAN

Foreword by Philip L. Wickeri

☙PICKWICK *Publications* · Eugene, Oregon

NO STRANGERS HERE
Christian Hospitality and Refugee Ministry in Twenty-First-Century Hong Kong

Copyright © 2017 Judy Chan. All rights reserved. Except for brief quotations in critical publications or reviews, no part of this book may be reproduced in any manner without prior written permission from the publisher. Write: Permissions, Wipf and Stock Publishers, 199 W. 8th Ave., Suite 3, Eugene, OR 97401.

Pickwick Publications
An Imprint of Wipf and Stock Publishers
199 W. 8th Ave., Suite 3
Eugene, OR 97401

www.wipfandstock.com

PAPERBACK ISBN: 978-1-5326-0415-7
HARDCOVER ISBN: 978-1-5326-0417-1
EBOOK ISBN: 978-1-5326-0416-4

Cataloguing-in-Publication data:

Names: Chan, Judy.

Title: No strangers here : Christian hospitality and refugee ministry in twenty-first-century Hong Kong / Judy Chan.

Description: Eugene, OR: Pickwick Publications, 2017 | Includes bibliographical references and index.

Identifiers: ISBN 978-1-5326-0415-7 (paperback) | ISBN 978-1-5326-0417-1 (hardcover) | ISBN 978-1-5326-0416-4 (ebook)

Subjects: LCSH: Hospitality—Religious Aspects—Christianity | Church work with refugees | Church work with refugees—Case studies | Church work with immigrants | Refugees—China—Hong Kong | Humanitarianism—Religious aspects—Case studies.

Classification: BV4466. C36 2017 (paperback) | BV4466 (ebook)

Manufactured in the U.S.A.   10/09/17

Scripture quotations are from *New Revised Standard Version Bible*, copyright © 1989 National Council of the Churches of Christ in the United States of America. Used by permission. All rights reserved worldwide.

To Dorothy McMahon Kwok
With gratitude for our precious friendship on both sides of the world

Contents

Foreword by Philip L. Wickeri | ix
Preface | xiii
Introduction | xv

Part One—The Concept of Christian Hospitality to Strangers

Chapter 1
The Religious Tradition of Hospitality | 3

Chapter 2
The Biblical and Historical Roots of Christian Hospitality | 21

Chapter 3
Christian Hospitality in Contemporary Theology | 44

Part Two—The Practice of Christian Hospitality to Refugees and Asylum Seekers

Chapter 4
Care for Refugees and Asylum Seekers | 71

Chapter 5
Welcoming the Stranger: The Hong Kong Context | 85

Chapter 6
Refugees and Asylum Seekers: The Hong Kong Situation | 109

Chapter 7
Refugee Ministry in Twenty-First-Century Hong Kong | 138

Chapter 8
Putting It All Together | 173

Bibliography | 193
General Index | 205
Scripture Index | 217

Foreword

HOSPITALITY TO STRANGERS WAS a common practice in the ancient world, from ancient China and India, to the Greco-Roman world, to Africa, Austral-Asia, and the Americas. It was an almost universal value, and a practice which helped to build up and protect the community in pre-modern societies. Hospitality was part of the ethic and identity of a people, and welcoming the stranger was inviolable in many cultures. It provided a means to alleviate danger and welcome strangers through the embrace of the other. With the development of modernity, and the increasing ease of travel and communications, the value of hospitality was little by little overshadowed by commercial interests, nationalism, and other factors. It is only in recent years that we have become aware of what has been lost.

Religious communities have led the way in the revival of interest in the cultural practice of hospitality over the last decades. For Christians of all traditions, hospitality has become a key understanding for the understanding of mission. Christian hospitality was developed in New Testament times, but has its background in the Old Testament and the traditions of the ancient Near East. For the people of Israel, it was based above all on the memory of God's provision when they were sojourners in the wilderness. This memory was extended to the church from our earliest history. And so, the importance of Christian hospitality has been rediscovered again and again in our own history. Eucharistic hospitality and the fellowship of the table. Welcoming strangers and receiving travelers. Church hospitality extended to the poor, the marginalized, and the migrant. Working for justice for all peoples. Hospitality as a way of defining who we are as a Church, and what we stand for as followers of Jesus.

Judy Chan has written a timely and engaging book on the practice of Christian hospitality. It is actually two books in one, interconnected, the one following the other. Part One is on the concept and theology of Christian hospitality, and Part Two presents a case study of Christian hospitality for asylum seekers in Hong Kong. In a highly readable and accessible style, she surveys the work that has been done on Christian hospitality, and applies this understanding to a case study of Hong Kong. Hong Kong is her context, but her study will be of interest to readers in other places. Given the enormity of our current global refugee crisis brought on by forced migration, this study is especially important at this time. Chan's work sheds light on what hospitality means for particular churches and parishes in one place. As refugees enter our cities, the global becomes the local.

In good Reformed perspective, Chan sees Christian hospitality as both a gift and a task to churches. Churches have inherited a role in caring for the needy in Jesus' name, but at the same time they have a great deal to learn about hospitality in practice, as she shows in her study of Hong Kong churches. Churches tend to be open to *the idea* of hospitality, but welcoming the stranger can be difficult *in practice* for congregations. This is especially so in the case of refugees and asylum seekers, where there may be questions of legal status alongside the ever-present challenge of accepting differences in the other.

Hong Kong has historically been an important city for refugees and asylum seekers. Up until the first decades of the nineteenth century, Hong Kong was a collection of fishing villages and agricultural lands far from the centers of power. In 1841, following its occupation by the British, it was described as a "barren rock with hardly a house upon it." In the years since, the city has become a haven for Chinese from Guangdong and farther north, seeking their fortunes or simply trying to survive. Hong Kong welcomed Chinese refugees and asylum seekers during the Chinese Civil War, both before and after the founding of the People's Republic of China. Beginning in 1975, Hong Kong became a center for the settlement of Vietnamese "boat people." And over the last twenty years, it has become a place for asylum seekers from South Asia, Africa, and other countries. Today, Hong Kong is recognized as a modern cityscape with skyscrapers and a dense population, where the refugees and asylum seekers are often hidden from view.

Chan focuses her study on the "special place" of international and expatriate congregations in extending hospitality to asylum seekers. Although some of these groups have worked in partnership with local Chinese churches, other churches and NGOs have acted on their own initiative in helping local refugees. Members of international churches have themselves been recipients of hospitality in their life and work far away from their countries of origin. This experience has perhaps made it easier for them to identify with people from other countries who find themselves lost and alone in Hong Kong. Chan's detailed studies of three major refugee programs and her consideration of several others help us to understand the important role that international churches and other organizations play in Hong Kong. But they also serve as a challenge to churches in the majority Chinese population of Hong Kong to pay more attention to the displaced persons in our midst.

Refugees and asylum seekers present a special case for extending Christian hospitality, as Chan notes. But it is this special case that shows how seriously churches and other organizations must take their commitment to hospitality. For this reason, she argues that hospitality itself is a radical practice, when we consider its ancient origins, its historical practice, and its relevance for the most pressing social issues of our time. She rightly understands that this is not without difficulty. Public opposition, compassion fatigue, and our sometimes unrealistic hopes of easy success are among the difficulties she addresses. Therefore, hospitality for migrants and asylum seekers must involve a long-term commitment on the part of churches and organizations who undertake this important mission, and this is itself a challenge for a sometimes transient population.

Chan challenges Christians all over the world to take our faith more seriously as we practice hospitality in our own mission and ministry. She wants us to be prepared to fight for a fairer system, as we deal with the concrete issues that we face in our churches. Her challenge cannot go unheeded. It is for this reason that the book which lies before you must be read by all who are concerned with our present migration crisis and our calling as Christians. We need to better understand our Christian response to asylum seekers and refugees, and be prepared to do something about it.

Philip L. Wickeri
Hong Kong
Epiphany 2017

Preface

THIS BOOK IS ABOUT people out of place. In other words, strangers. This book is also about people who help strangers find a place. In other words, the church. The strangers in this case are refugees and asylum seekers. The church that is helping them is in Hong Kong, China. What brings those strangers and that church together is hospitality.

I came to write this book because I live in Hong Kong and attend a church that welcomes refugees and asylum seekers into its fellowship. That first-hand exposure convinced me that something bigger was happening than I could see. Something significant was going on in the mission of the Hong Kong church beyond the relatively small number of strangers and local congregations involved. What could we learn from listening to their stories? What do we discover about mission in the church of the strangers? What happens when God changes our hearts of stone to hearts of flesh for refugees and asylum seekers? These were questions that I needed to answer for myself as well as for a wider audience.

No Strangers Here is both a theological and practical resource on Christian hospitality. The division into two parts is intentional. I could not write about what the church was doing or ought to be doing without first asking what God has already done. That is why I begin with the concept of hospitality to strangers from biblical and historical perspectives in Part One. Then in Part Two I focus on Hong Kong's experience of strangers in general and refugees and asylum seekers in particular. This order is somewhat different from other works in practical theology, moving from general to specific rather than the other way around. I am convinced that the argument for Christian hospitality in any setting is clearer and stronger when we start with God rather than ourselves. Yet, the practice of hospitality is best demonstrated in a real-life case study where theory meets experience. So, each part requires the other, and together they make a whole. As a result, this book will be useful to readers who are interested in theological hospitality, refugee ministry, Hong Kong church mission, and multicultural international congregations.

I wish to acknowledge those who have been a part of bringing this book to publication. First, I thank the Divinity School of Chung Chi College of the Chinese University of Hong Kong, ATESEA Theological Union, Lo Lung-kwong, Ying Fuk-tsang, and Limuel Equina for the opportunity to complete the doctoral dissertation on which this book is based. A special word of appreciation is given to Tobias Brandner, my teacher and supervisor. Through the many revisions of these chapters, he always expressed confidence in my ability to do the job right and to do it well. Under his expert guidance and steady encouragement, I was inspired and enabled to do my very best in every academic endeavor.

I am of course indebted to all the persons seeking asylum in Hong Kong who shared their stories and to all the interviewees in churches, Christian agencies, NGOs and elsewhere who welcomed me and patiently answered my questions. Without them, the book would not exist. Rose Chue and Rune Marie Nielsen provided invaluable assistance in proofreading and giving comments to improve the text. All errors that remain are my own.

Many others gave generously of their time and friendship, and their names are listed in part here: Hope Antone, Connie Au, Jeanne Brenneis, Michael Brenneis, Bud Carroll, Chan Kim-kwong, Paul Cheung, Amelia Chua, Gemma Tulud Cruz, Tjeerd de Boer, Rita Ferrone, Lakshmi Jacota, Kung Lap-yan, Kathleen LaCamera, Peter K.H. Lee, Ralph Lee, Chris Loughlin, Hans Lutz, Ambrose Mong, Jerry Moye, Ruth Moye, Po Kam-cheong, Eric So, Philip Swoboda, Nancy Tan, Tso Man-king, Janice Wickeri, Philip Wickeri, Shelley Wong, Franklin Woo, Jean Woo, and Mary Yuen. I must also give sincere thanks to Global Ministries of the United Church of Christ and the Christian Church (Disciples of Christ), Presbyterian World Mission of the Presbyterian Church USA, and the Hong Kong Christian Council for their faithful support of my mission work in the city that I have been blessed to call home with my family for the past twenty years. And finally, it has been my happy experience and good fortune to work with the outstanding team at Pickwick Publications under the editorial direction of Robin Parry. To God be all the glory!

Introduction

No Strangers Here grew out of questions about the church's ministry to refugees and asylum seekers in twenty-first-century Hong Kong. With the city as the author's place of residence since 1994, I became friends with several persons from Africa who were seeking asylum in a metropolis that branded itself as "Asia's world city." However, from what I observed of their situation in Hong Kong, they were living lives of poverty and quiet desperation.

Here is one refugee's story. "Steve" is a human rights lawyer from East Africa. He fled his country in 2004. Some of his colleagues had already been jailed or killed. He knew it was only a matter of time before his repressive government would come after him. With the warning that his life was in immediate danger, Steve had no time to prepare or to say goodbye to his family. He boarded a nighttime flight to Hong Kong with the expectation of returning home as soon as the situation was safe. As of 2017, he is still in Hong Kong.

When Steve arrived at the Hong Kong airport, he went to the immigration authorities and requested asylum. He knew his rights for international protection through the United Nations High Commissioner for Refugees. Instead of being helped, he was put into detention by skeptical immigration officials. They questioned him around the clock for five days in what he described as the worst experience of his life. "Can you give me the number of the UNHCR?" he pleaded. "There is no UN office here," was the harsh reply. Steve knew that was a lie. He finally got the phone number through miraculous intervention when another immigration official quietly passed the information to him. The UN processed his case within days to grant refugee status. He was released. But his problems were not over.

With no right to permanently stay or to work in Hong Kong, he had to find a way to survive. The UNHCR and the Social Welfare Department provided minimal support for housing and food, but it was barely enough for such an expensive city. When it became apparent that his time in Hong Kong would be much longer, he fought for his rights in the courts. He was not given the right to settle in Hong Kong, but he became the first recognized refugee in recent years to be granted permission to take up legal employment. Since then, he has been working at a service center for refugees to advocate for the 10,000 persons seeking asylum in the city. He longs for the day when he can go home to his family and country.

Steve is a devoted Christian. I asked him what was the most important thing that refugees and asylum seekers needed from the church. His answer? "Having the feeling that you are welcome. That's better than material things." And indeed in his own life, the experience of being accepted and trusted as a stranger in a foreign land was the greatest gift that he received. In other words, the most important thing that is needed is the gift of hospitality.

This book argues that Christian hospitality is a both a gift and a challenge to the body of Christ. Churches play a special role in caring for needy strangers in Jesus' name, yet churches still have much to learn about what is Christian hospitality and how to welcome weary travelers in search of safety and a place to belong. This book explores the many dimensions of hospitality, specifically from a Christian perspective, and then applies the findings to evaluate Hong Kong's refugee ministry over the past fifteen years. The goal is to help churches everywhere to more faithfully serve people seeking asylum in their land.

So what exactly is hospitality? The dictionary defines hospitality as "the friendly and generous reception of guests, visitors, or strangers." The adjective *hospitable* is linked to the word *hospital*, which is then linked to the word *host*, meaning "a person who receives or entertains other people as guests" or "a person, place, or organization that holds an event to which others are invited."[1] These definitions and links bring out essential elements of hospitality, such as the players (guest and host) and positive action (friendly and generous reception). They also suggest possible elements such as the care for vulnerable persons (hospital, strangers) and community-wide involvement (place, organization, event).

Besides the positive aspects, however, there is a dark side as well. Modern scholars have brought attention to the fact that hospitality is always shadowed by its "linguistic twin" —*hostility*. The ongoing tension between hospitality and hostility in any host-guest encounter is often exposed when communities are confronted with the arrival of strangers. This significant dimension of the dynamics of hospitality is evident in the unfavorable treatment of foreigners, outsiders, and migrants around the globe and certainly

---

1. *Oxford English Dictionary*, s.vv. "hospitality," "hospital," "host."

in Hong Kong. The surprising relationship between hospitality and hostility helps to explain why welcoming strangers is much harder than we expect it to be.

Hospitality thus provides an appropriate framework to study not only how refugees and asylum seekers should be received, but also how the church as God's host and guest in Jesus Christ should welcome vulnerable strangers in need of protection and provision. With the aim to help churches to become more hospitable to marginalized strangers in their midst, this book is organized along the following three lines of enquiry:

1. What is the nature and meaning of Christian hospitality to needy strangers?
2. What is the distinct situation of refugees and asylum seekers that calls for hospitality?
3. What witness and service through Christian hospitality do Hong Kong churches offer to displaced persons and to the wider community?

Part One lays out the conceptual framework of Christian hospitality, beginning with an exploration of the religious tradition of hospitality in antiquity. Since hospitality is a universal phenomenon, the focus is on the two ancient cultures that were foundational to the development of Christian hospitality, namely a) the Semitic culture of the ancient Near East, which was the setting of the Old Testament, and b) the Greco-Roman culture that was the setting of the birth of Christianity and the church in the New Testament (chapter 1). From there we engage in an in-depth study of the biblical foundations of Christian hospitality. We examine the role of strangers in the Old Testament in shaping the identity and ethics of the Jewish people and their forebears, followed by the New Testament witness of hospitality's importance to strangers in the life of Jesus and the early church. A survey of a number of major developments in Western Christian hospitality concludes chapter 2. Next we explore some contemporary theologies of hospitality that address the situation of modern strangers in the context of globalization, migration, and world politics. Besides utilizing biblical and historical sources, these theologies draw upon hospitality theory in other fields, such as social sciences and philosophy, in order to detect ongoing tensions for the praxis of the church. This is followed by three recent theological approaches that have been formulated to interpret the role of the church in caring for refugees and asylum seekers (chapter 3).

Part Two covers the practice of Christian hospitality to strangers with reference to refugees and asylum seekers. We start with an overview of the global issue of forced migration along with background information on the evolution of the modern refugee protection system. Subsequently, we look at the religious roots of the institution of asylum and the Christian church's practice of sanctuary. Examples from urban refugee ministry around the world highlight common issues of concern that are relevant for our study (chapter 4). Moving to the Hong Kong context, we examine how the city welcomed strangers from the perspective of three major components of its identity—Chinese tradition, British colonialism, and local Hong Kong culture. Accordingly we look at hospitality in the Hong Kong church and its role in welcoming strangers, highlighting the special place of international (non-Chinese) congregations in partnership with local Chinese churches (chapter 5). In chapter 6, we review three major waves of refugees and asylum seekers in Hong Kong's history—Chinese refugees from 1945 to 1954, Vietnamese refugees from 1975 to 2000, and the current group of asylum seekers and refugees from South Asia and Africa, among other places. The subject of chapter 7 is a case study of the Christian response to refugees and asylum seekers from 2000 to 2014 in Hong Kong, focusing on churches, Christian NGOs, and social service agencies with Christian backgrounds. Lastly, we summarize and analyze the findings of our study and make recommendations for further action (chapter 8).

Many excellent works have been written on Christian hospitality, such as Christine Pohl's landmark *Making Room: Recovering Hospitality as a Christian Tradition* (1999), John Koenig's *New Testament Hospitality: Partnership with Strangers as Promise and Mission* (1985), and Thomas Ogletree's *Hospitality to the Stranger: Dimensions of Moral Understanding* (1985). I am indebted to those scholars who are also cited in this study. Nonetheless, this book presents a more integrated, cross-disciplinary study of hospitality that draws upon other valuable insights that have been published in the anthropological, linguistic, and social science fields. These many rich resources enhance our understanding of hospitality and its critical role in the life of the church. We learn that hospitality has both enduring sacred and secular purposes that converge most indispensably in the care for the vulnerable, such as unprotected persons in need of safety and security.

Other authors have also written about refugees and asylum seekers in Hong Kong in recent years. Regarding book-length research on the current group of protection claimants in Hong Kong, two works have been useful to this author. Gordon Mathews's *Ghetto at the Center of the World: Chungking Mansions, Hong Kong* (2011) is an anthropological study with several sections specifically addressing the situation of asylum seekers. Francesco Vecchio's *Asylum Seeking and the Global City* (2015) is an examination of asylum seeker lives and their contribution to the informal local and global economies of Hong Kong. Again, both are cited in this book. However, *No*

Strangers Here is the first comprehensive study of church ministry and mission to this particular population through the theological lens of Christian hospitality. Information pertaining to the Hong Kong situation was collected from interviews, author visits and observation, journal articles, media reports, archival materials from print and online sources, and the websites of refugee agencies and churches. All participants in the interviews were informed of the nature and purpose of the study and gave their permission to be quoted in this book. For the purpose of protecting their identities, the real names of asylum seekers and refugees have not been used, except where indicated.

Throughout my research, I repeatedly came across the phrase "radical hospitality." The writers appear to be arguing for hospitality that goes far beyond the bland or narrow expressions that pass for welcome these days. I argue that hospitality itself at its core is already radical when we grasp its ancient origins, its historical practice, and its applicability to some of the most pressing social issues of our time. If anything, what we should aim for is *genuine* hospitality which theologian and educator Lester Ruiz says offers "both the Stranger and the giver of hospitality the opportunity to live well together in the context of their shared differences."[2] That is the dream of refugees and asylum seekers around the world. It is my hope that this book may contribute in some small way to helping that dream come true for strangers in the city through the witness and welcome of a faithful Christian community in Hong Kong and throughout the whole wide earth.

2. Ruiz, "Race, Power, and Migration," 218.

PART ONE

The Concept of Christian Hospitality to Strangers

Chapter 1

The Religious Tradition of Hospitality

SACRED ELEMENTS HAVE SHAPED hospitality since its ancient beginnings. Two prime examples are the major cultures in antiquity that influenced the development of Christian hospitality. The first is the Semitic culture of the ancient Near East as illustrated by the model of Abrahamic hospitality. Our focal text of Genesis 18:1–16 is one of the most accessible stories which scholars have drawn upon to reconstruct some beliefs and practices of the region. The second culture under study is the Greco-Roman hospitality drawn from the writings of the poet Homer and practices in the civic sphere during the time of the Roman Empire. Given the immense scope and diversity of these two cultures, we do not attempt to give a comprehensive description of ancient Near Eastern or Greco-Roman hospitality. Rather, the purpose is to sketch in broad strokes some of the religious elements of these two traditions that helped shape hospitality in the East and West, and ultimately in Christianity. The phenomenon of "divine visitation" features prominently in all three. After our historical exploration, we present valuable research on the roles of hosts and guests from the fields of anthropology and linguistics. This cross-disciplinary expedition will shed more light on the nature and purposes of ancient hospitality along with demonstrating its integral relationship to the sacred in antiquity.

HOSPITALITY IN THE ANCIENT NEAR EAST

The term "ancient Near East" is not a precise geographic region, but can be used to describe the area demarcated by the Black Sea, the Caucasus, and the Caspian Sea in the north, the Indian Ocean in the southeast, and the Red Sea and Sinai Peninsula in the south. Historically, beginning around 3000 BCE, this area included ancient Mesopotamia, Asia Minor, Syria-Palestine, and Egypt and corresponds roughly to what is called the Middle East in modern times.[1]

The traditional society of the ancient Near East has been described as agonistic. This means that defensive or aggressive social interaction was used in order to counter natural elements beyond human control or hostile groups outside one's own community. In such a context, the custom of hospitality provided a means of taking care of travelers in the harsh desert and nomadic settings while providing protection and honor for the household of the host in receiving guests from afar. Water, food, and shelter were essential provisions for those who were out of place, that is, away from their home base and without benefit of kith and kin.

Undoubtedly, traveling was dangerous in antiquity. The hostile environment was due not only to topography and climate but also to the need for travelers to move across ambiguous territory on friendly terms. Hospitality was a functional institution that allowed travelers safe passage from one location to the next, from daytime to nighttime, from exterior to interior spaces in a non-homogenous society.[2] Strangers could expect the right to be hosted for up to three days. Afterwards, protection might be provided for a limited time, which for some tribes was "until the salt he has eaten has left his stomach."

However, hospitality was not offered to every traveler or stranger. Certain groups like armies and traders, who were intentional wanderers with no fixed home base, were regarded with suspicion. Armies were considered a destructive threat while traders moved goods from one place to another. These transient groups who traveled in large numbers for protection were excluded from traditional hospitality. Instead, it was given usually to those with whom there was some extended kinship or tribal connection and from whom hospitality might be needed in the future.[3]

Besides providing safe passage for travelers, hospitality offered another significant benefit—hearing from strangers who could share information

---

1. Soden, *The Ancient Orient*, 1–3.
2. Liverani, *Myth and Politics*, 179–82.
3. Hobbs, "Hospitality in the First Testament," 7, 17–18.

about the different world from which they came. This broadening of horizons through welcoming strangers would have even greater consequences if it were discovered that the visitor came from another realm altogether, that is, from the heavenly places. Such is the case in the story of Abraham and the three visitors by the oaks of Mamre.

The ancient biblical figure of Abraham as a model of hospitality is shared by the three monotheistic religions of Judaism, Christianity, and Islam.[4] Abraham's own background as a nomadic foreigner is remembered in his obedience to the call of God to leave behind his country and his people to go to an unknown land (Gen 12). As a stranger living in a foreign land thereafter, he is depicted as both the recipient and giver of hospitality. Moreover, the story of divine visitation to Abraham and his wife Sarah, found in Genesis 18:1–16, illustrates customs of hospitality in the ancient Near East and reveals its religious significance in Hebrew tradition.

> The Lord appeared to Abraham by the oaks of Mamre, as he sat at the entrance of his tent in the heat of the day. He looked up and saw three men standing near him. When he saw them, he ran from the tent entrance to meet them, and bowed down to the ground. He said, 'My lord, if I find favor with you, do not pass by your servant. Let a little water be brought, and wash your feet, and rest yourselves under the tree. Let me bring a little bread, that you may refresh yourselves, and after that you may pass on—since you have come to your servant.' So they said, 'Do as you have said.' And Abraham hastened into the tent to Sarah, and said, 'Make ready quickly three measures of choice flour, knead it, and make cakes.' Abraham ran to the herd, and took a calf, tender and good, and gave it to the servant, who hastened to prepare it. Then he took curds and milk and the calf that he had prepared, and set it before them; and he stood by them under the tree while they ate. They said to him, 'Where is your wife Sarah?' And he said, 'There, in the tent.' Then one said, 'I will surely return to you in due season, and your wife Sarah shall have a son.' And Sarah was listening at the tent entrance behind him. (Gen 18:1–10)

In this passage, one vividly sees elements of ancient Near Eastern hospitality, which had been transformed by necessity into a highly esteemed virtue. Abraham shows eagerness to host by his running to meet the guests at the entrance to his tent. He uses formal language to invite the visitors to

---

4. The story of Abraham in Islam is not included in this chapter on hospitality in antiquity. The Qur'anic version will be discussed in chapter 3 under the topic of interfaith hospitality.

be his guests and he bows as a gesture of respect. Not only does he provide them with a place to rest, but he also gives them bread to eat and water for drinking and washing their feet. For the host to wash the feet of a visitor was to elevate the stranger to the status of guest. The guest was then under the complete care and protection of the host.[5] Following these customary courtesies, Abraham assures them that he will not detain them further although they are welcome to remain as his guests. Upon learning that they will stay longer, he rushes to prepare a feast for them with the speedy assistance of his wife and servants. Next he brings out generous portions of the finest food and serves them personally, standing as a sign of honor while they eat.

Matthews constructs a model of protocol in ancient Near Eastern hospitality based on the story of Abraham and other Old Testament narratives, with the following features:

a. Hospitality offered by individuals or a community is based on a "zone of obligation," or geographical boundaries within which a host is responsible for hospitality to strangers.

b. The initial invitation to hospitality is offered for a specified period of time by the male head of household or a male representative of the town, and this can be extended if mutually agreed upon by both host and guest.

c. The stranger may decline the offer of hospitality, but to do so may be considered an offense to the host's honor and lead to hostility or conflict.

d. After hospitality is accepted, hosts and guests must follow customary rules of behavior.

- The guest cannot make any requests.
- The host must give the finest provisions available.
- The guest will reciprocate with a counter-gift of lavish praise of the host, giving of good news, or making predictions of good fortune.
- The host cannot ask any personal questions until the guest volunteers the information.
- Protection and provision are accorded to guests until they depart the host's zone of obligation.[6]

---

5. Matthews and Benjamin, *Social World of Ancient Israel*, 85.
6. Matthews, "Hospitality and Hostility in Judges 4," 13–15.

In the case of Abraham, the visitors are outside the entrance of his tent, which is within his zone of obligation. An invitation to hospitality is offered, accepted, and extended to include a meal. Reciprocity for this lavish welcome comes in the form of good news that Sarah would bear a son the following year. Both Abraham and Sarah are elderly so the news is received with surprise. The story indicates that it is the Lord God—in the guise of three mysterious guests—who brings this blessing and fulfillment of the promise that Abraham would be the father of a great nation (Gen 12:1–3; 15:1–6; 17:15–21). In the verses that follow, Sarah laughs at the idea of pregnancy in her advanced age, but the guests' final words are confirmation of the divine blessing: "Is anything too wonderful for the Lord?" Following the visit, Abraham accompanies the men to set them on their way to their next destination. The good news comes to pass as Sarah becomes pregnant and bears a male child in due season (Gen 21:1–7).

The story of Abraham and the three visitors depicts divine presence through the arrival of unknown guests. The narratives of Abraham in Hebron can be understood as folktales from among the oldest traditions of the patriarchal sagas. Letellier explains the folklore elements.

> The unexpected and unannounced arrival of divine visitors in the midst of everyday human activities had a widespread currency in the ancient world. Bound up with visitation is the concern of generosity and hospitality. The secret advent of a deity tests the responses of the recipients and explores the extent of their goodness.[7]

The sacred nature of the visit is confirmed through generous welcome and the provision of food, which Letellier calls "the sacramental exchange." He notes that the motif of divine visitation has been combined with another common motif of a miraculous annunciation to a childless couple. A "numinous reciprocity" has been set in motion as the guests return a favor to their host by conveying the message of the impending birth of Isaac.[8] An act of hospitality becomes the means by which Abraham and Sarah are reassured that the earlier promise of a son will be fulfilled. It is a message of life and posterity. Here, the good news of a firstborn son is a gift from the guests and not a reward for Abraham's generous actions. Hospitality would normally have been expected and offered in the time of Genesis 18:1–16.[9]

The tradition of Abrahamic hospitality affirms the high social value of hospitality in antiquity, its practice as a religious duty, and unexpected

---

7. Letellier, *Day in Mamre, Night in Sodom*, 210.
8. Koenig, "Hospitality," *Anchor Bible Dictionary*, 299.
9. Westermann, *Genesis 12–36*, 276.

divine presence and blessing in its observance. These established protocols and sacred aspects meant that non-observance or violation of hospitality would be a serious offense in the ancient Near East, where according to Walton, "All experience was religious experience, all law was spiritual in nature, all duties were duties to the gods, all events had deity as their cause."[10] Indeed, heaven and earth were two different realms but events in both might be interconnected or parallel. We will explore this interconnection further in the next chapter when looking at the Abrahamic tradition's direct influence on Jewish and Christian hospitality.

CLASSICAL GRECO-ROMAN HOSPITALITY

The geographical boundaries of the region known as the Mediterranean world could be described as all the countries and lands that touch the shores of the Mediterranean Sea. It overlaps the area known as the ancient Near East and was home to other ancient cultures, notably Greek and Roman. Greco-Roman political and social culture influenced the entire region for over a thousand years. The period of classical antiquity dates from the writings of Homer (eighth to seventh century BCE) to the decline of the Roman Empire (fifth century CE).[11]

One of the best sources of knowledge about ancient Greek hospitality are the writings of Homer in his epic poems the *Iliad* and the *Odyssey*. Homer's works are believed to reflect the actual social practices of ancient Greece and were major influences in the education system and culture of the Greco-Roman period. The *Iliad* tells the story of the Trojan War when the city of Troy was under a ten-year siege by Greek states. The *Odyssey* is a sequel recounting the story of the warrior Odysseus in his ten-year journey to return home after the war. The theme of hospitality is prominent due to the storyline.

In his comprehensive study of hospitality scenes in Homer's writings, Reece examines each action from the approach of the visitor to the house to the time of his or her taking leave. These actions include "arrival, reception, seating, feasting, identification, bedding down, bathing, gift giving, and departure" depicted with highly conventional language in a recognizable pattern.[12] Suspense is created as the hero waits at the threshold to see whether hospitality will be offered. Lavish arrangements are made for the guest's total comfort and enjoyment. Only after the stranger has been given hospitality

---

10. Walton, *Ancient Near Eastern Thought*, 87.
11. Griffin, "Introduction," 1.
12. Reece, *The Stranger's Welcome*, 5.

with food and drink does the host ask questions of identity, destination, and purpose. The host is obliged to give hospitality no matter who the person is, and the guest may safely reveal his or her identity and intention only within the context of a hospitality relationship. The guest is then expected to provide entertainment in the form of news from the outside world. If the host learns that there are previous ties to the guest through one's father or son, the stranger is no longer a *xenos*[13] or foreigner, but instead called a *philos* or dear friend. A promise of future hospitality is guaranteed as host and guest are now bound by family ties. The guest is now obliged to return hospitality should the opportunity arise for the roles to be reversed. Upon the establishment of the new guest-friendship, the guest is sent off with precious gifts and provision for the rest of the journey.[14]

As with hospitality in the ancient Near East, Greek hospitality involved the kind treatment of travelers and strangers by provision of welcome, food, shelter, and protection as a sacred obligation. Hospitality was a demonstration of reverence for the gods, proper piety, and high civilization. There existed a "law of hospitality" based on honor rather than enforcement by legal codes. This unwritten obligation was upheld by the gods. Zeus was the chief Greek god of hospitality and the protector of strangers and wanderers.

The presence of the divine in guests was acknowledged with a drink offering poured out in the name of Zeus each time when a visitor arrived. The belief in a god who accompanies strangers was not an indication of general kindness to outsiders in ancient Greece, but rather an indication of the need for safeguards to protect them in an inhospitable society and age.[15] Taylor observes the following about the triangle of host, guest, and divine visitor.

> The religious obligation is especially binding when the stranger comes in the intensified form of a suppliant (*hiketês*, literally 'arriver') seeking sanctuary, or a beggar seeking sustenance. Every visitor has a claim on those to whom he comes, but the heightened vulnerability of a suppliant or beggar puts him particularly in need of divine protection, and makes any breach of appropriate treatment correspondingly culpable.[16]

---

13. The Greek word *xenos* can carry various meanings such as foreigner, stranger, enemy, or guest-friend, depending on the context and period.
14. Jipp, *Divine Visitations*, 62–72.
15. Hocart, *The Life-Giving Myth*, 78–80.
16. Taylor, *Classics and the Bible*, 2–3.

Through the intervention of the gods, the primitive fear and distrust of uninvited strangers was transformed into a moral obligation of hospitality, especially expected of a king.

In Homeric literature, there are numerous occasions when gods take on the appearance of someone known or of a stranger. Stories of a god in disguise seeking human reception are found throughout Greco-Roman literature. While these may be literary accounts, they do in fact reflect actual religious belief—the conviction that there was a "permeable membrane" separating the divine and human worlds in which travel could take place in both directions.[17]

The Greek term "theoxeny" (*theoxenia*) describes this phenomenon of divine visitation. Louden says, "Theoxeny is a specific subset of hospitality myth in which, unknown to the host, his guest (*xenos*) is a god (*theos*) in disguise."[18] He further distinguishes two sub-types of theoxeny—positive or negative—depending on the response of the community. When the community responds properly, the outcome is divine blessing. When the community fails to respond properly, the result is divine punishment. Examples of both positive and negative theoxenies are found in the *Odyssey*.

The role of hospitality in establishing both symbolic and concrete ties with foreigners in Greco-Roman society was recognized in Latin literature as well. Livy emphasized the duty of welcoming traveling strangers, both as a Roman virtue and as a tribute to hospitality's role in the founding of Rome. Cicero called hospitality "a most hallowed thing" that the gods devised for human benefit, while fellow philosopher Seneca wrote that the two most sacred things among people were hospitality and close relationships. The sanctity of the guest-friendship bond (*hospes, hospitium*) was enforced by the gods, most notably Jupiter, who was the Roman counterpart of Zeus. Thus, religious and ethical sanctions for the right of hospitality were in full force in Greco-Roman society.

Roman *hospitium* was highly valued by both Romans and foreigners. It was mutually advantageous in providing friendly relations that offered services such as safe lodging, food, protection, legal aid, medical care, and even burial arrangements if needed for the traveler or visitor in a *hospes* relationship. Hospitality relationships in Roman culture might also co-exist

---

17. Johnson, *The Acts of the Apostles*, 248, n.11.

18. Louden, *Homer's Odyssey and the Near East*, 31. He defines hospitality myth as "a mortal host entertaining or receiving a guest (usually a stranger of unknown identity) into his dwelling" (30); and he defines myth as "a sacred, traditional, narrative, that depicts the interrelations of mortals and gods, is especially concerned with defining what is moral or ethical behavior for a given culture, and passes on key information about the culture's traditions and institutions" (7).

with patronage relationships. However, the term *hospes* usually designated relations between equals while the terms *cliens/patronus* indicated inequality with the patron, who was normally superior to the client in terms of rank, wealth, and social status. Romans did not regard hospitality and patronage as mutually exclusive, but rather were flexible so that circumstances determined whether one responded as a guest-friend, a patron, or a client.[19] In terms of obligations in Roman society, however, Stock says, "The generally accepted order of claimants . . . was this: parents, wards, clients, guest-friends, kinsmen, connexions."[20] It is against this background of Greco-Roman hospitality that Christian hospitality with its Jewish roots sought both to emulate and to distinguish itself from the surrounding cultures.

ANTHROPOLOGICAL AND LINGUISTIC PERSPECTIVES ON ANCIENT HOSPITALITY

Having explored some basic features of ancient Near Eastern and Greco-Roman hospitality, we turn our attention to some notable contributions from the fields of modern anthropology and linguistics to see how they affect our understanding of both secular and sacred aspects of ancient hospitality. We begin with Marcel Mauss whose theories on gift-giving have been highly influential in anthropology on the role of exchange and reciprocity in establishing social relationships in archaic cultures. Next we engage the work of linguist Émile Benveniste and others to observe the semantic evolution of the Indo-European root words for hospitality—*hostis* and *hospes*—that reveal inherent tensions in the practice. Then we turn to the work of Julian Pitt-Rivers whose studies of hospitality and honor in Mediterranean culture shed light on the underlying dynamics of the host-guest relationship as well as the possibility of grace that seems to confound all human logic.

Reciprocity and gift exchange

The esteemed place of Mauss's work *The Gift* in the fields of anthropology and sociology is unmatched. The French anthropologist based his theories on fieldwork in Polynesia, Melanesia, and the American Northwest. His classic essay, originally published in French in 1925, explores the role of gift exchange as a foundation of archaic societies. He proposes that the ritual of gift exchange is much more than a voluntary giving and receiving between

---

19. Nicols, "Hospitality among the Romans," 433.
20. Stock, "Hospitality (Greek and Roman)," 810.

two parties. In fact, there is no such thing as a "free gift." There always exists the obligation to reciprocate whenever a gift is received. He astutely asks, "What power resides in the object given that causes its recipient to pay it back?"[21]

Mauss first seeks to uncover the mysterious nature of the gift itself. He explains it through the notion of *hau* or the spirit of a thing as revealed in Maori culture. In the Polynesian world, gifts are not simply inanimate objects or material possessions. Gifts carry a spiritual essence so even when they are given away, abandoned, or stolen, there is still something of the owner attached to them. This spirit of the object bonds the receiver with the giver. It also compels the recipient to pass on or return the gift because keeping it would be morally wrong and spiritually dangerous since these gifts possess a magical or religious power over the holder. Mauss says

> [E]verything—food, women, children, property, talismans, land, labour services, priestly functions, and ranks—is there for passing on, and for balancing accounts. Everything passes to and fro as if there were a constant exchange of a spiritual matter, including things and men, between clans and individuals, distributed between social ranks, the sexes, and the generations.[22]

This process of passing on and balancing accounts involves the three obligations of giving, receiving, and reciprocating. Mauss observed these obligations in the institution of potlatch as demonstrated in Native American culture. Potlatch consists of elaborate rounds of feasts and gift-giving among tribes in the ritual sharing of food and wealth. The American Northwest practice goes to extremes as tribal chiefs engage in fierce competition for dominance and prestige. As each seeks to outdo the other in ever larger displays of generosity, the intense rivalry could result in destruction or even death. After discovering similar but less competitive versions of potlatch in Polynesia and other parts of the world, Mauss concludes that the obligations to give, receive, and reciprocate are fundamental to the basic structures of human relations. He explains, "To refuse to give, to fail to invite, just as to refuse to accept, is tantamount to declaring war; it is to reject the bond of alliance and commonality."[23] Thus, all gifts and counter-gifts are part of an intricate system of reciprocity in which honor is engaged in order to build human solidarity. Mauss places gift exchange among those total social phenomena in which "all kinds of institutions are given expression at one

---

21. Mauss, *The Gift*, 4.
22. Ibid., 18.
23. Ibid., 17.

and the same time—religious, juridical, and moral . . . likewise, economic ones."[24]

Mauss's theory of gift exchange and reciprocity has been widely debated. Scholars generally applaud his brilliant contribution to the field of anthropology while making their own critiques, corrections, and expansions. The connection of hospitality to the notion of gift-giving is alluded to by Mauss, but not so clearly spelled out. Others such as Friese make a more direct link between the two.

> Hospitality, its offering, receiving and sharing . . . cannot be enforced, its (inaugural) gestures are given voluntarily. A return cannot be sued . . . As such, it is connected to sacrifice and what is established, is a relation between hospitality and the gift.[25]

For the purposes of this book, we comment on two aspects of Mauss's gift theory that are relevant to a cross-cultural model of ancient hospitality. One aspect is the need for reciprocity in human relations in order to build enduring social bonds. The other aspect is the claim that there is no such thing as a free gift. First, as we have seen in ancient Near Eastern and Greco-Roman cultures, hospitality was offered with the expectation of a return of the gift by the guest either in the present encounter or in future encounters. The expectation of reciprocation was a way of establishing temporary or permanent bonds for mutual benefit and protection. Ideally, the exchange of gifts, services, and honor through hospitality balanced the scales as long as both sides followed conventional rules of behavior so neither side was overburdened. In this way, one motive for hospitality could be considered enlightened self-interest. However, the potential for hospitality to degenerate into hostility was always present, whether breaking the rules as the suitors did at Odysseus's homecoming or even following the rules as seen in the Native American potlach. Thus, the reciprocity required in hospitality also carries an unavoidable tension which requires further explanation. Secondly, if there are no gifts without strings attached, as Mauss insists, then there is no truly altruistic category of hospitality. Every act of hospitality has ulterior motives, whether acknowledged or not. Every hospitable deed has its own reward, whether recognized or not. This would be the case whether the guests were mortals or gods; this would be true whether the hosts were human or divine. But, we may ask, is this in fact always the case? Are there any occasions in which gifts are freely given without obligation of return? If yes, when and how do they happen?

24. Ibid., 3.
25. Friese, "The Limits of Hospitality," 52.

In order to address the issues arising, we now turn to a linguistic analysis of the words host, hostility, and hospitality by Benveniste in his ground-breaking work *Indo-European Language and Society*. His perceptive study of the evolution of the Latin root words has been a rich source that complements previous studies and serves as a launching point for further reflection on the nature and paradox of hospitality.

A vocabulary of hospitality

The root of the English word "hospitality" can be traced back to two related Latin words—*hostis* and *hospes*. Although *hostis* is the root of negative words such as hostility and hostage, it originally carried a positive meaning of "guest." How do we explain its evolution into the negative meaning of "enemy," while *hospes* always carried hospitality's positive reference to a guest? Benveniste argues that *hostis* is actually the older of the two Latin terms and carried the meaning of guest in more primitive times. It subsequently acquired an additional negative meaning of enemy after hospitality evolved from personal relationships of trust between equals to impersonal and possibly threatening relations between sovereign states.[26]

This double meaning of *hostis* as guest or enemy continued to be relevant as the rules of hospitality developed. Outsiders in antiquity could not carry a neutral status. It must be determined whether the stranger was a friend or a foe, to be welcomed into the community or expelled as a threat. A favorable stranger would become a guest while the hostile stranger turned into an enemy. Over time, the word *hostis* came to have only the negative meaning of enemy.

In order to accommodate this linguistic development, a new term for guest in Latin was coined in the word *hospes*, a compound of the ancient *hostis* and the root of *pet* or *potis* (from which we derive the word "power"). *Hospes* carries the positive meaning of guest, host, or stranger and conveys the image of guest-master. Benveniste concludes that *hospes* (or **hosti-pet-*) "consequently meant 'he who predominantly personifies hospitality,' is hospitality itself."[27]

The fact that host, guest, and stranger all derive from common root words suggests that the emphasis is not so much on the individuals per se but rather on the bond between them. Mathews observes that the notion of stranger was vital to the identity of both host and guest in ancient

26. Benveniste, *Indo-European Language and Society*, 71.
27. Ibid.

hospitality, essentially an act that took place between two strangers.[28] The reciprocity of host and guest meant that one word could be used to describe both parties (*xenos, hospes*) like the English terms brother or cousin. The eventual shift toward using two words in English—host and guest—shows that this relationship was no longer as easily convertible as it was in ancient times.[29]

Furthermore, Browner proposes that the Greek concept of hospitality gave primary emphasis to the role of the guest and the obligation to care for strangers, while the Latin concept gave primary emphasis to the role of the host who is the master of the guest. Whether this hypothesis can be proven or not, it is apparent that the root word *xenos* has only survived in ordinary English usage in a few words, mostly negative, such as xenophobia, meaning fear of strangers, while *hospes* has lived on in positive vocabulary words such as hospital, hostel, and hospice.[30] These positive words describe historic institutions of hospitality (which we will look at in chapter 2), so the common root word is not surprising. Yet, it can be argued that studies of hospitality have for the most part focused on the host's perspective. To understand why this was a logical development, we turn to the work of Pitt-Rivers and the impact of his studies of hospitality in Mediterranean cultures.

The law of hospitality

The term "law of hospitality" is used by various scholars to formulate a more universal rule of how the phenomenon operates. Pitt-Rivers uses it in his research on ancient hospitality focusing on the Mediterranean region but suggests it has a general application to hospitality more broadly. He begins and ends his illuminating essay with reference to Homer's *Odyssey*, which he claims may be viewed as a study of the law of hospitality itself. His 1968 essay "The Law of Hospitality" is examined below.[31]

Pitt-Rivers proposes that a law of hospitality exists across cultures to address the problem of how to deal with strangers. Customs such as welcome feasts and contests of strength developed from the need to measure the stranger against the standards of the community. If a stranger passed the test or entered into a relationship with a patron, one's status changed from stranger to guest. The status of guest is in-between that of a hostile stranger and a full member of the community.

28. J. B. Mathews, "Hospitality and the New Testament Church," 73–75.
29. Stock, "Hospitality (Greek and Roman)," 808.
30. Browner, *The Duchess Who Wouldn't Sit Down*, 49–50.
31. Pitt-Rivers, *The Fate of Shechem*, 94–112.

Since antiquity, hospitality to strangers has been a sacred as well as practical duty. Pitt-Rivers hypothesizes that the association of strangers with the sacred is based on ancient fear of the divine as the unknown and the unknowable. Since strangers are in essence unknown, their presence represents a manifestation of the divine into the secular world. The mystery surrounding strangers from the "extra-ordinary" world connects them to the sacred, making the stranger a fitting medium for the appearance of a god or divine revelation. However, in order to deal with the danger that strangers as sacred visitors may pose to a community, they must either be refused recognition or transformed into guests in a process of inversion from sacred to secular, from hostile stranger (*hostis*) to welcomed guest (*hospes*).

Pitt-Rivers further draws upon the root meanings of *hostis* and *hospes* to point out the difference between reciprocal hostility and reciprocal hospitality. Reciprocal hostility is simultaneous, but reciprocal hospitality cannot take place at the same time. In order to successfully achieve reciprocal hospitality, each side must perform its proper role in exchanging honor. Both sides have to acknowledge the hierarchical structure in which the host is in the superior role and the guest is in the subordinate role. "It is always the host who ordains, the guest who complies" in an alternation of roles.[32]

Citing sociological necessity rather than any divine revelation, Pitt-Rivers argues that a natural law of hospitality exists in order for the institution to function smoothly across cultures. This law dictates that hosts must do their best to protect and honor their guests and do so without hostility, rivalry, or reluctance. Likewise, guests are compelled to show honor to the hosts by not displaying any signs of aggression, competition, or ingratitude for what is or is not offered. Thus, the distinction of roles and the proper behavior of hosts and guests ensure order and peace in the community. Any violation of this law of hospitality upsets the complementarity upon which the institution is built. In such cases of violation, the suppressed hostility returns and the parties concerned are no longer host and guest or strangers, but rather enemies.

Pitt-Rivers aptly summarizes his interpretation of the law of hospitality in terms of how it brings order and peace to situations of potential disorder and chaos.

> The law of hospitality is founded upon ambivalence. It imposes order through an appeal to the sacred, makes the unknown knowable, and replaces conflict by reciprocal honour. It does

---

32. Ibid., 107.

not eliminate the conflict altogether but places it in abeyance and prohibits its expression.³³

Tensions in hospitality

The distinct possibility of guests choosing not to follow expected protocol has always posed a threat. As mentioned above, there is tension lurking in any act of hospitality. Selwyn explains

> [T]he possibility of rebellion, betrayal, upset and sudden reversals of status are, by definition, always present . . . This only reinforces the fact that the honour of hosts is ultimately dependent on the will of guests, and that, inter alia, the status of guest is fundamentally ambivalent—a friend who brings honour and to whom honour is accorded, but who, in the end, might turn out to be, or turn into, a deadly foe.³⁴

When this infringement of the code of hospitality occurs, the parties revert to being enemies. Acts of hospitality can become occasions for acts of hostility. As the linguistic roots suggest, the tension is always present so one cannot speak about one without the other. Hospitality can turn into hostility and back again. Kearney describes the ethical dilemma that hospitality presents:

> When faced with the stranger, do we open or close the door? Do we reach for a weapon or extend an open hand? This is one of the inaugural dramas of human ethics. Hosting the stranger is not just some abstract virtue, however, but a living existential struggle—a struggle with crucial contemporary implications. The ethos of hospitality is never guaranteed; it is always shadowed by the twin of *hostility*. In this sense, hosting others—aliens and foreigners—is an on-going task, never a *fait accompli* . . . Hospitality is never a given; it is always a challenge and a choice.³⁵

Hospitality and hostility therefore are not truly polar opposites. Rather they are two sides of the same coin or twin sisters. Selwyn says, "[B]oth are alternative means of asserting a relationship with another. In this view the 'opposite' of giving hospitality is not so much making war but choosing

---

33. Ibid.
34. Selwyn, "An Anthropology of Hospitality," 34–35.
35. Kearney, "Guest or Enemy? Welcoming the Stranger."

simply to ignore the other's existence."³⁶ For Selwyn, the greatest danger lies not in the evil intentions of a potential guest. The worse thing that could happen would be for the stranger to remain a stranger, thereby losing the opportunity for transformation that hospitality can bring to relationships. We will explore the relationship between hospitality and hostility further in chapter 3 when examining the philosophical contributions of Jacques Derrida, who coined the word "hostipitality" to provoke a deeper discussion on the meaning and conditions of true hospitality.

The place of grace

Having addressed the tensions in hospitality, finally we must deal with the question of reciprocity and the concept of free gifts. Interestingly, Pitt-Rivers alludes to the possibility of free gifts in "The Law of Hospitality" when looking at the special status of beggars who are unable and are not expected to reciprocate the kindness that is shown. Here he makes a connection between the beggar and the deity in discussing the exchange. The beggar makes his request for assistance not with the promise to return the same but by invoking the name of God. Phrases such as "May God repay you" uttered by the (aspiring) guest imply that the host will be repaid one day in heaven, but not here on earth.³⁷

In a 1992 essay, Pitt-Rivers expands on the same idea by asking if the concept of grace (and the return of grace—thanks) has a role in anthropology alongside its prominent place among religions. He characterizes grace as that which "is always something extra, over and above 'what counts,' what is obligatory or predictable; it belongs on the register of the extraordinary (hence its association with the sacred)."³⁸ After acknowledging and discussing the religious foundations of grace, he suggests that the notion of gratuity which is derived from grace is also immensely important in everyday life. In fact, he poses it as a response to the problem of reciprocity. "Can one explain systems of reciprocity adequately without considering the possibility of non-reciprocity, i.e., gratuity?"³⁹

Pitt-Rivers argues that there are different ways of measuring reciprocity beyond Mauss's contractual model. An obligatory exchange of gifts or service of equivalent value between persons of equal status is not the only possibility. One may give freely to another without counting the cost,

---

36. Selwyn, "An Anthropology of Hospitality," 26.
37. Pitt-Rivers, *The Fate of Shechem*, 102–3.
38. Pitt-Rivers, "Postscript: The Place of Grace," 217.
39. Ibid., 216.

without demanding a return except perhaps a word of thanks. This is an exchange of grace. One may freely perform a favor out of the desire to bring pleasure, not to receive back a favor. This is the reciprocity of the heart. One may freely offer one's hearth and home to welcome another without calculation but with an unaccountable love. This is divine hospitality.

Hence, there is such a thing as a free gift. Its existence is demonstrated over and over outside the system of reciprocal services in manifestations of grace that Pitt-Rivers calls an unfathomable mystery which extends far beyond the boundaries of theology. He says, "If God is the source of grace, this does not mean that humans cannot generate it, and dispense it to others."[40] Indeed, twenty-first-century anthropologists Candea and Da Col point out how Pitt-Rivers's invitation to grace brings balance to the tensions of reciprocity as he accounts for the overflow in hospitality beyond its structural functions.[41] Thus the possibility of grace in any act of hospitality reminds us that its sacred elements are still present and active, that every encounter between host and guest is still an opportunity to experience extraordinary moments of divine and human blessings.

CONCLUSION

The study of Christian hospitality properly begins with an investigation of the wider contexts from which it emerged. This includes recognition of the tradition of hospitality in cultures of the ancient Near East and Mediterranean region and the high esteem in which it was held. Of special interest to our study are a) Semitic hospitality practices as demonstrated in the Abrahamic tradition and b) Mediterranean hospitality practices as illustrated in the Homeric literature of Greco-Roman culture. The kind and generous treatment of strangers was regarded as a moral as well as religious obligation that protected guests and hosts in potentially dangerous encounters. It was enforced by the gods and regulated by a standard protocol of behavior based on reciprocity. The possibility of divine visitation or theoxeny was a recurrent theme, whereby humans received guests who were gods in disguise as a test of hospitality. Thus sanctions were in place for violation of the divine right of the guest and the divine duty of the host. Political developments in the Roman Empire led to more permanent and public forms of *hospitium*, which were highly valued and mutually advantageous for hosts and guests alike.

40. Ibid., 224.
41. Candea and Da Col, "The Return to Hospitality," S5.

Anthropological and linguistic studies shed more light on the nature and purposes of ancient hospitality and its link with the sacred. Mauss's theory of gift exchange suggests that reciprocity is an essential feature of all human relations as a way to build solidarity and enduring social bonds. Hospitality, as a form of gift, also requires some gesture of reciprocity in order to function smoothly. Benveniste, in his study of the Latin root words *hostis* and *hospes*, reveals that tensions are inherent in the relationship between hosts and guests and must be resolved either positively or negatively—either as friends or as enemies. Numerous scholars have drawn upon this insight, including Pitt-Rivers who formulated a law of hospitality. He describes how the customs and rituals of welcoming strangers helped to alleviate primitive fear and potential danger by appealing to the sacred, making the unknown known, and relying on reciprocal honor. He later ponders the possibility of non-reciprocal relations as demonstrated by gratuitous acts of kindness and generosity that do not demand a return. These are acts of grace, beyond obligation or calculation, revealing a mysterious endowment that alters the standard exchange between giver and receiver.

The story of Christian hospitality likewise gives an account of the spiritual abundance that endows every exchange between hosts and guests taking place in Jesus' name. It is a story that stretches from the tents of ancient Israel in the desert to the eucharistic table in the early church to the confines of institutions of charitable care. It is a story that explains why Christians are expected to welcome the stranger and how they faced the challenges that inevitably rose up in every era. This is the story to which we turn now.

Chapter 2

The Biblical and Historical Roots of Christian Hospitality

SINCE ITS BEGINNINGS 2,000 years ago, the Christian church has recognized the obligation to provide hospitality to strangers. While emerging from hospitality traditions in ancient Near Eastern culture and Greco-Roman Mediterranean society, Christians developed their distinctive practices based on the belief that a) God in Christ is present in their host-guest encounters as a community and b) the church's mission is to share the good news that all people are welcome in the kingdom of God. We situate these distinctive practices in a framework drawn from scriptural evidence and biblical scholarship. Key narratives and teachings on hospitality are examined in the Hebrew Bible, in the practice of Jewish hospitality in the first century CE, in the life of Jesus in the Gospels, and in the early church as recorded in the New Testament. Then, we take a brief survey of the development of Christian hospitality in the following centuries in the Western church through its successes and failings as the body of Christ. This overview of the biblical origins and historical development of Christian hospitality will make clear why welcoming the stranger was central to Christian identity and faithful discipleship since the founding of the church.

HEBREW AND JEWISH HOSPITALITY

While biblical Hebrew has no exact word for hospitality as we employ it in English, the term usually associated with stranger is *gēr*, which could be more precisely translated as sojourner.[1] In the Old Testament, the Israelites used the word to describe themselves when they lived among foreigners or to speak of non-Israelites who lived among them. A distinction can be made between *gēr* and the term *nokhrî*. Both are strangers, but the former has settled in the land while the latter is just passing by. A *gēr* is in-between a native (*'ezrach*) and a foreigner (*nokhrî*).

During the Old Testament period, traditional hospitality would not have been offered to the *gēr* or the *nokhrî*. The *gēr* had legal status and protection in Israelite society as a resident alien while the *nokhrî* was regarded as a complete stranger who posed a threat. Instead, hospitality was reserved for those outside one's immediate household who had some connection to the host's moral community. Welcome, food, and shelter in one's private dwelling could be extended to a relatively unfamiliar traveler, who was more like an unknown friend to be transformed into a guest or "fictive kin" through the convention of hospitality.[2] Nevertheless, while the practice of traditional hospitality was extended primarily to traveling strangers according to ancient custom, the potent language of hospitality is evoked again and again in the Old Testament to express the deepest truths of Israel's identity and responsibility before God.

Narratives and teachings about hospitality are found throughout the Old Testament. For the Hebrew people, hospitality had deep spiritual significance in terms of their faith. The following motives are prominent:

Hospitality and blessing

Besides the major theoxeny story of Abraham and the three visitors (Gen 18:1–16), there are other stories where hospitality to strangers brings unexpected blessings, such as Abraham's servant and Rebekah at the well (Gen 24:1–49), Elijah and the widow of Zarephath (1 Kgs 17:1–24), and Elisha and the Shunammite woman (2 Kgs 4:8–37). Hospitality on other occasions provided opportunities for outsiders to demonstrate loyalty to Israel's God. One example is the story of Rahab who hid two Israelite spies from the King

---

1. *gēr* is derived from the root *gwr*. It is a common root word appearing in other Semitic languages. The word applies to someone not native to the area. As a verb it can mean to travel, to sojourn, or to stay in a foreign place. Spencer, "Sojourner," 103.

2. Hobbs, "Hospitality in the First Testament," 19–21.

of Jericho (Josh 2) and was promised future safety for herself and her family. As seen in most stories in which hospitality was offered and received, both host and guest obtained benefits which were attributed to God's blessings. Other Old Testament stories involving hospitality include Joseph and his brothers in Egypt (Gen 43:16–34), Moses and the priest of Midian (Exod 2:15–22), and Saul and Samuel (1 Sam 9:18–27).

God as host

Besides divine blessings, another motive for hospitality in Hebrew culture was the Israelites' understanding of their own history as aliens, strangers, and sojourners. As descendants of a "wandering Aramean" (Deut 26:5–11), slaves under the cruel Egyptian pharaoh, and wanderers for forty years in the wilderness after the Exodus, the Israelites forged an identity as God's aliens and sojourners even after they entered the "promised land." The Israelites regarded God as the true owner of the land. Leviticus 25:23 reads: "The land shall not be sold in perpetuity, for the land is mine; with me you are but aliens and tenants." God was their host and they were God's guests in perpetuity until the day when they would feast at the eschatological banquet table of the Lord. The prophetic vision of the fulfillment of righteousness and peace was also described as an endless feast hosted by God (Amos 9:13–15, Joel 3:18, Isa 25:6–9). Another beloved image of God as host is found in Psalm 23 in which the Lord prepares a table and anoints the guest's head with oil in the house where one will dwell with God forever (vv. 5–6).

Care for the stranger

In gratitude for God's loving care during their long sojourn, Israel too must show kindness to strangers in their midst who were homeless just as they once were. "You shall not oppress a resident alien; you know the heart of an alien, for you were aliens in the land of Egypt" (Exod 23:9). Concern for the *gēr* is mentioned over ninety times in the Hebrew Bible. The harsh memory of slavery compelled the Israelites to create a new society that was the exact opposite of what they had experienced as strangers in a foreign land. Due to their outsider status, resident aliens in agrarian societies were often left without access to land and were vulnerable to exploitation and marginalization. They were dependent on the goodwill of the community for survival and were frequently mentioned alongside the poor, widows, and orphans. These needy groups were to be given special protection (Exod 20:10, Exod 23:12, Deut 5:14–15). Their inclusion in the Israelite community as a matter of justice and love was one of the supreme signs of holiness in God's covenant people.

FIRST-CENTURY JEWISH HOSPITALITY

As the Israelites moved from nomadic life to settlement in villages and towns, the Hebrew customs of hospitality had to be adapted to new cultural settings. Some Jews also moved from Palestine into the Disapora. All these changes affected Jewish social relations in the first century CE, the period of the Christian New Testament. Yet the tradition of sacred hospitality remained significant in the life of the community.

Jewish hospitality in an urban setting

The virtue of hospitality was still held in highest esteem in Jewish hospitality even as the social surroundings changed. Abraham's status as the model of hospitality was legendary among both Palestinian and Diaspora Jews. As Koenig describes from examples in the rabbinic literature, Abraham was portrayed as the founder of inns for travelers, the inventor of grace after meals, and a host who insisted that guests praise the God of Israel in order to get their meal.[3] While Jews by the first century may have placed greater emphasis on the land of Israel and their special role living there, they always remembered their nomadic roots and God's provision as host. Hospitality remained a highly regarded practice that looked forward to the never-ending feast at the end of time which God would host for Israel and all people.

Jewish institutions of hospitality

The Jews of the Second Temple and rabbinic periods held up hospitality as a virtue even more than did their Greek and Roman neighbors. Three Jewish religious institutions were instrumental in the practice of hospitality in the first century: the Sabbath, the synagogue, and traveling pairs of wisdom teachers. The Sabbath eve was a traditional time to invite guests, especially the needy, into the home for supper while synagogues were known to welcome Jewish visitors and travelers needing accommodation. Traveling Jewish scholars were honored guests in private homes where they gave religious teaching in exchange for provision.[4] Through the extension of welcome to

---

3. Koenig, "Hospitality," *Anchor Bible Dictionary*, 300.
4. Koenig, *New Testament Hospitality*, 16–17.

travelers, to teachers of the Torah, and to those who came to listen to them, the provision of hospitality became one of the characteristic ideals of the Jewish people.[5]

Restrictions and advances in Jewish hospitality

Some potentially divisive hospitality practices were evident in Palestinian Judaism at the time of Jesus. Among them was the existence of "associates" (*haberim*), groups that sought to duplicate the strict piety of temple regulations in Jewish homes in daily life. This divided those who were members of the associations (*haburoth*) from those who would not or could not join. Being guests in each other's homes was almost impossible as the associates dared not to dine with the ritually unclean. The various social, economic, political, and religious forces in place prevented mixing among different classes and parties. According to Koenig, this led to a tendency toward exclusivism in Palestinian Judaism prior to 70 CE.[6]

Stählin likewise takes note of advances and restrictions in the Jewish hospitality of the period. Hellenistic Jews borrowed two things from the pagans: a) the custom of standing hospitality (though not likely offered to non-Jews) and b) the establishment of inns for guests. The evolution of the spiritual understanding and practice of hospitality is evident in the rabbinic writings.

> In the Rabb. writings hospitableness is often commended as a work of mercy, and extolled in lofty terms. It is more than a vision of the Shekinah . . . it is one of the most meritorious works, of which one enjoys the interest in this world and the capital in the next . . . But it is worth noting that what was once practised spontaneously and [unremunerated] now has to be commanded (cf. already Isa 58.7) and also made acceptable with a promise of a reward. The worst limitation, however, is that the legitimate recipients of [hospitality] are to be Jews rather than [strangers, foreigners].[7]

Sanders offers a different explanation for the exclusivist tendencies which Koenig and Stählin criticize in first-century Judaism. He says it is

---

5. Jewish travelers tended to avoid commercial hospitality because of lack of ritually clean (kosher) food, the immoral reputation of public inns, and the hostile reception of Jewish guests due to prejudice in the society. Mathews, "Hospitality and the New Testament Church," 310–14.

6. Koenig, *New Testament Hospitality*, 17–20.

7. Stählin, "xenos," 20.

crucial to understand the Jewish theology of election and covenant which formed their national religion and way of life. Sanders calls this theology "covenantal nomism"—"the *common* Jewish understanding of 'getting in and staying in' the people of God."[8] He explains this covenantal nomism as follows:

> Although Jews maintained various kinds of relations with Gentiles, exclusivism was part and parcel of Judaism. Breaking down all barriers would have finally meant accepting idolatry, and this was strongly resisted . . . The theology of exclusivism was not that snobbery was good, but that God set Israel apart so that they would be 'preserved from false beliefs' and worship 'the only God'. . . As Philo put it, Jews do not mix with others 'to depart from the ways of their fathers'. . . Josephus pointed out that, while Jews welcomed converts, they did not admit 'casual visitors' to the 'intimacies of our daily life'. . . All these authors urged *philanthrōpia*, love of humanity, and 'equal treatment of everyone,' including Gentiles . . . Monotheism, however, required some degree of exclusivism.[9]

Sanders notes that Christians later would face the same issue of exclusivism, with some choosing to set themselves apart from pagans while others engaged more with the society.

NEW TESTAMENT HOSPITALITY

The Greek term for hospitality in the New Testament is *philoxenia*, derived from *philia* or brotherly love and *xenos* meaning stranger or foreigner. Often translated as "love of strangers," *philoxenia* "refers literally not to a love of strangers per se but to a delight in the whole guest-host relationship, in the mysterious reversals and gains for all parties which may take place."[10] While the term *philoxenia* is not found in the Gospels, hospitality played a significant role in the ministry of Jesus with numerous stories of encounters between hosts, guests, and strangers. Hospitality also features prominently in the Acts of the Apostles.

Variations of *philoxenos* (lover of strangers) or *philoxenia* (the virtue of loving strangers) are found in the teachings of the New Testament church:

---

8. "In this term 'covenant' stands for God's grace in election ('getting in'), 'nomism' for the requirement obedience to the law (*nomos* in Greek; 'staying in')." Sanders, *Judaism*, 262.

9. Ibid., 266.

10. Koenig, *New Testament Hospitality*, 8.

- Rom 12:13: "Contribute to the needs of the saints; extend hospitality to strangers."
- 1 Tim 3:2: "Now a bishop must be above reproach, married only once, temperate, sensible, respectable, hospitable, an apt teacher, not a drunkard, not violent but gentle, not quarrelsome, and not a lover of money."
- Heb 13:2: "Do not neglect to show hospitality to strangers, for by doing that some have entertained angels without knowing it."
- 1 Pet 4:9: "Be hospitable to one another without complaining."

The association of hospitality with love is found in Judaism as well. According to rabbinic teaching, hospitality to wayfarers, the rearing of orphaned children, the ransoming of prisoners, visiting the sick, burying the dead, and comforting the grieving were "deeds of lovingkindness" to be practiced by Israel as direct ministry to the needy.[11] However, these deeds of lovingkindness were more than simply benevolent actions. They reflected a theological understanding of the obligations of a people in a covenant relationship with God. As Mathews observes about Judaism and subsequently Christianity, hospitality to the needy was practiced in imitation of the divine love poured out on the faithful and on all people in this world and the next.

> To take the part of the host, then, is to act as God acts, and for this very reason such imitation constitutes a means of making God known to others . . . This is a reflection of the prevalent rabbinic idea that Israel, by imitating God's *hesed*, heeds the call to become holy as her Lord is holy, and in so doing fulfills her primary mission of hallowing the name of God, that is, of acting in ways 'that men shall see and say that the God of Israel is the true God.'[12]

As we will see, New Testament hospitality takes that divine love all the way to the cross of Jesus. Through God's sacrificial love as both host and guest on earth, the possibility of theoxeny or divine visitation becomes an integral part of the Christian understanding of hospitality and mission. Let us explore further the role of hospitality in the Gospels and the New Testament church.

---

11. Mathews, "Hospitality and the New Testament Church," 238–39.
12. Ibid., 255.

HOSPITALITY IN THE GOSPELS

Ministry of Jesus

The stories of Jesus as told in the New Testament show him in the roles of host and guest, giving and receiving hospitality in a variety of settings. For example, he serves as host in the feeding miracles (Matt 14:13–21, Mark 6:30–44, Luke 9:10–17, John 6:1–14), in the washing of the disciples' feet (John 13:1–11), at the Last Supper (Matt 26:26–29, Mark 14:22–26, Luke 22:14–20), and at breakfast by the Sea of Tiberias (John 21:1–14). At other times, he is a guest in the homes belonging to Levi, a tax collector (Matt 9:9–13, Mark 2:13–17, Luke 5:27–32), Simon the Pharisee (Luke 7:36–50), Martha and Mary (Luke 10:38–42), Zacchaeus, another tax collector (Luke 19:1–10), at a wedding in Cana (John 2:1–11), and with two disciples in Emmaus after his resurrection (Luke 24:28–32).

Several themes emerge from these hospitality stories. One is Jesus' use of table fellowship to break down religious and social barriers. By gladly dining with tax-collectors and sinners, he demonstrates God's love for the marginalized and excluded in Jewish society. He challenges Jewish purity laws by turning the rules upside down. Bretherton says, "Jesus relates hospitality and holiness by inverting their relations: hospitality becomes the means of holiness."[13] When criticized by the Pharisees and others for the bad company he kept, Jesus responds that these outcasts who repented were in fact closer to the kingdom of God than the righteous accusers were.

A second theme is the use of shared meals to anticipate the glory of the coming kingdom of God, symbolized by an abundance of food and drink at a grand banquet. The feeding of the 5,000 is the only miracle attributed to Jesus that is told in all four Gospels, indicating its significance in the memory of the early church. The spiritual message conveyed is that when God is host, there would always be more than enough to satisfy the hunger and thirst of the crowds.

A third theme is the reversal of roles of host and guest in biblical hospitality. Jesus enters situations as a guest and ends up serving as the host. At the village home of two sisters, Martha is depicted as the dutiful host; yet, it is Mary whom Jesus praises for taking an even better role—that of guest—and sitting at his feet to learn from him. As a guest with his mother and disciples at a wedding in Cana, he miraculously provides the finest wine for the bridegroom's feast when the supply runs out. This reversal of roles is perhaps most striking in the post-resurrection account of Jesus and two

---

13. Bretherton, *Hospitality as Holiness*, 130.

disciples on the Emmaus road when their guest is transformed to being the host around the table.

A fourth theme is the establishment of a sacred bond between Jesus and his disciples, instituted in the breaking of bread and the drinking of wine. Through the ultimate act of hospitality through his death on the cross, God in Christ welcomes the world to the heavenly table of the Lord and is revealed anew whenever his followers share a meal in his honor. This recognition of Jesus as the risen Lord through a holy meal, such as with the two Emmaus disciples, can be understood as an anticipation of the Eucharist and the final banquet in the kingdom of heaven.

Teachings of Jesus

Jesus' teachings also address the subject of hospitality, echoing some of the same themes that have been mentioned above. There are numerous passages related to hospitality in the kingdom of God. These include parables on being a good neighbor (Luke 10:25–37), divine guest lists (Luke 14:15–24), divine welcome in repentance (Luke 15:11–32), divine presence in disguise (Matt 25:31–46); revelations of the in-breaking of God's feast (Luke 7:31–35, Mark 2:18–22, and parallels); instructions to the disciples on receiving hospitality (Mark 6:8–11, Luke 10:1–12); teaching on prayer for daily bread (Luke 11:2–3); teaching for hosts and guests at a banquet (Luke 14:1–14); encouragement for welcoming God's messengers (Matt 10:40–42); and Jesus' christological designation of himself as the bread of life (John 6:25–59).

Three of these passages are among those highlighted by recent scholars as crucial in the development of a Christian understanding of hospitality: Luke 10:25–37, Luke 14:1–24, and Matthew 25:31–46. In these scripture texts, the themes of fellowship with outcasts, God as host at the heavenly banquet, and reversal of roles for host and guest appear again. An element of surprise is central to all three.

a. The Good Samaritan (Luke 10:25–37)

This parable is told by Jesus in response to a lawyer seeking to test the teacher and to justify himself. The lawyer initially questions Jesus about the requirements for inheriting eternal life. After agreeing that Jewish law gave the answer in the commands to love God and to love one's neighbor as oneself (Deut 6.5, Lev 19:18), the lawyer follows up with another question: "And who is my neighbor?"

Instead of answering directly, Jesus tells a story of an unfortunate man traveling from Jerusalem to Jericho. The man, presumably Jewish, was robbed, beaten, and left half-dead. Three persons passed by the victim: a priest, a Levite, and a Samaritan. Only the Samaritan—a foreigner and despised enemy of the Jews— stopped to care for the man.

> But a Samaritan while traveling came near him; and when he saw him, he was moved with pity. He went to him and bandaged his wounds, having poured oil and wine on them. Then he put him on his own animal, brought him to an inn, and took care of him. The next day he took out two denarii, gave them to the innkeeper, and said, 'Take care of him; and when I come back, I will repay you whatever more you spend.' (Luke 10:33–35)

After telling this parable featuring a surprising Samaritan hero, Jesus asks the lawyer which of the three in the story was a neighbor to the injured man. The lawyer is forced to admit that it was "the one who showed him mercy" (v. 37), in other words, the hated Samaritan. Jesus' final instruction for the lawyer is to "Go and do likewise."

There are various ways to interpret the parable of the Good Samaritan, particularly regarding which character should be identified with Jesus. One interpretation is to see the Samaritan figure as Christ the Savior, a view which goes all the way back to ancient Christianity in the first centuries. Roukema observes that "before Christians were ready to identify themselves with the Samaritan, they first, before their conversion, had identified themselves with the wounded man helped by the Samaritan, who was represented by other Christians."[14] In other words, a christological interpretation necessarily preceded the ability to go and do likewise as an ethical principle. A different approach is to see Christ the Savior as the victim who is injured on his journey from Jerusalem (representing heaven) to Jericho (representing earth). This would be particularly noteworthy in the light of the teaching of Matthew 25.

In terms of Christian hospitality to strangers, the parable shows the Samaritan as the embodiment of divine hospitality poured out to any who are in need regardless of differences in religion, ethnicity, or culture. Byrne sums up the parable well: "In the ministry of Jesus, which the Church has to continue, God offers extravagant, life-giving hospitality to wounded and half-dead humanity. The way to eternal life is to allow oneself to become an active instrument and channel of that same boundary-breaking hospitality."[15]

14. Roukema, "The Good Samaritan," 56.
15. Byrne, *The Hospitality of God*, 102.

b. Banquet hospitality (Luke 14:1–24)

The passage is set in the home of a leading Pharisee where Jesus is invited to share a Sabbath meal. After observing guests scrambling for prestigious seats near the host, he advises them of the need for humility and for allowing the host to determine who is worthy of honor (see Prov 25:6–7). Then in Luke 14:12–14, Jesus turns to the host with instructions about hospitality pleasing to God.

> He said also to the one who had invited him, 'When you give a luncheon or a dinner, do not invite your friends or your brothers or your relatives or rich neighbors, in case they may invite you in return, and you would be repaid. But when you give a banquet, invite the poor, the crippled, the lame, and the blind. And you will be blessed, because they cannot repay you, for you will be repaid at the resurrection of the righteous.'

The suggestion to invite guests from the bottom of society who were unable to reciprocate would have been surprising. This concept ran contrary to established rules in Greco-Roman society for hosting a proper dinner or feast. Jesus rebukes both guests and hosts who seek honor for themselves through hospitality. He emphasizes the blessing that comes with welcoming those who could never repay, here represented by the poor, the crippled, the lame, and the blind. It is no coincidence that the four groups that Jesus put at the top of a holy guest list are the same as those who would sit at the great feast of the kingdom of God in the parable that follows in Luke 14:15–24. The parable is a challenge to any limitations on God's hospitality and a warning that there will be exclusion and rejection of those who fail to respond properly to the gracious divine invitation.

Bretherton remarks that the hospitality displayed in the parable undergoes a conversion from an "economy of gift exchange" to an "economy of blessing." The host in the story had no obligation or prior relationships with any of those who were final guests at the feast and expects nothing in return. The guests likewise receive no tangible benefits in terms of social, economic, or political status. Yet, something transformative happens between host and guests.

> [T]he host of this parable . . . actively pursues relationships with others, and it is pursued in such a way that the host is rendered vulnerable to rejection, while the recipients are blessed by participation in the feast. The host does not simply give a gift (the meal), nor does he identify or show solidarity with the poor and outcast in some notional or distant manner, rather, the host

parties with them. Moreover, his actions are expressive of his need for and dependence on these people: a party, by definition, requires others. Thus the fruit of this feast is a communion of giver and receiver.[16]

c. Last Judgment (Matt 25:31–46)

In the parable of the judgment of the nations, the Son of Man as king is shown at the end times separating people into two groups like a shepherd dividing sheep and goats. The righteous are those whom he praises for taking care of him in his time of greatest need. They are welcomed into the kingdom.

> Come, you that are blessed by my Father, inherit the kingdom prepared for you from the foundation of the world; for I was hungry and you gave me food, I was thirsty and you gave me something to drink, I was a stranger and you welcomed me, I was naked and you gave me clothing, I was sick and you took care of me, I was in prison and you visited me. (Matt 25: 34–36)

When those on his right hand express surprise, asking when these reported acts of mercy were performed, the king responds, "Truly I tell you, just as you did it to one of the least of these who are members of my family, you did it to me" (v. 40). Likewise, those on the left side who are sent to eternal punishment are accused of refusing to help the king in his time of greatest need. They too express surprise and claim never to have encountered him in such circumstances. The king answers, "Truly I tell you, just as you did not do it to one of the least of these, you did not do it to me" (v. 45).

According to Louden, this passage is remarkable in its depiction of a full theoxeny, simultaneously positive and negative. Christ comes as a needy guest to test the character of mortals, who are later judged according to their earlier treatment of him when he was in disguise.

> In a considerable expansion of a traditional motif, as is characteristic of Christianity, the outcomes of both types of theoxeny are extended into eternity. Those who were hospitable, a positive theoxeny, will receive not merely a miraculous reward, but eternal life. While those who failed to be hospitable, a negative theoxeny, will not only be destroyed, in an apocalypse, but will receive eternal punishment (Matt 25:46). In an additional expansion of the mythic genre, Christ declares that anyone who

---

16. Bretherton, *Hospitality as Holiness*, 133.

acted this way toward one of his followers will also be so judged (Matt 25:45). In so doing, he figures all of them in a virtual theoxeny, mortals playing the role of the disguised immortal to test a host's hospitality and morality.[17]

The identities of the sheep, goats, and "the least of these" have been subject to debate in interpreting the story. Who are the ones being judged here—Christians, non-Christians, or both? Who are the least of these—the suffering disciples of Christ or suffering humanity? There is evidence that the early church understood "the least of these" to be traveling Christian missionaries or fellow Christians in need of food, shelter, clothing, nursing, and visitation. The nations of the world, including Christians, would be judged according to their reception or rejection of these itinerant brothers and sisters in faith. This could be regarded as the classical interpretation. Later, a more universalistic interpretation prevailed whereby "the least of these" were identified as any needy person, non-Christian as well as Christian.[18]

Certainly the belief that serving the needy was the same as serving Christ himself inspired the church to give special attention to these acts of mercy. Pohl rightly identifies Matthew 25:31–46 as the most important biblical passage in the tradition of Christian hospitality that "personally and powerfully connects hospitality toward human beings with care for Jesus."[19] Furthermore, this passage was the basis of acts of charity or service to feed the hungry, give drink to the thirsty, clothe the naked, shelter the homeless, visit the sick, ransom the prisoners, and additionally to bury the dead as part of the practice of Christian hospitality.

HOSPITALITY IN THE NEW TESTAMENT CHURCH

Hospitality continued to be a mark of the New Testament church as it claimed a new identity as followers of Jesus Christ. Like the ancient Israelites, the early Christians saw themselves as God's aliens and pilgrims in the world with their true citizenship in another. In 1 Peter, Christians are addressed as exiles (*parepidēmois*) in 1:1 and aliens and exiles (*paroikous*

---

17. Louden, *Homer's Odyssey and the Near East*, 55.

18. For an extended discussion of the history of interpretation of Matthew 25:31–46, see Luz, *Matthew 21–28*, 263–96. Luz makes a strong argument that the classical interpretation of the passage is closest to Matthew's original intention, but he allows that the universalistic interpretation is valid if one takes "the crucified interpreter, Jesus" as the guiding principle.

19. Pohl, *Making Room*, 22.

and *parepidēmois*) in the world in 2:11. Elliott argues that the use of these Greek words is socially significant. The *paroikos* or resident alien was not a figurative, spiritualized identity to contrast the Christian's earthly journey with one's heavenly home. Rather, he says, being a resident alien was the real political and legal situation of the believers in Asia Minor being addressed in 1 Peter. Early Christians were called to keep their distinctive identity and practice, their loyalty to God, and not to fall back in the old life of paganism like the Gentiles.[20]

This claim of stranger status was understandable given the early church's position as a minority in the Roman Empire. Mathews explains that Christian persecution was related to the animosity that Jews experienced as they separated themselves from the Gentile world.

> Early Christianity, as a sectarian group within the larger framework of Judaism, not only was born into this environment of growing Jewish-Gentile hostility, but also inherited much of the animus existing between the two groups. As had been the case with the parent community, so too the Church's withdrawal from and condemnation of the life of the pagan world provoked a corresponding feeling of resentment and mistrust. Already in the apostolic age this feeling led, either spontaneously . . . or as a result of Jewish instigation, to incidents of violence between Gentiles and Christians. Here were sown the seeds that led to open persecution in the second Christian generation.[21]

This dislocation, alienation, and persecution that Christians experienced meant that they were still seeking a hospitable home (*oikos*) in the world. A "home for the homeless" would ultimately be found in the Christian community established as the household of God (1 Pet 2:4–5). The suffering of the faithful was a necessary trial for followers of Christ and members of God's household. Nevertheless, these new family members and living arrangements presented unexpected and often painful challenges in terms of Christian hospitality. We look at three of those challenges in the areas of almsgiving, reception of traveling missionaries and fellow believers, and communal life.

---

20. Elliott, *A Home for the Homeless*, 21–49.
21. Mathews, "Hospitality and the New Testament Church," 315.

Alms for the poor

The giving of alms represents an important dimension of Christian hospitality inherited from the Jewish tradition. It not only fulfilled an obligation to care for needy strangers but also displayed one's attitudes about wealth, sharing, and community. While the first Christians eventually abandoned Jewish practices of circumcision, Sabbath observance, and food laws, they continued the duties of prayer, fasting, and almsgiving.[22] Almsgiving is featured in the story of Peter's healing of a crippled beggar (Acts 3:1–10) and noted as indication of the righteousness of the disciple Dorcas (Acts 9:36) and the Roman centurion Cornelius (Acts 10:2).

As described in Acts, members of the early church voluntarily shared their personal wealth as a sign of Christian love. Acts 4:32 says, "Now the whole group of those who believed were of one heart and soul, and no one claimed private ownership of any possessions, but everything they owned was held in common." From time to time, wealthier Christians sold their land or houses and offered the money to the church to give to any in need. One such believer was Barnabas, a Levite from Cyprus who sold a field he owned and laid all the money at the feet of the apostles (Acts 4:36–37). Two other believers, Ananias and his wife Sapphira, also sold a piece of their property but did not lay all the money at the apostles' feet. Their sin was not the refusal to give all the money to the church, but rather their deception in pretending that they had. Peter condemned their actions not only as a lie against the apostles but even more as a lie against the Holy Spirit of God. Their guilt resulted in the shocking sudden deaths of both husband and wife (Acts 5:1–10).

Hospitality partnerships

As the Christian faith spread outside Jerusalem, hospitality went beyond the local community and was extended to Christians from other churches. Traveling missionaries and fellow believers under persecution expected welcome and protection from other Christian communities around the Roman Empire. The early church's mobility reflected the mobility of Greco-Roman society in general, with the first churches established in urban cities along major trade routes. Traveling Christians, like their Jewish counterparts, preferred private hospitality in homes of fellow believers rather than staying in public inns, which could have questionable hosts as well as questionable

---

22. Greer, *Broken Lights and Mended Lives*, 121.

guests.²³ According to Malherbe, Christian hospitality in the New Testament church was not just for practical reasons but also was a concrete expression of Christian love (see Heb 13:1–2, Rom 12:13, 1 Pet 4:9). Traveling Christians contributed to the formation of a church communication network, thereby making a valuable contribution to early church unity.

In fact, the whole book of Acts could be read as a collection of host-guest stories showing how Christians could support each other in the church's worldwide mission. Koenig highlights two persons in particular—Joseph the Levite (called Barnabas) in Acts 4:36 and Ananias, a believer in Damascus in Acts 9:10. Both men take risks to welcome Saul (later called Paul) even though he is a feared stranger and known persecutor of the church. Ananias and Barnabas are prime examples of "bridge-builders" for God's mission through their courageous hospitality.[24] Koenig maintains that this partnership with strangers is God's intention, "where members learn to know one another as coparticipants in the power of the kingdom and companion-builders of God's home on earth, where hospitality becomes the generative foundation for ethics."[25]

Arterbury also sees hospitality as the key to interpreting the story of Peter and Cornelius (Acts 9:43—11:18), albeit with twists on Jewish and Mediterranean social conventions. After being tested in a series of hospitality encounters with strangers, Peter accepts hospitality from a Roman soldier and Gentile despite the Jewish aversion to being hosted by foreigners. By establishing a reciprocal relationship with Cornelius as his social and religious equal, Peter then is able to offer the Christian God's hospitality to all those gathered in Cornelius's home. This is sealed with the gift of the Holy Spirit. By so doing, Luke makes clear that God is the main actor throughout the story and is the true God of Hospitality over and above Zeus, the Greek god of hospitality. Further, the author of Acts demonstrates time and time again how Christian hospitality can be an effective means of evangelizing non-Christians and bringing unity between Jews and Gentiles within the church in obedience to God's continuing revelation in Jesus Christ.[26]

---

23. Malherbe, *Social Aspects of Early Christianity*, 63–66. He notes that inns in the New Testament period had a bad reputation among the upper class because of poor facilities. Also, innkeepers were associated with the practice of magic, and it was commonly understood that prostitutes were available at these inns.

24. Koenig, *New Testament Hospitality*, 87.

25. Ibid., 125.

26. Arterbury, *Entertaining Angels*, 11–12, 15–191.

Table fellowship in community

Shared meals were significant opportunities for a fresh understanding of divine hospitality in the New Testament church. Many of these meals took place in the setting of family households since the early church gathered in private homes for worship and fellowship. The house churches were composed of a fairly wide cross-section of society. This stratification was due not only to the nature of extended households living together under one roof, but also to converts coming from both upper and lower ranks of society. Thus, worship and fellowship around the Lord's Supper provided a key arena for believers to welcome one another with the extravagant welcome of God in Jesus Christ as Paul taught in Romans 15:7.

However, from Paul's letter to the Corinthian church (1 Cor 11:17–34), it was apparent that controversy erupted over food and table manners in some gatherings. Instead of demonstrating unity in Christ, the Lord's Supper became an occasion to divide the church between those who had money and status in society and those who did not. Class distinctions from outside the church had seeped inside the church. Congregational meals became a source of humiliation for poorer Corinthians who arrived later, had less food to offer for the common meal, and were left hungrier than the richer members. All this was contrary to what the Lord's Supper and Christian hospitality should have meant as a demonstration of equality and reciprocity in the kingdom of God.[27] Paul urged the Corinthians not to bring judgment upon themselves. Instead, they should wait for all to come to the table, examine themselves carefully before partaking of Christ's body and blood, and then feast together as grateful guests of God.

BRIEF SURVEY OF CHRISTIAN HOSPITALITY IN CHURCH HISTORY

In the centuries following the New Testament era, Christians had to address new situations internally and externally in order to serve "the least of these." Changing church-state relations, social pressures of urban migration, and the rise of secular institutions providing public welfare all impacted the Western church's practice of hospitality. We discuss these developments below.

---

27. Koenig, *New Testament Hospitality*, 65–71.

a. Strangers still welcoming strangers

The success of the church in welcoming strangers in the second and third centuries can be attributed to its own continuing identity as strangers and aliens in a pagan world. Oden says, "It is not so far a step from understanding oneself to be a stranger in the world to identifying with other political, economic, and social strangers, nor vice versa."[28] This naturally led to solidarity with those marginalized in the society and with the uprooted and ethnically diverse peoples in the Roman Empire. The real-life experience of being an outsider was crucial to the church's ability to reach out and welcome others in the name of Christ.

b. Ecumenical unity through hospitality

In its care for the poor, stranger, and sick, the church began ministering more and more to non-Christians. Greer emphasizes how hospitality became a catalyst for ecumenical unity, yet "unity . . . opened outward rather than closed upon itself."[29] The rapid growth of the Christian faith was in part attributed to people's attraction to the community life of the early church, which perhaps was even more persuasive to converts than the church's preaching. Christians remained faithful and united in visiting the sick and dying, even to the point of sacrificing their own lives. Epidemics and other disasters helped to fuel the growth of Christianity in the first centuries. The church offered care, community, and meaning for urban dwellers in chaotic times, resulting in increased conversions.[30]

c. Undeserving strangers

One issue that the church had to confront early on was abuse of the standing invitation of hospitality to itinerant missionaries. Apparently, some visiting servants of God took unfair advantage of the hospitality of Christian communities. The early second-century treatise known as the *Didache* gave rules about discerning false prophets based on their teaching, length of stay, and request for support. This points to an ongoing dilemma in Christian hospitality: "the tension between recognizing Jesus in every stranger and the prudential consideration of discriminating between deserving and

---

28. Oden, *And You Welcomed Me*, 38.
29. Greer, *Broken Lights and Mended Lives*, 124.
30. Stark, *The Rise of Christianity*, 73–94.

undeserving strangers."[31] The problem of false prophets was the major reason for the disappearance of itinerant Christian missionaries. Bishops would become the primary agents of administering hospitality with assistance from the deacons.

d. Witness through non-discrimination

With the conversion of Emperor Constantine to Christianity in the early fourth century, the church's role in providing hospitality changed dramatically. No longer a persecuted minority, Christianity was officially recognized and lauded for its contribution to welfare provision in the Roman Empire. The church was given substantial financial resources to carry out its charitable works. This meant that Christian hospitality in essence became a civic duty as well as a public service that the church was obliged to perform for society. Churches were noted for their excellence in carrying out this task and for their care for all persons, whether Christian or not. This non-discriminatory commitment to care for the needy did not escape the notice of pagans, who used the example to goad their own people to carry out similar levels of good works.[32]

e. Institutionalization of hospitality

In order to meet the ever-growing demands of such a vast population, it was perhaps inevitable that Christian hospitality would need to be further institutionalized. By creating separate establishments to shelter, feed, and care for needy groups, the church was able to provide higher quality service for a greater number of people. During the fourth century, there was a movement from informal to formal practices of hospitality in the establishment of hostels for strangers, hospitals for the sick and poor, and monasteries where pilgrims were welcomed.[33] From generation to generation, these institutions continued to be vital centers of Christian hospitality to receive needy guests as the embodiment of Christ himself.

---

31. Bretherton, *Hospitality as Holiness*, 139.
32. Pohl, *Making Room*, 43–44.
33. Ibid.

f. Personal loss in hospitality

One unforeseen consequence of this institutionalization, however, was the loss of personal responsibility for hospitality as well as the isolation of the needy from the Christian community and the community at large. The great Greek Father John Chrysostom famously preached on the matter in Homily 45 on the Acts of the Apostles. "'Why, has not the Church means' you will say? She has: but what is that to you? That they should be fed from the common funds of the Church, can that benefit you? If another man prays, does it follow that you are not bound to pray?"[34] Chrysostom was not opposed to institutionalized charity. However, he insisted that solidarity with the poor and suffering required one's physical presence and sacrifice to gain any spiritual benefit. Hospitality is an essential Christian virtue that allows the faithful to receive Christ himself in the poor and the stranger. Chrysostom exhorted his followers to receive these honored guests with their own hands and in their own homes.

g. Hospitality as a shared duty

Despite the efforts of the church to retain the biblical foundations of Christian hospitality, it became increasingly difficult as the church grew in power, wealth, and influence and as society's needs escalated during the Middle Ages. Church and state had become mutually dependent for survival and carrying out works of mercy. Pohl sums up the state of Christian hospitality at the end of this period: "In the diversity of institutions, in the loss of the worshipping community as a significant site for hospitality, and in the differentiation of care among recipients, the socially transformative potential of hospitality was lost."[35] Nevertheless, the failure of the church's hospitality opened the door for wider involvement by other players. By the late eleventh and twelfth centuries, the carrying out of Matthew's "six merciful acts" had moved beyond the exclusive domain of the church and into the arena for contribution by the laity. The rapid increase in poverty in the eleventh century with the huge influx of thousands of refugees into the cities required more than the traditional approach of clergy and monks to address the problem of poverty. The institutionalization of social welfare was inevitable.[36]

---

34. Chrysostom, *Homily XLV*, Acts 20:32.
35. Pohl, *Making Room*, 51.
36. Risse, *Mending Bodies, Saving Souls*, 109.

h. Hospitality reformed and always reforming

Protestant reformers in the sixteenth century sought to restore the biblical and patristic understanding of hospitality. They called for a return to the basics of care for the needy poor and those in exile, such as religious refugees fleeing persecution. The duty of care for the stranger and the needy, however, belonged to the entire community. Nonetheless, Pohl astutely observes that the long-term consequences of separating hospitality from the church setting were significant losses for Christian practice. Gone was the sense of mystery and divine presence in encounters with strangers. The public and institutional settings of hospitality detached their care from Christian identity. Society was moving more and more towards secularization. As Protestant denominations increased and diversified, there were no longer any institutional settings for Christians to welcome those who were not more or less like themselves.[37] Christian hospitality continued to be carried out mostly by charities, missions, and intentional communities, but rarely by local congregations. The best solution would be a combination of home, church, institution, and government working together to welcome the stranger in an increasingly complex world.

CONCLUSION

The biblical view of hospitality shows how central the concept was in establishing both a moral framework for relationships and a theological basis for the existence of the Israelite nation and the Christian church. The model for all host-guest encounters is the experience of God as true host and of God's people as grateful recipients of divine lovingkindness. In the Gospels, Jesus welcomed strangers and outcasts into his life as a sign of the in-breaking of God's kingdom. Through his life, death, and resurrection, Jesus welcomed the world to be reconciled with God and one another. The first Christians joyfully claimed their new roles as guests and hosts of God's love in Jesus Christ. Although Christians would continue to regard themselves as God's aliens and strangers on earth, hospitality became a means of receiving the risen Christ himself in the breaking of bread and in caring for "the least of these." Partnership with strangers also made it possible for the gospel to spread to the ends of the earth through the work of the Holy Spirit. The New Testament witness proved that the risks inherent in hospitality were necessary in order to experience its blessings, and that the greater the sacrifice required, the greater the divine blessings of hospitality to be received.

---

37. Pohl, *Making Room*, 53.

Our historical exploration reveals how the Christian mandate to welcome the stranger was a continuous challenge to the church's theology and practice. The New Testament expectation of personal involvement and sacrifice in offering hospitality gave way to ecclesial and corporate models as the status of the church changed and the demands from the society increased. Hence, the space for hospitality moved from private homes and church buildings to the bishop's residence and monasteries and finally to institutions and the public arena. The divine nature of giving and receiving hospitality was not lost but rather obscured. While the massive social problems of urbanization required cooperation with secular forces, it was still vital for the church that the host could see Christ in the stranger if the stranger were to see Christ in the host.[38]

As the church sought to address this dilemma of the sacred-profane divide in hospitality, a number of issues arose. At times, it was a question of identity. How far could the church go in welcoming strangers without compromising its own distinctiveness as the body of Christ? At other times, it was a question of limits. What was the church's role in tending bodies as well as souls on a large-scale, long-term basis? And still yet at other times, it was a question of integrity. How could Christian hospitality transform social relations and structures if the church itself were perceived to be a part of the hierarchy of earthly power and prestige? The answers to these questions required the church to return again and again in humility to scripture, prayer, parish, and community to discern the way forward. There were successes and there were failures, but the religious conviction that hospitality was a key indicator of spiritual health never truly waned. Admittedly, its practice as a Christian virtue was lacking or distorted at times. Yet, hospitality was so central to the gospel message that recovery of its theological importance was not only essential but also inevitable. For as long as there were travelers, strangers, and outcasts who were not welcome (and there always were), the church knew that it must respond or be guilty of rejecting Christ himself. That Christ seemed to come so often in the form of a beggar is an inconvenient truth that tested the church's spiritual depth and maturity.

In the next chapter we move to contemporary theological models of hospitality. While these models are based on the biblical and historical foundations discussed above, they are a further response to the challenges of a modern era in which there are more strangers than ever before due to international migration, economic globalization, world politics, and

---

38. "Did we see Christ in them? Did they see Christ in us?" De Waal, *Seeking God*, 121. Quoted in Pohl, *Making Room*, 173.

multi-faith collisions.[39] Nevertheless, the church faces many of the same questions of identity, limits, and integrity as it seeks to be a faithful host and guest of God in Jesus Christ. Let us now explore current theological issues and constructs in our study of hospitality.

---

39. The term "multi-faith collision" is taken from Marty, *When Faiths Collide*.

Chapter 3

Christian Hospitality in Contemporary Theology

BEGINNING IN THE LATE twentieth century, the topic of hospitality experienced an explosion of renewed interest across disciplines, including philosophy, social science, cultural studies, political science, and religion. Critical studies in these fields recognized the versatility of hospitality as a lens to analyze dramatic changes taking place worldwide in the past thirty to forty years and to develop solidarity with marginalized groups on both macro and micro levels.

The concept of hospitality as a theological framework experienced a similar renaissance. The resurgence of writings on Christian hospitality retrieved and reinterpreted traditional sources while incorporating insights from philosophy and the humanities for fresh perspectives. Therefore, a discussion of contemporary theologies of Christian hospitality encompasses not only the teachings and praxis of the church, but also acknowledges the contributions of other disciplines in shaping a response to the stranger in the twenty-first century. We examine these developments via some of the theological tensions that have arisen and the shifts that have taken place as the church continues to wrestle with its own identity, integrity, and limits as God's host and guest. Then we conclude by examining three theologies of hospitality that particularly focus on refugees and asylum seekers.

TENSIONS IN CHRISTIAN HOSPITALITY

Spirituality vs. charity

With a legacy of church-founded humanitarian institutions to serve the poor and needy, there remains the problem of lack of personal Christian involvement in welcoming the stranger. This problem is even more pronounced in hectic modern life in which we have had to "unlearn" hospitality because time is precious and space is limited.[1] We leave the care of needy strangers to social welfare agencies and charities, though the result may be help that "fills their hands but breaks their hearts."[2] Christian hospitality should be at its heart a spiritual practice that enables the church to receive others as they themselves have been received by God through Jesus Christ. Like in ancient times, the church must be reclaimed as a sacred center and training ground for hospitality.

The writings of Nouwen have been formative in recovering hospitality for the church's spiritual life. His 1975 book *Reaching Out* made a significant contribution in his description of the spiritual movement from "hostility to hospitality." He urges the church to recall hospitality as a biblical practice and a means whereby hosts and guests can reveal their most precious gifts and give new life to each other. Nouwen emphasizes that hospitality involves both friendship and freedom for the guest. Thus, there is the need to create safe spaces where people can find spirituality relevant to their life experiences. His emphasis on "creating space" aims for a welcoming place where guests are naturally expected and included.[3] Later in his life, Nouwen was profoundly influenced by his friendship with Jean Vanier and participation in the L'Arche communities for persons with intellectual disabilities. There he experienced hospitality in the context of the day-to-day life of a Christian community.

Vanier, the founder of L'Arche, acknowledges that strangers disrupt people's lives by introducing the unexpected and different. Yet, he says it is precisely through welcoming the stranger into the home of one's heart that one meets Jesus, and lives are changed. Vanier observes that a common reaction to those who are different is fear and labeling. Those persons who are different can be marginalized and excluded en masse by society, as he tragically has seen happen with people who are intellectually disabled. He offers a divine solution.

---

1. Ben Jelloun, *French Hospitality*, 37.
2. Hallie, *Tales of Good and Evil*, 207.
3. Nouwen, *Reaching Out*, 51.

> The frontiers that separate people from each other can come down if we open our hearts to this vulnerable God. Jesus sent us the Spirit, to change our hearts of stone into hearts of flesh. He became weak and was crucified and died on the cross. The message of Jesus is transformation. He calls us to open up to others. So the big question will always be, 'Do we want to change? Do we want to open our hearts to the different?'[4]

While service to the needy is important, Vanier says that the basic calling as Christians is not to do things *for* them but to *be with* them. In this way we enter into a heart to heart relationship and become their friend and God's friend.[5] Our own incarnational presence is required in order for hosts and guests to be transformed from strangers to friends.

In the embodiment of Christian hospitality, Newman reminds us of the primacy of corporate worship as the starting point. She declares that hospitality is first and foremost our participation in the triune life of God through the liturgy and sacraments. "To say that worship itself is our participation in divine hospitality is also to say that worship is the primary ritualized place where we learn to be guests and hosts in the kingdom of God."[6] This priority of classical worship centering on the celebration of the Eucharist sets Christian hospitality apart from every other kind of hospitality in its trinitarian formulation and expression.

Wrobleski agrees that Christian hospitality takes its distinctive nature from the church's worship and partnership with God who is "ultimately host, guest, and home."[7] She names the church as the place where Christians must first learn to practice hospitality to God and to other Christians before extending it to the world. In the fullness of time, churches must become three-dimensional places of hospitality in which a) hospitality to God shows their *depth*, b) hospitality to one another indicates their *length*, and c) hospitality to strangers measures their *width*. In order to fill out all three dimensions, the church must draw upon the spiritual disciplines that make space for God, such as prayer, fellowship, celebration, rest, and confession. Without these basic practices, which are rooted in the virtues of gratitude and humility, the ministry of Christian hospitality is unsustainable.[8]

---

4. Vanier, *Encountering 'the Other,'* 61–62.
5. Vanier, *Befriending the Stranger*, 42–43.
6. Newman, *Untamed Hospitality*, 17.
7. Wrobleski, *The Limits of Hospitality*, 18. See Massignon, *L'hospitalité sacrée*, 121: "This mystery touches the very bottom of the mystery of the Trinity, where God is at once Guest [*Hôte*], Host [*Hospitalier*], and Home [*Foyer*]." Quoted in Derrida, *Acts of Religion*, 373.
8. Ibid., xv, 87–88.

Hospitality vs. holiness

The tension that Christians experience between separation versus engagement with the world was seen in the early church and in monastic life. The first Christians embraced their identity as resident aliens in this world with their true home in heaven while simultaneously expanding their earthly mission. Monks lived in seclusion from the world yet extended hospitality as a concrete way to welcome Christ through the welcome of strangers. This tension between hospitality and holiness still exists for the church in modern times. The separation is not as stark as with ascetic seclusion, but still it involves a degree of spiritual segregation to protect distinctive Christian beliefs and the Christian way of life. The struggle to be both holy and hospitable remains a challenge.

The embracing of both hospitality and holiness as faithful aims of the Christian church is affirmed by Jacobsen. He describes them as opposite virtues, quoting the thinking of philosopher Blaise Pascal. Hospitality is an essential characteristic of the church in its life as the body of Christ and its witness in the world. However, hospitality by itself is not enough to guide Christian life and practice. The opposite virtue—holiness—is needed. To be holy, Jacobsen says, is to be set apart. Holiness is total dedication to God alone and the opposition to every evil that stands in contrast to what is good and honorable. The pairing of these two virtues keeps the church from sliding into meaningless inclusivity on the one hand and self-righteousness on the other hand. "Hospitality reminds us of the wonder of God's open-armed grace; holiness reminds us that grace is not cheap."[9]

Whereas Jacobsen pairs hospitality with holiness, Bretherton stresses the need to formulate a distinctly christological model of hospitality in order to avoid triumphalism. Drawing on the writings of Oliver O'Donovan, he points to Christ's ascension and the coming of the Spirit at Pentecost as events that shape the eschatological tension inherent in Christian hospitality. In other words, the mark of hospitality witnesses to both the present and future aspects of the kingdom of God, the "already but not yet" reality of the inaugurated eschaton. Pentecost allows the church to genuinely engage with non-Christians in celebration of the presence of God through the Holy Spirit. The ascension, however, reminds us that Christ is absent on earth, so all the church's thoughts and actions must still be guided by him alone until he returns in glory at the end of time.

The church acknowledges this tension sacramentally through its seasons of feasting and fasting in the liturgical calendar. Christians live out

---

9. Jacobsen, "Hospitality and Holiness," 56.

the challenge practically by reaching out to their neighbors with a cross-shaped love in the power of the resurrection. In that way, the body of Christ proclaims its faith with the same hospitality and holiness of their Lord and Savior. The church can do no more than that, but it can do no less as well. Bretherton concludes, "As an eschatological social practice, Christian hospitality is inspired and empowered by the Holy Spirit, who enables the church to host the life of its neighbours without the church being assimilated to, colonized by, or having to withdraw from its neighbours."[10]

Center vs. margins

While Christian hospitality has its foundations in God's hospitality to the world through Jesus Christ, questions arise concerning the church's role as host to strangers and those who are different from oneself. As we saw earlier, the structure of hospitality by design is hierarchical, with the host in the superior position and the guest in the subordinate position. This arrangement raises critical issues of identity and control. Contemporary philosophers and theologians have asked whether there are ways to reconceptualize what is taking place when a stranger stands at the threshold. Their provocative writings have stimulated the church to think more deeply on the morality and ethics of hospitality, especially in light of increased international migration, expansion of multicultural societies, and the rise of xenophobia.

The dynamics of hospitality display a new dimension with philosophical reflections on the concept of the Other. This term was introduced to distinguish that which is alien to the Self but also fundamental to understanding the relational nature of human existence. Levinas asserts that Western philosophy has been held in bondage to the Self or "I" in its construction of categories in which everything is reduced to analogies to the Self (the Same). He argues that rather than starting with "being as existence," one must begin with the face-to-face encounters between the Self and the Other. It is in these encounters with radical exteriority that we eschatologically experience the inbreaking of the Infinite.[11]

Drawing on Levinas's writings, Ogletree turns to hospitality as a way of distinguishing between the Self and the Other in Christian moral understanding. The metaphor of hospitality forces a de-centering of perspective from the one who offers hospitality to the one who receives it. The primacy of the Other in moral experience is correct, but he says that Levinas may have gone too far in taking the side of the Other in moral encounters.

---

10. Bretherton, *Hospitality as Holiness*, 143. See also 142–51.
11. Levinas, *Totality and Infinity*.

Mutual respect and care are required. Nonetheless, in locating one's readiness to welcome the Other and show hospitality to the stranger as the beginning of moral experience, Levinas has offered "a profound corrective to the cultural imperialism which is embodied in the ethnocentric character of so much of our thinking."[12]

Ogletree describes the results of this profound corrective in the prologue of his book *Hospitality to the Stranger*.

> To offer hospitality to a stranger is to welcome something new, unfamiliar, and unknown into our life-world. On the one hand, hospitality requires a recognition of the stranger's vulnerability in an alien social world . . . On the other hand, hospitality designates occasions of potential discovery which can open up our narrow, provincial worlds. Strangers have stories to tell which we have never heard before, stories which can redirect our seeing and stimulate our imaginations . . . The stranger does not simply challenge or subvert our assumed world of meaning; she may enrich, even transform that world.[13]

Strangers also play a vital role in the transformation of the public life of the church. Palmer contends that Christians need to interact with strangers in order for the church to break out of its insular and self-satisfied existence. Hospitality best captures the quality of relationships that we should seek with strangers, and as a practice makes a bridge to link the private and public life. He goes as far as to say that the stranger of public life becomes the spiritual guide of our private life. It is through the stranger that we are able to see ourselves, the world, and God more clearly, remembering in truth that God is a stranger to us. This enlarged view is a divine gift and an opportunity to find wholeness amid our estranged lives through a public ministry that not only welcomes strangers into the church but is willing to go outside the church to meet them.[14]

In this welcome of the stranger, however, Christians must be alert when strangers' stories reveal the social oppression present in a society. In such cases, Ogletree claims the moral response of the host is beyond offering "merely hospitality." There must be repentance in the knowledge that the host is often a beneficiary of the oppressive system. Ogletree calls for the host-stranger dialectic to be a catalyst for liberation.

Russell likewise seeks liberation for the stranger. However, she chooses a different route. She moves away from the hermeneutic of the Other, which

12. Ogletree, *Hospitality to the Stranger*, 58.
13. Ibid., 2–3.
14. Palmer, *The Company of Strangers*, 79.

she says is dualistic, distancing, and non-existent in God's eyes. Instead, she employs a hermeneutic of hospitality which she defines as the practice of God's welcome achieved "by reaching across difference to participate in God's actions." Such deeds are used to bring justice and healing to a suffering world and to confront our fear of the ones we call "other."[15] Furthermore, she employs postcolonial feminist theory to reframe hospitality as an opportunity to celebrate "riotous difference" as God's gift to the church seen in the events at Pentecost. Calling for the church to decolonize its mind and the Christian worldview of election, she believes these changes require reaching out to strangers so that people from all faiths, cultures, races, sexual orientations, and nationalities are welcome at God's kitchen table as well as the eucharistic table. It is only through "just hospitality" that the church can be an authentic witness in a divided world in crisis.[16]

In the move from "mere hospitality" to "just hospitality," Min offers an alternative strategy for an authentic Christian witness in a divided world. He seeks a change in paradigm by proposing not a solidarity *with* strangers but rather a solidarity *of* strangers. This theological model, which Min calls a "solidarity of others," perfectly conveys his conviction that none of us is in a privileged position to enter into solidarity with "others" of our choice. That is an elitist perspective. We are all others to one another and therefore all equally responsible to one another. There are no subjects and objects—all are subjects. Min calls for a theology of *others* insofar as it is rooted in particularity, yet encompassed within a theology of *solidarity* of others insofar as it extends its concern to all humanity and creation.[17]

Lastly, the questions of identity and otherness are powerfully addressed by Volf in his book *Exclusion and Embrace,* which continues to impact Christian communities around the world, including those in Asia. He argues that theologians should not focus primarily on correct social arrangements to accommodate differences in society, but rather on what kind of social agents or selves we need to be in order to live in peace and harmony. Christian faith and community provide a response to the politics of difference by acknowledging the need for both distance and belonging in terms of identity. "Belonging without distance destroys," but "distance without belonging isolates."[18] If distance to our own culture or particular background comes from allegiance to God, then we can create space to include others unlike ourselves and to judge evil in every culture, starting

---

15. Russell, *Just Hospitality,* 19–20.
16. Ibid., 53–54. Russell, *Church in the Round,* 173.
17. Min, *The Solidarity of Others,* 82, 138.
18. Volf, *Exclusion and Embrace,* 50.

with our own. For Volf, the ultimate goal of this inclusion and judgment is reconciliation. The biblical gestures of reconciliation serve as the model whereby Christians must also open their arms and themselves to receive those they have excluded, including those they regard as bitter enemies. By following the example of Jesus Christ in the power of the Holy Spirit, the church pursues justice for both victims and perpetrators in mutual repentance and forgiveness through the mercy of God.

Boundlessness vs. boundaries

Within the Christian tradition, the boundless hospitality of God is the model for the church's practice of welcoming the stranger. Nevertheless, the need to establish boundaries or set limits in the human expression of hospitality always arises. How does a Christian community make responsible decisions regarding its finite resources of time, space, funds, and personnel without setting up undue barriers?

The philosophical writings of French phenomenologist Derrida prove to be instructive on this point. In his influential works on hospitality, he challenges the juridical nature of modern hospitality with the "im(possibility)" of unconditional welcome. The tensions that potentially keep both host and guest on edge are brought out into the open and allowed to implode in his deconstructive methodology. He disputes everything that we presume to know about hospitality, insisting that in fact we do not know what hospitality is. Calling for a new perspective, he proceeds to expose the paradoxes that ultimately make true hospitality impossible to achieve and yet impel us to never give up trying to welcome unconditionally.[19]

To formulate his critique, Derrida draws upon a wide variety of texts. The most significant reference is to Benveniste's classic etymological study on the root words *hostis* and *hospes*. Derrida says that the underlying hostility in hospitality that turns a stranger into an enemy rather than guest is due to the power exercised by the host. The whole structure of hospitality guarantees that guests are never truly welcomed because they are under the control of the host, who arbitrarily establishes all the rules by which the encounter will take place, if at all. Hospitality can potentially lead to acts of violence against the guest, and in some cases violate those under the despot's care. Thus, he coins the word "hostipitality" to describe this contradiction.[20]

---

19. Derrida, "Hostipitality," 3–18.
20. Derrida and Dufourmantelle, *Of Hospitality*, 45.

For Derrida, pure hospitality would be a hospitality of visitation rather than a hospitality of invitation. That means the host would not even know in advance who the guest is, when the guest will arrive, or what the guest will require. This unconditional hospitality recalls ancient practices in which the guest would not be required to reveal his or her name, identity, or purpose in order to receive entry and welcome. He even goes as far as to say that the guest becomes the master of the house, so that the host must give up his or her domain according to the guest's needs.

Derrida acknowledges that the demand for the host to surrender control over his or her home may lead to chaos which makes it impossible for hospitality to even be offered. After all, how can hospitality be extended unless one has possession of the home in the first place and the ability to protect and provide for guests? This "double law of hospitality" recognizes that an unconditional welcome (the Law of hospitality) requires some conditions on that welcome (the laws of hospitality) in order to function. Nonetheless, unconditional hospitality "fundamentally confounds the distinction between guest and host, since we can no longer be certain who in fact has the final say in an encounter," notes one commentator.[21] Derrida argues that unconditional hospitality is the ideal by which one should measure true hospitality in its purest form beyond debt and economy. This impossible possibility is an aporia that keeps the tension alive between the goal of perfect hospitality and the reality of our imperfect efforts to act justly toward the stranger.

While the church seeks to follow this model of unconditional hospitality, some theologians offer a critique of Derrida's strict categories by engaging in some deconstruction of their own. For example, Wrobleski maintains that the conditions of Christian hospitality need not be a negative, limiting force. In fact, the stipulating of conditions can be a positive act in that "'conditions' may entail those features of a situation that are necessary for the possibility of a certain result, apart from any decision or volition of those involved—such as when we speak of oxygen, sunlight, and water as necessary conditions for plant growth."[22]

In terms of the conditions required for hospitality, she names a) the separate identities of host and guest and b) the possession of a safe place for a host to offer to guests. These conditions mark out boundaries which make hospitality possible in the first place, though boundaries can be moved or crossed over as relationships develop. For her, unconditional hospitality is better named as the "spirit of hospitality" that stands in tension with the

---

21. Farrer, "Cosmopolitanism as Virtue."
22. Wrobleski, *The Limits of Hospitality*, 29.

limiting conditions that are required to welcome others. She makes clear that she is speaking of the positive limits *of* hospitality, not the negative limits *to* hospitality.[23]

Wrobleski lays out positive limits or boundaries in terms of three polarities—identity/indeterminacy, possession/gift, and security/risk. She says, "[E]ach extreme must maintain an influence or 'pull' on the other if hospitality is to maintain its integrity as such. The most adequate way of describing the ongoing influence of the spirit of hospitality is to say that such a spirit strives to form boundaries *nonviolently.*"[24]

That said, the daily challenges of becoming intentionally vulnerable for the sake of the gospel require equal measures of compassion and common sense on behalf of both hosts and guests. For instance, when making hard choices about capacity and limits in serving the homeless, a staff was quoted as saying, "One theory is that when a stranger comes to the door, it's Christ and you let him in. And the other theory is that if you're going to let Christ in, you don't want to have Christ sleep under the sink, and you don't want Christ to crowd out all the other Christs that are already in there."[25] So even when a Christian community must set a quota for how many guests can be safely hosted at one time, the residents will always be looking for alternatives that expand capacity and communicate the love of God. Even when a host must say no to the stranger at the door, it is still possible to say yes in some way that leaves the person better off than he or she was before.

The matter of capacity and limits also raises the issue of discerning which guests should be given priority. Screening criteria may need to be established, though again, Christian hospitality seeks to be as flexible as possible. Human judgment about who is deserving or undeserving is always subject to revision when a change of circumstances or a change of heart occurs. Granted, as we saw in chapter 2, the church throughout its history always retained the right to dismiss visitors or guests who are deemed dishonest, parasitical, or a danger to others. Still, churches have traditionally been among the first responders to people on the margins of society, many of whom already suffer from poverty, isolation, rejection, or trauma. Houses of hospitality must not add the loss of human dignity to the stranger's list of woes in these encounters.

---

23. Ibid., 29–31.
24. Ibid., 32.
25. Richard McSorley, quoted in Troester, *Voices from the Catholic Worker*, 164.

Evangelism vs. interfaith friendship

The paradigm of hospitality has been applied to the subject of interfaith relations with great enthusiasm among some religious scholars and faith leaders. They are persuaded that world faiths can achieve peaceful co-existence and mutual understanding rather than allow hostility and conflict to prevail among adherents of different religions. Within Christianity, hospitality has been extensively employed to develop alternative approaches to interfaith relations beyond the traditional missionary mandate to convert the religious other, yet still preserve the uniqueness of Christian revelation and witness at some level. Here we give an overview of some significant ways in which Christian hospitality to other faiths has been conceptualized in the various settings in which it has taken place: inside the church, in the sacred spaces and texts of other religions, in the public arena, and across the spiritual map of whole regions.

a. Hospitality and mission

Generous hospitality is a means whereby one witnesses to being a disciple of Christ. However, it may also be the means by which one can make disciples of Christ by introducing non-Christians to the gospel message through friendship and service. While this has always been the case in the history of the church, modern mission has often been conceived of as an outward or centrifugal movement taking the gospel from the church to the ends of the earth. Arias observes how evangelization could take place as an inward or centripetal movement through hospitality. Centripetal mission is an opportunity for evangelization when churches attract guests through incarnational Christian witness and open their doors to strangers in worship, fellowship, and ministry. The traditional pattern of mission from center to periphery has shifted to multi-directional and even reverse mission.[26]

However, others caution against hospitality being offered with the ultimate aim of religious conversion, especially for adherents of other faiths. Drawing on Nouwen's writings, Ross uses his metaphor of "creating space" to insist that hospitality should never be an occasion for proselytizing. From a missiological perspective, she affirms that Christian mission is a divine invitation to be in a relationship with a loving God through Jesus Christ. Yet, she says, mission is also about giving people the space for change to take place and accepting the possibility that some persons may not want to change.

---

26. Arias, "Centripetal Mission," 69–81.

> We invite people in on their own terms—this is real hospitality, the divine invitation. We do not invite people in and say, 'You can come in if you believe what I believe and behave as I do.' This would be manipulation and exploitation... Rather creating space means allowing for a spaciousness in all our encounters. This is what genuinely humble hospitality can offer and this is what mission is all about—an encounter with the other in the name of Christ.[27]

Ross adds that the most effective hosts are those who recognize their own poverty of heart and mind, especially when welcoming people on the margins of society. She observes that true hospitality as well as true engagement in mission happen as we acknowledge our own emptiness and need for God.

b. Sharing hospitality in sacred spaces

Interreligious hospitality is a means to welcome and be welcomed by others with the desire to learn from the diversity of spiritual expressions of divine presence in the universe. Reciprocity requires that one is able to receive as well as to give hospitality. Interreligious hospitality goes beyond interfaith dialogue as a means of bringing understanding among religions. Instead, it promotes hospitality in the sacred spaces of each other's faith, as in the practice advocated by Béthune, one of the pioneers in Benedictine-Buddhist monastic hospitality. He testifies how this openness to an immersion in the sacred experiences of another faith immeasurably enriched, even transformed, his own Christian faith.

> It is in the eyes of others that we come to know ourselves better ... Christians who like myself have accepted unreservedly the hospitality offered to them have been profoundly challenged. I can verify this with the example of Christian monks and nuns who have lived in the Buddhist monastery. They have been called to live their own monastic life and their own Christian faith more coherently. It seems to me that this is the most important experience given by an interreligious encounter. It is an invitation to develop more fully our own commitment in response to the witness that challenges us.[28]

---

27. Ross, "Creating Space," 174–75.
28. Béthune, "Interreligious Dialogue and Sacred Hospitality," 19.

The sharing of sacred spaces and rituals of worship with others mirrors the opening of one's home to guests in the intimacy of family life. Depending on the particular religion, there may be issues of boundaries in terms of what outsiders may participate in (such as the Eucharist in Christian churches), or what outsiders may not participate in (such as prayers or religious gestures that indicate allegiance to another religion's gods). There must be a willingness to respect differences as well as the desire to develop friendships on a mutual journey of spiritual discovery. Hospitality to adherents of other faiths carries the possibility of challenge and change to one's own religious understanding, and that is both the risk and the blessing for Christians in welcoming the other with the open arms of Jesus Christ.

c. Abrahamic faiths and hospitality

Since the terrorist attacks that occurred in the USA on September 11, 2001, there have been renewed efforts to promote interfaith understanding and peace-building, especially among the three monotheistic religions of Judaism, Christianity, and Islam. Reynolds calls attention to the shared correlation of loving God and loving neighbor present in all three faiths. He calls for retrieving the ethic of hospitality that is a vital part of the Abrahamic faiths in order that they may not be strangers to each other.[29]

The tale of Abraham as told in Genesis 18 and Qur'an 51 demonstrates the interdependent nature of hospitality when guests and hosts become vulnerable to one other. This vulnerability is even more striking in the language used in the Qur'anic version.

> Has the story reached thee, of the honoured guests of Abraham? Behold, they entered his presence and said: 'Peace!' He said, "Peace!' (and thought, 'These seem) unusual people.' Then he turned quickly to his household, brought out a fatted calf, and placed it before them . . . He said, 'Will ye not eat?' (When they did not eat), he conceived a fear of them. They said, 'Fear not,' and they gave him glad tidings of a son endowed with knowledge.[30]

Commenting on the text, Ali notes, "According to the laws of hospitality, a stranger under your roof is under your protection, but if he refuses to eat, he refuses your hospitality and keeps himself free from any ties of

---

29. Reynolds, "Toward a Wider Hospitality," 176.
30. Ali, *The Holy Qur'an,* 1424.

guest and host."³¹ Hospitality requires both sides to perform in Islam what Akpinar calls "an act of unconditional surrender to the needs of others,"³² a notion also present in Christianity. Allard builds on this notion of unconditional surrender and open invitation to suggest ways that hospitality could be the basis of political dialogue. He says

> To give or receive hospitality is to open oneself to the grace of God that comes in the visage of a stranger . . . The stranger sent by God is God's offer of grace. Our invitation to the stranger is an acceptance of grace . . . A theology of hospitality calls us to the 'unconditional surrender,' which creates an interdependent relationship between ourselves and the stranger where productive, transformative dialogue is possible.³³

A comparative study of other ancient texts of the three Abrahamic faiths may yield even more resources for interfaith hospitality. Scenes from the stories of Abraham are discussed by Michel to illustrate models of interreligious encounter.³⁴ This intertextual approach recalls Ricoeur's hermeneutic model of linguistic hospitality, derived from the creative process of translation from one language to another. When the task is carried out faithfully, a happy translation results in hospitality "where the pleasure of dwelling in the other's language is balanced by the pleasure of receiving the foreign word at home, in one's own welcoming house."³⁵ By working on the premise that communication and relationship are possible, even if imperfect, Ricoeur opens a path for host and guest to travel together via a symbolic text that conveys a desire to share what is most precious with another. The use of a translation paradigm has rich connotations pointing to the importance of symbols, signs, and language to interpret others and ourselves.

---

31. Ibid.
32. Akpinar, "Hospitality in Islam," 23.
33. Allard, "In the Shade of the Oaks of Mamre," 422.
34. Michel, "Where to Now?," 530–38. Besides the story of the three visitors in Genesis 18, he discusses the call of Abraham (Gen 12:1), the encounter with Melkizedek, king of Salem (Gen 14.8), Abraham and Lot dividing the land (Gen 13:18), Abraham and Nimrod (Jewish midrash and Islamic tradition), Hagar and Ishmail (Gen 16:7–15, Gen 21:14–21), and the death of Abraham (Gen 25:9).
35. Ricoeur, *On Translation*, 10.

d. Hospitality and a theology of religions

In the 2006 document "Religious Plurality and Christian Self-understanding," the World Council of Churches (WCC) utilizes the theme of hospitality to sketch a Christian theology of religions. The statement was not issued as the official view of WCC but rather as a background document to stimulate further discussion and debate. The starting point is faith in one Creator God who graciously extends hospitality to the world as witnessed in the Hebrew Bible narratives. In the New Testament, the ministry of Jesus demonstrates hospitality as radical openness to others that affirms human dignity for all. This is shown supremely in his incarnation, his kenotic love, and his sacrifice on the cross. Christians testify to salvation through Jesus Christ in the power of the Holy Spirit. At the same time, Christians should accept that the same Holy Spirit is present in other living faiths in which their followers also testify to spiritual enlightenment and divine guidance. The plurality of religious traditions invites Christians to affirm their "openness to the possibility that the God we know in Jesus Christ may encounter us also in the lives of our neighbours of other faiths."[36] Christian mission thus has no room for triumphalism, says the document, but instead is a ministry of reconciliation with strangers and others through hospitality for mutual transformation.

The WCC acknowledges that formulating a theological approach to religious plurality is a difficult and controversial task. Nonetheless, in its efforts to address the tension between the Christian confession of salvation through Jesus Christ alone and the concession that no one can put a limit on the saving power of God, the WCC has moved further toward its inevitable conclusion that Christianity is only one among many expressions of authentic religious faith. Hence, Christians and churches should welcome opportunities for interfaith dialogue, friendship, and joint action as far as possible in order to promote peace and justice in our communities.

This position of a broad interfaith hospitality is especially relevant to Christianity in Asia as some theologians have long advocated for recognition of the rich spiritual heritage of Asian religions. One creative approach to religious pluralism comes from the Pentecostal theologian Yong. He formulates a robust pneumatological theology of hospitality with an emphasis on the "many tongues, many practices" arising from the Pentecost event.[37] Theology infused with the Holy Spirit is lived out in "dramatic performances" whereby the church can improvise in new settings while keeping

---

36. World Council of Churches, "Religious Plurality and Christian Self-understanding," par. 34.

37. Yong, *Hospitality and the Other*, 62–64.

true to the script of the Bible in a pluralistic, postmodern world. He takes his scriptural inspiration for interfaith hospitality primarily from stories in Luke-Acts such as the parable of the Good Samaritan. Yong comments

> If the Samaritans were those of the other religion to the Jews of the first century, what implications does this parable hold regarding those in other faiths for Christians in the twenty-first century? Might people of other faiths not only be instruments through which God's revelation comes afresh to the people of God, but also perhaps be able to fulfill the requirements for inheriting eternal life (10:25) precisely through the hospitality that they show to their neighbors (which includes Christians)?[38]

With Jesus as the ultimate paradigm of both divine host and divine guest, Yong argues that the trinitarian logic of God as "Giver, Given, and Giving" allows the church to experience the superabundant hospitality of God that never runs out. This excessive, overflowing gift of the Spirit inaugurated on the day of Pentecost cancels an economy of scarcity and exchange. Christians can freely perform as hosts and guests for their religious neighbors. By employing various tongues and diverse practices in interfaith and interreligious settings, the church can fulfill its mission to bring divine reconciliation and healing in a fractured, violent world.[39]

Other Asian theologians go even further in the call for hospitality among religious traditions. Ariarajah points out a critical difference between Semitic religions and Asian religions in terms of their stance toward plurality. The nature of the belief structure of Semitic religions such as Christianity and Islam is based on revelation that is unique and of universal significance. This makes them resistant to accepting a plurality of beliefs. Asian religions, in contrast, are generally tolerant and even welcoming of plurality as a natural, healthy state of religious affairs. Ariarajah says that Christianity's missionary claim to be the only true religion alienated many Asians believers of other faiths who regarded Christians as "arrogant, ignorant, and intolerant." These early negative encounters, often in the context of colonization by Western powers, continue to be sources of distrust and animosity toward Christianity in some parts of Asia.[40]

Another characteristic of Asian spirituality that impacts hospitality is the existence of multi-religious belonging, whereby one could claim to be an adherent of two or even more religions at the same time. Models for interreligious dialogue that largely have been formulated in the West with

38. Ibid., 103.
39. Ibid., 118–28.
40. Ariarajah, "Changing Paradigms of Asian Christian Attitude," 353, 356.

a Christian starting point cannot do justice to the plural, multi-religious realities of Asian experience. Reflecting on the approach of some Asian theologians, Tang asks, "Can one be Christian and Buddhist at the same time? The starting point is accepting a 'real' experience of and relationship with both the Buddha and the Christ . . . What if multiple religious identity is a complex but authentic reality?"[41]

A plural religious identity for Asian Christians is not only possible but necessary, says Korean theologian Kim. Drawing on his own spiritual journey as a Confucianist-Christian, he insists that living religions like Taoism, Confucianism, Buddhism, and Shamanism are part of the cultural DNA of Asian people. For him, the urgent task of Asian theology is not a speculative discussion of religious pluralism, which he regards as a Western construct. Instead, there needs to be an articulation of Christian identity that helps Asian Christians show proper reverence for and ownership of all the ancient spiritual traditions of their culture.[42]

Kim takes up the task drawing on his Confucianist roots in an East Asian construction of what he calls a "relational theology of the Way (Tao)." In a theme presentation at the Seventh Congress of Asian Theologians (CATS VII) in Seoul in 2012, he said

> The Christian notion of hospitality, I may argue, endorses that a theology of the Tao (Way) is a more proper theological option [for Asia] than classical, dogmatic logos-theologies and modern, liberationist praxis-theologies . . . In contrast, the tao by definition refers to the unity of knowing and acting and transcends the dualism of logos and praxis . . . God in Jesus Christ is after all the hospitality of the Triune God toward us to enable us to return to the original humanity in harmony with the divinity and others . . . thus, the theology of the Tao focuses on the way of life together with a preferential option to the *yin* side of the universe including strangers, minjung, and *dalit*, which precisely means a radical humanization.[43]

The theme of hospitality in the Asian context was further addressed at CATS VII by Indian theologian Thangaraj. He reflects on the widespread conflicts and tensions, sometimes violent, between religious groups that in the past have lived in relative peace and harmony. In embracing God's hospitality to the religious other, he says Asian Christians should learn first how

---

41. Tang, "Identity and Marginality," 95–96.

42. Kim, *Christ and the Tao*, 130–31.

43. Kim, "Embracing and Embodying God's Hospitality Today in Asia," 9–10. See also Kim, *Christ and the Tao*, 124–76.

to be gracious guests at the "rich table of religious plurality" without dictating what should be on the menu or how much one is going to partake. A posture of openness and vulnerability as guests mirrors humanity's first role as God's guests in the bountiful created world. Then Christians can be called on to play the role of gracious hosts, but only after there is an invitation and a cry for help. Indeed, says Thangaraj, the aim of interreligious hospitality must always be to transform or change the particular social, economic, and political situation for greater freedom and liberation of those who suffer and are marginalized in the society.

He concludes with three possible outcomes when religions practice mutual hospitality: a) the guest may choose to be a member of the other's religious family, otherwise known as religious conversion, which was his family's own experience converting from Hinduism to Christianity; b) the host may experience change through positive encounters with guests who enrich family life and offer new perspectives, such as Gandhi who remained a Hindu but was profoundly influenced by the teachings of Jesus, especially the Sermon on the Mount; or c) host and guest become partners in spirituality and service, drawing on religious texts and practices from both sides for mutual enhancement and transformation, such as some Christians who practice meditation or yoga and some Hindus who regularly read the Christian scriptures.[44]

Lastly, Asian feminist theologians point out dimensions of gender and sexuality that are often missing from the discussion of religious pluralism and interreligious dialogue. Hong Kong-born theologian Kwok proposes a postcolonial theology of religious differences that focuses not on religious diversity but rather on "religious difference as it is constituted and produced in concrete situations, often with significant power differentials."[45] Women's voices at many major interfaith gatherings have been marginalized due to the dominance of men as official representatives of their faith. Feminist scholars have taken it upon themselves to organize meetings such as Asian women's interfaith conferences in Kuala Lumpur in 1989 and in Bandung in 2005. There they examined both the oppressive and liberating aspects for women in their respective faiths and explored how to build solidarity as Asian sisters across a multi-religious and multicultural continent.[46] Asian women's perspectives, experiences, and theological contributions should

---

44. Thangaraj, "Embodying God's Hospitality in a Multi-Religious World," 14–25.
45. Kwok, *Postcolonial Imagination and Feminist Theology*, 205.
46. Kwok, *Globalization, Gender, and Peacebuilding*, 30–33.

be welcomed at the dialogical table as a genuine sign of intrareligious and interreligious hospitality.[47]

RECENT THEOLOGICAL REFLECTIONS ON HOSPITALITY TO REFUGEES AND ASYLUM SEEKERS

After exploring some of the tensions in Christian hospitality in contemporary theology, we conclude with several recent theological models of hospitality to refugees and asylum seekers. These cover a range of approaches and are useful to stimulate further discussion in Part Two on the practice of hospitality to strangers.

Faithful hospitality

In analyzing the place of hospitality in international relations, Wilson argues that religious groups play a significant role in caring for refugees and asylum seekers in the twenty-first century through "faithful hospitality." According to Wilson, the religions of Islam, Christianity, and Judaism share a common religious motivation for pursuing social justice: "personal faith, experience of God's love and knowledge of the love of God for humanity."[48] She names two theological foundations of faithful hospitality at the core of these three religions, namely a) that all humans are separated from God by sin, and b) that God intervened in order to bring reconciliation between God and humanity. To illustrate her point, she shows how these concepts are understood in the respective teachings of each faith.

Wilson translates the above idea into the "language of hospitality" by drawing on both Levinas's and Derrida's philosophical concepts. The three Abrahamic faiths teach that everyone has become an "other" to God due to human sin or humanity's lowly origins, and thus everyone is unworthy before God in some way, not just a marginalized few. Likewise, when God intervened to bring reconciliation with humanity, "each of these interventions ... suggest that all are now welcome and included, rather than all being

---

47. Ibid., 27, 33. Over half of the participants at CATS VII were women, thanks to the organizer's attention to gender balance. Among the points made by women in the meeting was a reflection on the theme of "Embodying and Embracing God's Hospitality Today in Asia." They spoke of the possible danger of associating women with embodied hospitality in light of the problems of human trafficking, pornography, and commercial sex which are rampant in Asia. "Statement from the Women's Forum," Christian Conference of Asia, *CTC Bulletin* 28, no. 2, 113.

48. Wilson, "Be Welcome," 152.

marginalized and excluded."⁴⁹ Thus, faithful hospitality refuses to succumb to dualistic thinking that divides the world into believers and non-believers; us and them; self and other. Solidarity with the marginalized, including refugees and asylum seekers, arises out of a shared humanity redeemed by a loving God. Wilson characterizes the exercise of faithful hospitality as one way that Derrida's unconditional hospitality could be more realistically achieved. She attributes this to the worldview of religious actors who do not cling tightly to their possessions, including home, because everything belongs to God and is to be used in service to the divine. Besides, an eternal home awaits the faithful.⁵⁰

"Faithful hospitality" offers possibilities for developing an interfaith theology of refugee service that could be a strong intervening force to offset the power imbalance between the rights of states and the rights of unprotected individuals. However, Wilson draws rather heavily on Christian theology as the framework, despite her stated intention to be more broadly inclusive of other religions. In her attempt to find common theological ground among Muslims, Jews, and Christians, the unique contribution of each to faithful hospitality is diluted or even lost. The differences among the three monotheistic faiths need not block cooperation in advocacy for the most vulnerable in society. Yet, one must thoroughly understand the particular religious identity and beliefs of each faith before assessing their shared role and motivation in the international refugee protection system.

Hallowing bare life

Bretherton, whose work on hospitality and holiness was cited earlier, turns his attention specifically to the issue of refugees and the duty of care that Christians owe to this vulnerable population. He outlines the role of the church in a theological vision he calls "hallowing bare life." This vision views the stark existence of refugees, or bare life,⁵¹ through the petition of the Lord's Prayer to hallow the name of God (Matt 6:9, Luke 11:2). He says, "To hallow the name of God involves us in standing against that which

---

49. Ibid., 156.
50. Ibid., 147.
51. Bretherton takes the phrase "bare life" from the writings of philosopher Giorgio Agamben, who characterized it as "life exposed to death," especially due to state violence. See Agamben, *Homo Sacer*, 88. Bretherton, *Christianity and Contemporary Politics*, 138–39.

desecrates God's holy name. The rendering of creatures as bare life constitutes such a desecration."[52]

The church hallows bare life through acknowledging refugees near and far as God's gift, judgment, and promise. Hallowing bare life as *gift* recognizes that every human being is a unique individual with distinct identity, dignity, and the right to communicate and relate with others. Hallowing bare life as *judgment* calls into question the human tendency toward exclusion as a response to differentiation. This calls for a counter response of human hospitality to those who have been rendered bare life due to our sins of greed and idolatrous security. Hallowing bare life as *promise* includes the lives of refugees and asylum seekers in the hope of the kingdom of God. In living out this prayer of Jesus, the church reconfigures former social relationships and develops new public friendships to witness to the in-breaking of God's reign here and now. This promise requires mutual sacrifice and change on the part of both hosts and guests.[53]

A specific manifestation of hospitality in which the gift, judgment, and promise of bare life is fulfilled is the practice of church sanctuary. Here Bretherton sees the church's concrete witness to the sanctity of life by saving lives of vulnerable persons. Theologically, the claim that Christ is King means that all stand under divine judgment—"both accused and accuser, king and subject, outlaw and law-maker, violated and violator." Even more importantly, in the proclamation of the gospel, all stand under the mercy of the cross where forgiveness of sins and reconciliation with God are made possible.[54]

Bretherton's theological approach to the duty of care for refugees, sketched briefly here, is robust and creative. He pushes the church to move beyond humanitarian assistance to see the political and spiritual crisis clearly for what it is. He claims the riches of scripture, worship, and doctrine as primary sources for ordering a Christian response to asylum seekers and refugees. He never overestimates the power of churches to solve the refugee problem; yet at the same time he never underestimates the good that churches have done and can do when they fully utilize the moral force of their Christian faith. However, Bretherton's writing can be extremely complex as he seeks to integrate political theory, social science, philosophy, ethics, and theology. At times, it is difficult to follow his dense arguments although he does provide helpful summaries. In the wider scheme of guiding Christian participation in the public square, his framework of Christian

---

52. Bretherton, *Christianity and Contemporary Politics*, 145.
53. Ibid., 145–52.
54. Ibid., 157–58.

cosmopolitanism is valuable for the church, but perhaps less useful to states, governments, and non-religious actors as a basis for making policy decisions on forced migration.

Fear vs. faith

Snyder argues that fear among established populations in host countries is the biggest challenge to the acceptance of refugees and asylum seekers. The fear is based on multiple sources—political-cultural, socio-economic, and national and personal security. When these fears are fueled by politics of insecurity, public hostility, and negative media coverage, there emerges what she names as an ecology of fear. As an alternative, she proposes an ecology of faith rooted in generosity and compassion in encountering strangers.[55]

Stories of fear versus faith are found in biblical narratives that clearly demonstrate how Judeo-Christian tradition has used both exclusion and inclusion in dealing with foreigners in their midst. It is no coincidence that the three chosen narratives focus on the situation of women as outsiders in the Bible. Snyder intentionally employs a dialogical method through postcolonial and liberationist hermeneutical lenses to interpret scripture, emphasizing the need to tackle difficult texts with new eyes from multiple perspectives.

The focal text used to illustrate an ecology of fear comes from Ezra-Nehemiah which narrates the return of some of the Israelites to Judah from exile in Babylon. As Ezra and Nehemiah lead the people to rebuild the community and the temple in Jerusalem, there is a harsh prohibition against keeping foreign wives (Ezra 9:1–4, 10–12; 10:11, Neh 13:23–27) or mixing with the "peoples of the land" (Ezra 3:3, 4:4, Neh 13:3). Snyder contends that there is no way to avoid the xenophobic elements of this narrative. Those who use this text in the canon of their holy scriptures must acknowledge that this exclusionary policy for the sake of religious purity was both oppressive and unjust. Christians must also confess that the church at times used the argument of religious purity to exclude and oppress foreigners and strangers in the name of God.[56]

In contrast to Ezra-Nehemiah, Snyder offers two other biblical narratives that illustrate an ecology of faith—the story of Ruth in the Hebrew Bible and the story of the Syro-Phoenician woman in the Gospel of Mark 7:24–30. Here, both women are life-bringing strangers whose presence leads to unexpected blessings even as they seek help in desperate situations.

---

55. Snyder, *Asylum-Seeking, Migration and Church*, 13.
56. Ibid., 140–46.

In both stories, the women are portrayed as catalysts for positive change in the community of insiders as well as for future generations.[57]

In applying these texts to the modern situation of refugees and asylum seekers, Snyder affirms that hospitality to the stranger both then and now has been a key practice in an ecology of faith and the source of mutual blessings. Thus, she questions whether the mindset of "doing our duty" is adequate or appropriate as a church response to refugees and asylum seekers. She sees a danger of perpetuating a paternalistic attitude whereby churches are the main actors who do all the giving, while asylum seekers and refugees are passive recipients of this gracious service. Instead, she says, Christians are called to engage in mutual hospitality that involves *both* service to the neighbor in need *and* the distinct possibility of transformation of both parties.[58] She concurs with Ignatieff's point that "fulfilling people's *needs* is very different from helping strangers to *flourish*, something which involves the intangible qualities of love and belonging, dignity, respect, and ultimate meaning."[59]

Snyder's scriptural approach using feminist, postcolonial, and liberation theologies to enter into dialogue with the Bible text is admirable. She engages with a wide variety of experts in search of alternative scholarship that more closely speaks to the lived experiences of global refugees and asylum seekers. Additionally, Snyder takes on a bigger challenge than Wilson or Bretherton do by presenting her theological approach via a book-length study of refugee and asylum seeker ministry in the UK. However, while fear versus faith is a valid quandary for the church, the biblical illustrations of Ruth and the Syro-Phoenician woman rely on the courage of the stranger to bring about transformation in the community. Does this imply that refugees and asylum seekers must take on that burden as well? Surely not, but Snyder could have made it clearer what responsibilities belong to the host and what belong to the guest. Refugees and asylum seekers themselves may inhabit an ecology of fear that is vastly different from that of the host's. What would be required for hosts and guests to create an ecology of faith together where the church, community, and persons seeking protection can all flourish?

CONCLUSION

The current resurgence of hospitality as a theological interpretative lens exhibits a tension between recovering the riches of biblical and historic

---

57. Ibid., 167–74.
58. Snyder, "The Dangers of 'Doing Our Duty,'" 352–54.
59. Ibid., 355. Ignatieff, *The Needs of Strangers*, 10.

models and moving beyond them to address a multicultural, multi-religious postmodern world. Prominent biblical themes are the welcoming of Christ in the stranger, God's hospitality in the cross of Jesus, and the spiritual overflow and eschatological promise of Pentecost. With the Bible in one hand and a newspaper in the other, scholars and practitioners seek to formulate new models that could tackle the radical inhospitality evident in society's treatment of the "other," especially foreigners, migrants, and people of different races, cultures, and religions. The philosophical writings of Levinas and Derrida have been particularly influential in stimulating Christian thinking on the subject. By advocating a radical openness to the stranger, Christian hospitality promotes mutuality, equality, and responsibility in the host-guest relationship. At the same time, attention is given to appropriate boundaries that would allow hospitality to flourish under optimal conditions. These boundaries range anywhere from logistical requirements all the way to theological parameters in order to maintain the spirit of Christian hospitality.

Of special concern is the role of hospitality in promoting interfaith friendship as a corrective to the triumphalism of earlier missionary movements. We explored a range of approaches that began with Christians offering hospitality in the church as a form of reverse mission and then moved to more mutual encounters with religious faiths sharing spiritual practices in their sacred places. This was followed by the search for common ground in holy texts that would lead to joint advocacy for needy strangers. Lastly, we analyzed contributions by a number of Asian theologians who call for recognition of the positive value of Asian spiritual plurality and the existence of models of multi-religious belonging and cooperation as well as the necessity of including Asian women's experience in the quest for interreligious understanding.

Contemporary theological responses to the plight of refugees and asylum seekers through hospitality vary from an interreligious approach of faithful hospitality, to a christological approach of hallowing bare life, to a postcolonial approach contrasting an ecology of fear with an ecology of faith. Whichever approach is taken, it is evident that the most compelling theologies of refugee ministry put asylum seekers and refugees on equal footing with everyone else in the church, whether that is as sinners or the redeemed. In other words, there is no "us" or "them"—we are all the same before God in a solidarity *of* others. For Christians, through Jesus Christ, the fate of the marginalized and the fate of the church are unavoidably intertwined.

As we conclude Part One on "The Concept of Christian Hospitality to Strangers," what can be said as a concise summary of the lessons learned from this historical, biblical, and theological exploration? Perhaps the simplest way is to name three things that churches and Christians can expect when engaged in a fruitful ministry of hospitality: a) Expect and welcome difference as a gift from God the Creator, b) Expect that hospitality will be difficult yet ultimately rewarding as the call of Jesus Christ, and c) Expect surprises for both hosts and guests as the ongoing work of the Holy Spirit. These are lessons from the first-hand experience and best practices of Christian hospitality over the centuries, whether at the individual and congregational level or in the wider arena of institutions, religious bodies, and public policy.

PART TWO

The Practice of Christian Hospitality to Refugees and Asylum Seekers

Chapter 4

Care for Refugees and Asylum Seekers

WHILE THE UPROOTING OF persons from their native land is as old as the Bible itself, the issue of forced migration today is a pressing global matter with political, social, economic, and moral implications. To formulate an effective Christian response to refugees and asylum seekers in the twenty-first century, we must understand how the current situation came to be and what others have done in the past. This requires that we define our terminology and then chart the evolution of the international refugee protection system. Next, from historical and pastoral perspectives, we focus on the church's role in caring for refugees. An examination of the relationship between the institutions of asylum and sanctuary reveals the presence of religion early on in protecting those fleeing for their lives. The church's continuing ministry to persons seeking asylum raises common issues of concern and offers possible solutions in Christian outreach to this population. By looking at the broader picture of the refugee situation and the church's response, we are able to place the local situation in its proper context for analysis and action.

PEOPLE ON THE MOVE

Every era and geographic region is witness to persons leaving their homeland in search of opportunities for a better life. This is still true in the twenty-first century as international migration shows no sign of abatement. Migration studies use the terms "voluntary migrants" and "forced migrants" to distinguish between those who leave their homeland for economic or other reasons from those who are forced to flee due to persecution or conflict. However, some voluntary migrants may face a degree of coercion, while other forced migrants do possess resources that allow them choices about when and where to flee. Thus, the distinction between voluntary migrants and forced migrants is not always clear-cut.

While the term *refugee* has been popularly used to describe all forced migrants, the definition according to international refugee law is more precise. According to the 1951 Refugee Convention, a *refugee* is someone who

> . . . owing to a well-founded fear of being persecuted for reasons of race, religion, nationality, membership of a particular social group or political opinion, is outside the country of his nationality and is unable or, owing to such fear, is unwilling to avail himself of the protection of that country.[1]

The terms "refugee" and "asylum seeker" are closely related, but they are not exactly the same. According to the United Nations High Commissioner for Refugees (UNHCR), a refugee is one who has been recognized as meeting the requirements of the 1951 Convention and granted refugee status. Asylum seekers (with pending cases) are those who have applied for international protection but whose claim for refugee status has not yet been determined. International law recognizes refugees as "a unique category of human rights victims to whom special protection and benefits should be accorded."[2]

An international system to care for refugees has been in operation since the 1920s. The international refugee protection regime began during the interwar years (1921–1943) to address the plight of millions made homeless in Europe and Asia in the aftermath of World War I and the breakup of historic empires. After World War II in the 1940s, the contemporary refugee regime was put into place to manage the forty million persons displaced in Europe who resettled in Australia, North America, and elsewhere. The UNHCR was established in 1950 and the Refugee Convention was adopted the following year.

Under the 1951 Convention, refugees are guaranteed certain rights since they are no longer under the legal protection of their home country. The most significant right is "non-refoulement," or the right not to be returned to a country where a refugee may face persecution. Non-refoulement has

---

1. United Nations High Commissioner for Refugees, "1951 Convention Relating to the Status of Refugees," Article 1a(2).

2. Loescher, "The International Refugee Regime," 351.

been called the cornerstone of global refugee protection and is understood to be binding on all states under international law. This applies to states who have signed the Convention as well as those who have not.³ Other important refugee rights in the host country are the freedom to practice one's religion, access to courts, right to employment, right to education for children, and freedom of movement.

The Office of the United Nations High Commissioner for Refugees is the key multilateral institution with the mandate to provide protection and promote durable solutions for refugees. UNHCR includes refugees, asylum seekers, returnees, stateless people, and some internally displaced persons under its mandate for protection and assistance based on humanitarian grounds. Besides the UNHCR, other intergovernmental agencies and many non-government organizations (NGOs) are involved in serving refugees, such as the International Committee of the Red Cross, the World Food Programme, OXFAM, *Médecins sans Frontières,* and the International Rescue Committee.

While states have vested interests in resolving refugee and asylum seeker issues—e.g., national, regional, and international stability—the same governments have proven resistant to yielding their authority and independence to bodies like the UNHCR. This is likely due to fear that there is no end in sight for the refugee problem, and governments are unwilling to be tied to seemingly endless financial and social obligations on demand.⁴ Due to these fears, in the early 1990s, the issue of asylum became increasingly politicized with refugees and asylum seekers bearing the brunt of political backlash in the receiving countries. This led to heightened restrictions in Western countries as the public called for tighter border controls, detention of asylum seekers, and deportation of irregular migrants. Castles observes

> The refugee regime of Western countries has been fundamentally transformed over the last 30 years. It has changed from a system designed to welcome Cold War refugees from the East and to resettle them as permanent exiles in new homes, to an exclusionary regime, designed to keep out asylum seekers from the South.⁵

---

3. Loescher and Milner, "UNHRC and the Global Governance of Refugees," 193.
4. Loescher, "The International Refugee Regime," 352, 357.
5. Castles et al., *The Age of Migration,* 227.

THE CHURCH AND THE INSTITUTION OF ASYLUM

The word "asylum" is derived from the Greek word *asylos*, meaning invulnerable or inviolable. Historically, asylum was associated with protected physical spaces from which nothing could be taken and no one could be violated. While modern states hold the legal right to grant asylum to those seeking protection, the tradition of asylum and its religious counterpart—sanctuary—can be traced back to antiquity, including biblical times.

In the Hebrew scripture, there were six cities of refuge where those guilty of certain acts such as manslaughter (crimes without intention) could safely flee to in the region.[6] The sacred nature of refuge was applicable as well to the ancient sanctuaries of Greece and Rome. Marfleet notes, "In these spaces, protective power emanates from the deities; those who violate the *sacrum* challenge godly authority and subvert values associated with its guardians and the entire community, risking severe punishment."[7]

With Emperor Constantine's conversion to Christianity in the fourth century, the Roman Empire formally codified Christian sanctuary in 392. For approximately 1,300 years, churches in the West provided protection for those who had committed certain crimes and sought safety. One difference from Roman practice was that the church offered sanctuary even for those who were guilty of crimes with intention. However, some categories of persons and offenses were excluded, notably "[d]ebtors, embezzlers of state funds, Jews, heretics . . . apostates . . . tax officials, murderers, rapists, and adulterers."[8]

The institution of church sanctuary flourished in Europe from the fifth to fifteenth century. It was regulated by both secular law and Roman Catholic Church councils. Spiritual penance and punishment could be required for "[t]he church undertook to exercise mercy and dispense justice in a world that had little time for either."[9] The period of sanctuary granted to a person normally ranged from three to forty days.

In the church's eyes, the authority of secular rulers was given by the grace of God, and thus the right of Christian sanctuary was a divine prerogative. That meant that those who sought refuge in the church could not be pursued by secular officials since the authority of the church prevailed in this matter. However, increasing conflicts between the church and state

---

6. See Num 35:6–34, Josh 20:1–9, and Deut 4:41–43.
7. Marfleet, "Understanding 'Sanctuary,'" 442.
8. Rabben, *Give Refuge to the Stranger*, 55.
9. Ibid., 57.

over institutional power, including that of sanctuary, saw the church losing influence over time.

In the sixteenth century, King Henry VIII's break with the Roman Catholic Church signaled the end of church sanctuary in England. The English Parliament formally repealed all rights of church sanctuary in 1623. This coincided with the emergence of nation-states in the seventeenth century in which civil authorities sought to exercise exclusive power over granting asylum and protection. The opportunity soon arose when the persecuted Calvinist minority in France known as the Huguenots were offered permanent asylum in England by the Crown. This may have been the first use of the English term *refugee* as understood in modern international law. It also extended the concept of sanctuary beyond particular sites to include a whole nation-state.[10]

Even as the legal right of church sanctuary ended, the practice as a moral right did not. Christians and churches continued to follow their conscience by protecting those fleeing persecution, slavery, and extermination. The principle of Christian sanctuary was invoked in later centuries in the Underground Railroad that assisted black slaves in the southern USA to escape to freedom in the nineteenth century, in the protection of Jews in Europe during the Holocaust in World War II, and in the 1980s sanctuary movement in North America for undocumented refugees from Central America. A recent model that invokes the ancient principle is the UK's City of Sanctuary movement initiated by church leaders in Sheffield, England in 2005. The movement brings together a broad coalition of community groups and organizations, faith communities, and refugees and asylum seekers to influence the politics of asylum indirectly through a "culture of hospitality" at the grassroots level. Many other examples around the world testify to the enduring provision of divine protection within sacred spaces and through religious communities.

While official state asylum and unofficial church sanctuary continue to co-exist, Rabben points out a critical historical difference.

> It should be kept in mind that modern asylum came into formal existence as a universal right of *states* to grant, not of *individuals* to receive. In contrast to sanctuary, a religious institution . . . , asylum was a secular and political institution, a part of the modern international system of sovereign states.[11]

---

10. Marfleet, "Understanding 'Sanctuary,'" 448.
11. Rabben, *Give Refuge to the Stranger*, 73.

Nonetheless, even as a secular and political institution, asylum cannot be totally cut off from its moral and spiritual foundations. In fact, with its roots in the institution of sanctuary, asylum is by nature linked to hospitality and issues of character, attitude, and tradition. While Plaut sees hospitality as a variant of asylum,[12] it would be more accurate to view asylum as a variant of hospitality with potential to transform encounters between nation-states, communities, citizens, and unprotected persons.

PRACTICAL MODELS OF REFUGEE MINISTRY

The specific commitment to the well-being of refugees and asylum seekers is wide-ranging with implications for the overall ministry and mission of the church. According to Langmead, hospitality among refugees and asylum seekers includes

> . . . justice-seeking, political action, inclusion around our tables, intercultural friendship, pursuing a hospitable multicultural approach to church life, practical assistance, long-term commitment, learning from those who are different, sensitivity to the power dynamics of 'welcome,' a willingness to 'let go' as well as 'embrace,' interfaith dialogue, and discovering the intertwining of the guest and host roles which is embedded in biblical and theological understandings of God's activity amongst us.[13]

This rather comprehensive list touches on many important elements of refugee ministry. However, it is more helpful for our purposes to view the different components under specific working categories.

Wilson suggests three activities that encompass faithful hospitality: a) meeting of immediate needs, b) protection from harm, and c) advocacy against injustice and for shift in power.[14] Snyder offers somewhat different categories which she refers to as "encounters."

- Encounters of *grassroots service* involve personal and pastoral care to individuals or families.
- Encounters with *powers* designate activities such as advocacy and lobbying to change policies and attitudes in the established population.
- Encounters in *worship* describe ministry through Christian liturgy and prayer.

---

12. Plaut, *Asylum: A Moral Dilemma*, 11.
13. Langmead, "Refugees as Guests and Hosts," 1.
14. Wilson, "Be Welcome," 160–64.

- Encounters in *theology* engage with people seeking asylum through theological reflection and analysis.[15]

While Wilson's three activities are straightforward, Snyder's four encounters are more suggestive of dynamic relationships as well as the potential for service through religious activities. The many examples that she cites from the British context could be applied to the service of churches and Christian agencies in other places as well. There are multitudes of these encounters through churches and institutions around the world working in refugee and asylum seeker service. There is much we could learn from those on the front lines.

ISSUES IN REFUGEE MINISTRY

a. Strategic planning

How do churches and Christian organizations decide which services to provide, to what extent, and for how long? The international agency Jesuit Refugee Service emphasizes working with existing services rather than duplicating them, and filling in gaps to meet needs not being met by other groups. Sustainable collaboration with other NGOs and mainstream service providers is vital to ensure continuity. Involvement of refugees and asylum seekers in the planning, conducting, and evaluation of projects is built into the process as a means of promoting human dignity and cultural sensitivity. Jesuit Refugee Service warns against creating dependency and doing things for refugees and asylum seekers that they can do for themselves. When agencies give material assistance, expectations should be clear whether the aid is for emergency purposes, for a short-term period, or a part of ongoing service. Service providers also need to be aware of their limits "in terms of numbers, resources, time and the law."[16]

Within the limits of every organization, how do Christian NGOs and churches decide which persons should receive priority in their concern? It is tempting to categorize protection claimants using terms such as legal or illegal, genuine or bogus, deserving or undeserving. Those who have received refugee status under the UNHCR are usually regarded as legal, genuine, and deserving and thus should be accorded assistance. Others who are suspected to be economic migrants taking advantage of the refugee system might be regarded as illegal, bogus, and undeserving of aid. In reality, many

---

15. Snyder, *Asylum-Seeking, Migration and Church*, 35–45, 197–213.
16. Jesuit Refugee Service, *Working with Urban Refugees*, 12.

of those who became recognized refugees endured years of destitution and hostility in the long, drawn-out process of refugee status determination and resettlement. Even if asylum seekers cannot meet the requirements of the UNHCR or immigration law for refugee status, they are still vulnerable to poverty and exploitation while living far away from their culture and family. Whatever one's immigration status, every person deserves to be treated with respect based on his or her human identity (*imago Dei*) rather than judged based on a political label.[17]

Beyond the social services that Christian organizations and churches provide to refugee and asylum seeker clients, there is need for models of refugee ministry based on "the kind of long and patient friendships that nurture community, alter the national character of the church, and challenge the state's assumptions about citizenship and human identity."[18] The act of accompaniment involves walking alongside a person physically, emotionally, and spiritually. Christian agencies and congregations also involve themselves in "doxological politics" whereby they bless those seeking asylum through acts of neighborly listening, community organizing, offer of sanctuary, and worshipping together.[19]

At the same time, however, we must recognize that the primary need of the refugee or asylum seeker is political—a new state in which one can live without fear of persecution. That is why challenging unjust laws and practices is a key component of refugee ministry in places where advocacy and lobbying are allowed. Policy changes at the structural level can have a huge impact on the lives of all refugees and asylum seekers, far beyond the limited number that Christian organizations and churches can serve directly. Unless Christians also join forces with others in the community to work for justice for unprotected persons, churches may actually be doing more harm than good in administering humanitarian assistance that ignores the political dimension and maintains the status quo.[20]

b. Christian identity

In serving refugees and asylum seekers, the issue of Christian identity arises particularly related to working in a multi-faith context. Some faith-based refugee service agencies do not emphasize their distinct Christian identity or teachings while serving because many of those coming to them are

---

17. See Groody, "Crossing the Divide," 642–48.
18. Ralston, "Refugees and the Role of Religious Groups."
19. Ibid. See also Bretherton, *Christianity and Contemporary Politics*, 142–45.
20. Bretherton, *Christianity and Contemporary Politics*, 141.

adherents of other faiths such as Islam, Buddhism, or Hinduism. If staff spoke about religion at all, the stress would be on common core values of all faiths such as compassion and justice. Proselytizing, or attempting to convert others to Christianity, is seen as inappropriate and unethical since service should be given without any ulterior motives. The power imbalance between service providers and refugees is another reason given for avoiding proselytizing. Refugees and asylum seekers are already in a vulnerable position with limited control over their current situation. To press them on matters of faith in the context of giving aid could be seen as an abuse of power and even psychological and spiritual manipulation.[21]

The fact remains, however, that some churches and Christian agencies do evangelize among refugees and asylum seekers of other faiths. While this may be frowned upon by others, it is not illegal in many countries. Besides, religious freedom according to Christian principles includes the right to change one's religion as long as there is no coercion or deception involved. Local congregations in particular may view refugee ministry as both an obligation and an opportunity—an obligation to care for persons seeking asylum who are from a Christian background and an opportunity to share the message of Jesus Christ with those who have never been exposed to Christianity.

A story in the Baptist Press reported a touching case of Christian outreach to a refugee family in detention in Asia. The father, Rajeevan, recalled the kindness of church members who brought fresh food without imposing their beliefs on his family. He saw that Christians were doing this for everyone, regardless of background, without asking for anything back. This care moved the former Hindu to find out what motivated the visitors' unselfish actions and what kind of God they worshipped.

> Why would anyone come to such a depressing place and give strangers this precious gift? He soon realized the Christians' 'gift' involved more than time: it was one of peace and hope, something his war-torn family had never experienced. When . . . missionaries . . . shared the Gospel with Rajeevan, it was the first time he'd ever heard of Jesus. The information made his heart feel so peaceful, he knew he had to go to this church . . . 'I went to the church and never wanted to leave. I felt peace and . . . Love! I found love and forgiveness through Jesus Christ.'[22]

From a more cynical viewpoint, this story might represent a typical public relations ploy to raise funds for overseas missionaries and mission

21. Wilson, "Much to Be Proud of," 553–56.
22. Rain, "In Bangkok Detention."

boards. In other words, it is a heartwarming tale of how one's mission donations are changing lives and saving the lost through the power of the gospel. One could ask if the low-key ministry of other workers might also have led some refugees to inquire about Christianity and request baptism; but these stories intentionally go unreported in the press. And one need not search long before discovering stories of Christians who choose to convert to other religions through meaningful interfaith encounters. Thus, the issue of proselytizing is complex and multifaceted with no simple answers of right and wrong.

What should be of concern to those who work among refugees and asylum seekers is three-fold: i) whether conversion to Christianity puts the lives of refugees or asylum seekers in danger among their own people in the host country or in their homeland should they have to return; ii) whether those who choose to convert to Christianity do so in belief that it will improve their chances of gaining refugee status and resettlement in Western countries; and iii) whether those who apply for asylum on the grounds of religious persecution after converting to Christianity receive adequate support from churches when presenting their cases before immigration or UN officials.

The first concern requires that churches make sincere efforts to learn about other world faiths as well as what that faith means in the life of an individual refugee or asylum seeker. Christians should also seek to understand the cultures of those they serve and the role that religion plays in the culture. "Religious narratives and institutions . . . are at the core of the experience of the vast majority of communities facing crisis and, perhaps as crucially, of the majority of national humanitarian agency staff that typically constitute 90 per cent of the humanitarian workforce," argue Ager and Ager.[23] Thus, among the principles and recommendations for Christian witness in a multi-religious world endorsed by three major Christian bodies in 2011 are "to acknowledge and appreciate what is true and good in [other faiths]" and to "avoid misrepresenting the beliefs and practices of people of different religions."[24] For some refugees and asylum seekers, conversion to Christianity could lead to being disowned by family and community or even bring the threat of death for the crime of apostasy. In these potentially high risk situations, churches should proceed with utmost caution in order to ensure the well-being of refugees and asylum seekers and the integrity of the Christian witness.

---

23. Ager and Ager, "Faith and the Discourse of Secular Humanitarianism," 465–66.

24. World Council of Churches et al., "Christian Witness in a Multi-religious World."

The second concern of motivation for Christian conversion likewise requires sensitive handling and discernment. Churches may worry that asylum seekers and refugees convert for the wrong reason, that is, out of false hope that Christian identity will improve their chances of obtaining refugee status and resettlement to countries where Christianity is the majority religion. Given the strong cooperation of churches and Christian agencies in refugee resettlement in the Global North, it is not hard to see how persons seeking asylum might reasonably assume that becoming a Christian would be beneficial to their future prospects. However, one should keep in mind that there may be manifold reasons why a person or family chooses to change from one religion to another. Motivations can only be determined on a case-by-case basis with gracious and respectful treatment of all inquirers. To ensure personal discernment on behalf of persons wishing to convert, Christians should "acknowledge that changing one's religion is a decisive step that must be accompanied by sufficient time for adequate reflection and preparation, through a process ensuring full personal freedom."[25]

Once asylum seekers have converted to Christianity, they may seek the assistance of the church in presenting their case to immigration or UNHCR officers. This brings up the third concern of how churches can be supportive of converts, particularly if the claim for asylum is based on religious persecution, e.g., on grounds that the person cannot safely return to his or her country because he or she has converted to Christianity. Here, actions taken by churches in the UK are instructive. Church leaders such as the former Sub-Dean of Christ Church Cathedral in Oxford publicly challenged the poor handling of asylum cases involving Christian conversion in a letter printed in a prominent London newspaper.[26] The Evangelical Alliance published a full report on the issue, citing specific incidents of unfair procedure.

> [M]any of the questions used cannot give a true representation of the appellant's faith because they are: a) based on western Christian culture (e.g. 'How do you cook a turkey for Christmas?'); b) insensitive to the particular type of Christianity that the appellant has been exposed to (e.g. asking a Pentecostal convert about Anglican liturgy); c) asking things which aren't even in the Bible (e.g. such as knowing the names of the thieves crucified on the crosses alongside Jesus or the name of the forbidden fruit).[27]

---

25. Ibid.
26. Coulton, "Asylum Injustice."
27. Coton, *Alltogether for Asylum Justice*, 18.

Thus, even in countries where Christianity is well-established, it cannot be assumed that those presiding over asylum hearings are knowledgeable about religious practice or the differences among various churches. Officials are often skeptical of claims of religious persecution and may view conversion as a baptism of convenience to bolster chances of gaining refugee status. In response, the Methodist Church in Britain issued a briefing to prepare clergy who are called upon to give evidence in support of applications of asylum seekers who are members of their churches. Such evidence could be critical to the success of the application since a Christian minister would be regarded as an expert witness to the applicant's Christian faith including attendance at worship, participation in congregational activities, and formal church membership as indicated by profession of faith and baptism.[28]

c. Funding

Refugee ministries receive funding from a variety of sources such as donations, institutional church support, and grants from government or non-government agencies. Those that receive funds as operational partners of government departments or refugee agencies such as UNHCR will be subject to guidelines that may restrict their religious activities or limit their ability to criticize government and agency policies. One Christian refugee agency in Australia found itself facing such a situation. In earlier years it was not eligible for government funding for asylum seeker programs, and later it declined available funding in order to maintain its independent stance. While the agency took a leading role in developing the community detention model for refugees and asylum seekers, the organization turned down the government's invitation to be the primary manager of the program. The contract was subsequently given to the Australian Red Cross, a move that was seen as both practical and strategic. The Red Cross is a much larger organization in terms of national reputation and capacity. It also operates under a policy of neutrality and therefore refrains from criticizing government policies. Both factors work in the government's favor. Nonetheless, the Christian agency is an active partner in implementing the community detention program and relies on non-government sources of funding and in-kind support to carry out its work. This mission includes the right to criticize government policies on refugees and asylum seekers and to advocate for more just and humane laws.[29]

---

28. McDonald, "Asylum Application and Christian Belief."
29. Wilson, "Much to Be Proud of," 555, 557.

In terms of donations, faith-based organizations need to appeal to different bases in order to raise funds successfully. Faith-based organizations use the language of human rights, compassion, and multi-faith service to gain support from the broader community. Yet, among churches, these same organizations may need to employ more explicitly theological and biblical language to appeal to Christian communities. Christian refugee agencies could be caught between donors who think the organization's religious identity is too strong and others who think the organization's religious identity is too weak. It is worth noting that research on faith-based organizations in humanitarian work indicates that there may be greater differences between some Christian faith-based agencies themselves than between secular and faith-based agencies.[30] In any case, faith-based organizations need to be clear about their organization's vision and mission, both in promotion and practice. Christian supporters can provide valuable feedback when the mission becomes too wide; non-Christian supporters can offer helpful perspectives when the vision becomes too narrow.

CONCLUSION

The modern system of care for refugees and asylum seekers developed from the early to the mid-twentieth century to cope with the large numbers of displaced persons due to the two World Wars. The United Nations High Commissioner for Refugees is the most prominent international agency working in the field of forced migration. In cooperation with or at times in conflict with nation-states and other parties, the UNHCR has the mandate to provide protection and offer durable solutions to the protracted and complex global issue of refugees and asylum seekers.

The history of the institution of asylum reveals that it has been part of religious tradition since ancient times and was practiced in Hebraic, Greek, and Roman cultures. The right to provide protection to vulnerable persons fleeing persecution was officially taken up by the Christian church in the fourth century after Emperor Constantine's conversion. This privilege not only allowed the church to claim divine prerogative over civil authorities in the matter, but also heightened the power and prestige of the clergy and the premises over which they presided. With the rise of monarchies in fifteenth-century Europe, the church's exclusive right to offer sanctuary

---

30. See Thaut, "The Role of Faith in Christian Faith-Based Humanitarian Agencies," 319–50. She classifies Christian faith-based agencies in three broad categories of Accommodative–Humanitarian, Synthesis–Humanitarian, and Evangelistic–Humanitarian, based on their theological orientation.

in England was challenged by civil authorities until it was revoked in the early seventeenth century. As the modern nation-states began to emerge, the right of sanctuary was taken over by governments who granted protection to refugees within the bounds of a whole country rather than within the limits of a particular location. The church, however, asserted its moral right to offer sanctuary in certain situations and has even continued to do so into modern times.

In terms of Christian action on a practical and pastoral level, studies on urban refugee ministry demonstrate not only that churches worldwide are deeply committed to refugee and asylum seeker well-being in the long-term, but that manifold issues of strategic planning, Christian identity, and funding must be confronted and resolved. Nonetheless, even with multiple and diverse approaches to the matter, the conclusions are consistent. The church can make a difference and will become different when it is faithfully involved in the lives of vulnerable strangers.

With this background on the global situation of refugees and asylum seekers and urban refugee ministry, we are ready to turn to the local situation in Hong Kong. We look at Hong Kong's experience of welcoming the stranger from cultural and historical perspectives and the historic role of the church there in caring for strangers in their midst. Then we survey two earlier waves of refugees and asylum seekers coming from mainland China and Vietnam into Hong Kong and the church's response. This is followed by an in-depth study of the situation since the year 2000 with asylum seekers from South Asia, Africa, and other lands, and finally the Hong Kong church's response in caring for refugees and asylum seekers in the twenty-first century.

Chapter 5

Welcoming the Stranger
The Hong Kong Context

IF HOSPITALITY IS ESSENTIALLY concerned about a society's treatment of strangers, then Hong Kong offers a rich resource for investigation and analysis. The city has been variously described in its history as "a Chinese colony that happens to be run by Britain,"[1] "a borrowed place living on borrowed time,"[2] and "a Chinese global city in the world economy."[3] Indeed, Hong Kong's experience of hospitality as a community and in the church can be attributed in part to its shifting fortunes related to the socio-political, economic, and religious affairs of the motherland. Yet the fate of strangers in the former British Crown colony and present-day Special Administrative Region (HKSAR) of the People's Republic of China also lay, in many ways, in the hands and hearts of Hong Kong residents themselves. This chapter studies Hong Kong hospitality in its historical and cultural contexts to grasp the significance of the stranger in the social constructions that emerge from its Eastern and Western endowments. We examine the general situation of Hong Kong and strangers, analyzing multiple forces of Chinese, colonial, and local factors. Then we investigate the Hong Kong church and its hospitality to strangers starting from its missionary beginnings and concluding with the multicultural, multinational environment that now characterizes Christianity in the HKSAR.

1. Welsh, *A History of Hong Kong*, 8.
2. Hughes, *Borrowed Place, Borrowed Time*, 13.
3. Chiu and Lui, *Hong Kong: Becoming a Chinese Global City*.

This selective recounting of portions of the Hong Kong story sets the stage for our discussion of hospitality to refugees and asylum seekers.

HONG KONG AND STRANGERS

After over 150 years as a British colony (1841–1997), Hong Kong residents have an extensive history of dealing with strangers. In the early days, strangers arrived in forms as diverse as colonial masters, foreign missionaries, refugees from mainland China, Nepalese Gurkha soldiers, and businessmen from the Indian subcontinent. In more recent times they have come as Vietnamese boat people, migrant workers, imported labor, new arrivals and visitors from mainland China, and asylum seekers from South Asia and Africa. Although the city's population is overwhelmingly ethnic Chinese (94 percent), Hong Kongers are accustomed to living with difference and encountering the "other." The multiple influences of Chinese tradition, Western colonialism, and local Hong Kong culture have created an international metropolis of seven million that its tourism board proudly promotes as a city of "Fascinating Contrasts." Some social critics, however, are quick to point out that these strikingly different worlds in Hong Kong do not co-exist as peacefully as one might be led to believe.

> [M]ulticulturalism in Hong Kong merely describes the residence of people with different cultural backgrounds. Equal freedom and chances of survival; freedom from discrimination, mutual respect and reception; as well as other senses of worth contained in the ideal multiculturalism concept are still very thin and weak under Hong Kong's public policies. Minorities in the city can rarely enjoy their deserved rights and identity; on the contrary, discrimination and social exclusion are their common experiences.[4]

Accusations of discrimination and social exclusion in Hong Kong are nothing new. After all, the Chinese population in the city experienced discrimination and social exclusion under British colonialism, especially in the early years. For example, Chinese were not allowed to build homes in exclusive areas such as Victoria Peak and were required to carry a lantern and a pass when they went out at night. Nevertheless, as Hong Kong continues to come to terms with its own postcolonial identity, it is probably fair to say that many Hong Kongers' views of multiculturalism have been shaped by historical factors, particularly on the issue of race. As Law and Lee bluntly

---

4. Law and Lee, "The Myth of Multiculturalism," 120.

put it, an unfortunate legacy of 150 years of British colonial rule for Hong Kong people was the internalization of the "white superiority" of the British, particularly among the social élite. Colonialism by necessity classifies people according to skin color, and it is no accident that the highest class would belong to the white race. In Hong Kongers' minds, then, "The white people represent civilization, development, elegance, wisdom and rationality. In contrast, the coloured races represent cruelty, vulgarity, stupidity and irrationality."[5]

Those objecting to this unflattering portrayal of Hong Kong people could respond in several ways. One response would be to point out examples where this is not the case, such as the high status of some ethnic minorities in the city like the Harilela family of Indian descent, or the existence of "mixed marriages" in which Chinese have wedded persons of other races. Another response would be that many Hong Kong people have been exposed to other cultures through study, travel, or living abroad. Young people in particular are more open-minded about people of different backgrounds, and some study and work locally in multi-racial, multicultural settings. Hence, they do not necessarily hold the same views as their parents' or grandparents' generation. Third, since ethnic Chinese make up 94 percent of the population, it is natural that many Hong Kongers do not have the opportunities to interact with the other 6 percent, who may not speak the local dialect of Cantonese Chinese. A domestic worker from the Philippines or Indonesia may be the extent of some families' contact with persons unlike themselves, and the employer-employee situation does not easily lend itself to personal friendships.

It should be clear that when we speak of Hong Kong and strangers, it is difficult to make sweeping generalizations. At the same time, it is necessary to try to gain some insights on Hong Kong's self-understanding of what it means to be a hospitable people and city. To do that, we examine three major components of Hong Kong identity mentioned earlier: a) Chinese tradition, b) Western colonialism, and c) local Hong Kong culture. Since it is beyond the scope of this book to go in-depth into each area, we focus on what each component has contributed to the ways that strangers are viewed and treated, especially those of other nationalities, cultures, races, and ethnicities. In terms of Chinese tradition, we look specifically at the influence of Confucianism on social relations in Chinese society. Concerning Western colonialism, we investigate how Hong Kong was impacted by the imposition of foreign rule and racial separation with the arrival of the British presence. Then we explore how the emergence of a local Hong Kong

5. Ibid.

culture has altered the concept of "home" and who is an insider and who is an outsider in the postcolonial era.

THE INFLUENCE OF CHINESE TRADITION

The teachings of the Chinese philosopher Confucius (551–479 BCE) and the Confucian tradition carried on by his followers such as Mencius (372–289 BCE) are among the greatest cultural influences in East Asia. While Buddhism, Taoism, and folk or popular religion are the major spiritual traditions of China, one can best understand social relations and the place of the stranger through the perspectives of Confucianism.

> [I]t is beyond dispute that Confucian ethical and spiritual values have served, for well over twenty-five hundred years, as the source of inspiration as well as the court of appeal for human interaction at all levels—between individuals, communities, and nations in the Sinic world.[6]

Ancient Chinese culture gave prominence to developing and maintaining harmonious social relationships. Confucian ethics are relational ethics that guide behavior and customs in the fabric of daily life in a practical way. To that end, Confucianism emphasizes moral cultivation of virtues that lead persons, families, and society into right thought and right action. The concept of *ren*, which could be translated as "humanity" or "benevolence," is central to Confucian ethics. Confucius is credited with transforming *ren* into a general virtue for every person, not a particular virtue obtainable only by a special few.[7] His follower Mencius further taught that human nature is innately good, and thus humans possess the knowledge of and the ability to do what is good. He says, "For a man to give full realization of his heart is for him to understand his own nature, and a man who knows his own nature will know Heaven" (VII.A.1).[8]

Confucianism teaches that the five foundational relationships (*wu lun*) were between the emperor and minister, the father and son, the husband and wife, the elder brother and younger brother, and between friends. In these dyads, the first four are hierarchical while the fifth of friend to friend is between equals. Each party occupies a set social role defined by clear and

---

6. Tu, "Confucianism," 147.
7. Wing-tsit Chan, *A Source Book in Chinese Philosophy*, 16.
8. *Mencius*, 287.

complementary obligations. It has been pointed out "that only one of the five is biological, that all are defined in moral terms, and that all are reciprocal."[9]

In Chinese society, the center of identity is the family rather than the individual. One has the greatest responsibility to those in one's immediate family circle or bloodline, beginning with one's parents. Filial piety (*xiao*) or honoring and caring for one's father and mother is a sacred duty. The next closest relations would be one's neighbors, colleagues, schoolmates, and those with whom there is familiarity through village, work, school, or other daily connections. The most distant group would be strangers (*mo sheng ren*) with whom one has no prior relationship and who are unfamiliar to one's current social circles. Yang describes this scheme as a particularistic rather than a universalistic relational orientation. That is, one relates to persons according to the particular or special relationship between them, rather than from a universal orientation with the same standard of behavior toward everyone.[10] In the Chinese way of thinking, the universalistic approach makes no sense morally and would result in social chaos. According to Mencius, to treat someone else's father exactly the same as one's own father or to treat an ordinary person exactly the same as one's ruler would be "to ignore one's father on the one hand, and one's prince on the other," making humans the same as animals.[11]

It is not that the Chinese had no concern or sense of responsibility to others outside their immediate circle of family and acquaintances. Certainly they did. The moral self-cultivation that guides the individual's heart and mind and that regulates one's family relationships should have positive impacts in ever-widening circles to the community, the country, the world, and beyond.[12] Mencius's illustration of human compassion (without hesitation or calculation) to save an unknown child who was about to fall into a well is often cited as an example of universal love and moral goodness. However, Confucian teaching about the subject from one's personal perspective in everyday circumstances is more prescribed.

> One loves [the common people], but to a lesser degree, and perhaps, in a different manner. In Confucius' terminology, one should be generous (*hui*) to the common people (V.16). This is in keeping with Confucius' general attitude towards obligations.

---

9. Chan, *A Source Book in Chinese Philosophy*, 70.
10. Yang, "Chinese Social Orientation," 22, 28–29.
11. *Mencius*, III.B.9.
12. Tu, "Confucianism," 143–44.

> Our obligation towards others should be in proportion to the benefit we have received from them.[13]

Put another way, while Confucianism teaches that love is universal, it also insists that there must be an order of distinction to determine which relationships should have priority in what could be characterized as "a graded love for people, not impartial concern for all."[14] This means that one would naturally care for family and friends ahead of complete strangers.

In terms of strangers, then, what should be one's response? Regarding the traditional five relations (*wu lun*), Chan comments

> It is often said that these do not include the stranger and the enemy. But to Confucianists, no one is unrelated, and therefore a stranger is inconceivable. He is at least related as older or younger. As to the enemy, there should never be such a person, for all people should be friends.[15]

This is of course an ideal depiction of harmonious human relations in the Chinese philosophical worldview. Strangers did exist in China, and the same as everywhere, they could just as easily become an enemy rather than a friend. Nonetheless, Confucianism continually affirms that ordinary humans can attain the moral goodness of a sage through the cultivation of *ren* (benevolence) and *yi* (righteousness), and the observance of *li* (ritual propriety). In this belief, Chan notes two important principles: "One is that every person can be perfect, and the other is that all people are basically equal."[16] That evil exists or failures occur is not due to fallen human nature, but rather due to the "underdevelopment of one's original endowment."[17]

The virtue of propriety (*li*) in relationships also regulates the hospitality extended by hosts to any guests. The Chinese word for "hospitality" is *hao ke*, meaning to treat a guest well or to enjoy having guests. An oft-quoted saying from Confucius's *Analects* reflects this pleasure: "Is it not a joy to have like-minded friends come from afar?" The Chinese character for "guest" 客 (*ke*) depicts an individual (各) under one's roof (宀), while the word for "host" 主人 (*zhu ren*) carries the meaning of master or ruler. The

---

13. D.C. Lau, "Introduction," in Confucius, *The Analects*, xix.
14. Joseph Chan, "Giving Priority to the Worst Off," 244.
15. Chan, *A Source Book in Chinese Philosophy*, 70.
16. Ibid., 56. "'Natural equality' of [humans] refers primarily to the fact that all [persons] are capable of cultivating their innate goodness. But society is also a hierarchy of superordinates and subordinates, and social harmony depends on the recognition of and the conformity to this hierarchy of statuses and roles." Thomas Wong, "The Ethos of the Hong Kong Chinese Revisited," 363.
17. Ibid., 55.

hierarchical nature of Chinese hospitality is not unlike that in other cultures. This distinction in roles was seen as natural with a reciprocal gesture of hospitality forthcoming in an ongoing relationship.[18]

Hierarchy, harmony, and humility are clearly demonstrated in Chinese hospitality in the hosting of meals, which were central to the practice. Here hosts and guests are given their rightful social place at lavish, carefully orchestrated feasts or banquets which also carry spiritual meaning. While Confucianism is not an organized religion per se, its thought and practice have a profound spiritual dimension. "A defining characteristic of Confucian humanism is faith in the creative transformation of our human condition as a communal act and as a dialogical response to Heaven," says Tu.[19] Through following prescribed rites, the sharing of food and drink become occasions to foster peace and solidarity in the family, community, and kingdom as well as order in the cosmos. In fact, when the rituals of hospitality are properly observed at all levels, it is believed that universal forces come into harmony to produce great blessings for everyone.[20] In the Sino-centric worldview of ancient China, the blessings naturally fell first upon one's nearest and dearest, yet the benefits could be enjoyed by many others, including strangers, as long as Chinese tradition and customs were respected.

Lee, however, argues that traditional Confucian ethics with its emphasis on hierarchical relationships of state and family fail to address the modern situation of strangers in China in an age of urbanization, migration, and globalization. As she puts it, how should one "relate to a person with whom you share no past and cannot foresee or desire a common future"?[21] She contrasts the coziness of kinship sociality with the barrenness of stranger sociality, noting that the rhetoric of "fictive kin" has been employed to incorporate strangers who cannot be avoided and to serve the political interests of the state in mainland China. Lee observes that Chinese sociality rooted in consanguinity and familiarity differs from sociality in European and South Asian societies, which have been heavily influenced by strong religious institutions that loosen the bonds of clan and land and thus alter the moral landscape.[22]

In the context of modern Hong Kong, it can be said that the city is living in a "post-Confucian sociopolitical society." King describes this as a mixture of indigenous values and Western influences, a kind of Confucianism which

18. Berling, *A Pilgrim in Chinese Culture*, 101–3.
19. Tu, "Confucianism," 142.
20. Koenig, "Hospitality," *The Encyclopedia of Religion*, 472–73.
21. Haiyan Lee, *The Stranger and the Chinese Moral Imagination*, 1.
22. Ibid., 1–7, 13–16.

he calls "*rationalistic traditionalism* . . . a transformed value orientation of Confucianism."[23] Values such as ancestor veneration, filial piety, frugality, and respect for teachers are maintained as part of the Chinese familistic ethos. However, King notes

> Hong Kong Chinese have an active self-awareness in the sense that they are capable cognitively of assessing the practical utility of the various elements of Chinese tradition for achieving their social and economic goals. Chinese traditions are not always cherished as something intrinsically sacred or good; instead, they are more often than not treated as cultural resources to be tapped and utilized according to instrumental considerations.[24]

Therefore, what one finds in Hong Kong is "social Confucianism" or "Confucianism of everyday life" with a set of beliefs and values widely accepted by the common person to guide social relations in the family and outside the family.[25] The stranger or foreigner has a place in the system, and that place in the twenty-first century is largely determined by the Hong Kong Chinese majority according to a combination of social, cultural, economic, and political factors.

THE IMPACT OF WESTERN COLONIALISM

While the Chinese majority in Hong Kong today largely decide the fate of strangers in their midst, the situation was quite the opposite during the colonial period which began around 1841. Even though British expatriates were vastly outnumbered by the several thousand original inhabitants as well as the millions who later poured in over the border from China, the colonial administration was firmly in charge. With the aim of establishing Hong Kong as an imperial outpost for trade rather than settlement, the British took over the running of the colony with "self confidence and racial arrogance that came with the power of empire."[26]

The segregation between the British and the Chinese in Hong Kong was typical of colonial hierarchies. Although many of the British who arrived in the early days were not from the upper classes, they were able to enjoy a high status and superior lifestyle afforded by their position in the colonial administration. The local Chinese community at that time were not

---

23. King, "The Transformation of Confucianism," 267.
24. Ibid., 275.
25. Ibid.
26. Steve Tsang, *A Modern History of Hong Kong*, 62.

from the upper classes either, being mostly ordinary farmers and fisherfolk. Those Chinese coming later to Hong Kong, however, saw opportunities for economic gain and a more stable life than what could be had in the mainland. Thus, even with an alien government in place, many sought refuge in Hong Kong with plans to return home when conditions improved.

Divided by language, culture, social class, and clout, the "colonizers" and the "colonized" lived separate existences. While there may have been daily contact in which the Chinese primarily served the needs of the colonial or European population, they did not live side-by-side. The separation was mental as well as physical, with each side believing its customs and culture to be superior to the other. Local Chinese preferred to go their own way and do things in their own way as far as possible, and they did so rather effectively. It could be said that both British and Chinese were satisfied to have as little as possible to do with each other as long as they could lawfully co-exist and prosper in peace.[27]

The strict segregation would give way to more mixing as Hong Kong's fortunes began to rise. As Hong Kong prospered economically, there emerged a wealthy upper class of Chinese engaged in trade and finance who gained a place in colonial society through business partnerships, China government connections, Western education, and charitable endeavors.[28] For the Chinese élite in Hong Kong, an English-language education was the first step up the social ladder followed by a career path in government service as interpreters, in business as local agents for foreign firms, in capitalist ventures as financiers and investors, and finally as appointed members of the colonial Legislative Council or advisory boards.[29] A small middle class arose as well alongside the bulk of the population who were laborers in the lower class grassroots level. Over time, most Hong Kong residents would enjoy some benefits from the increasing prosperity and largely benevolent colonial rule, especially with the remarkable economic recovery following the Second World War.

Lau argues that Hong Kong's colonial experience is atypical and unique in many respects. He describes it in the early 1980s as follows:

> Basically, Hong Kong is a society where political power is concentrated in the hands of a particular racial/ethnic group, where different ethnic groups share certain assumptions about the importance of economic goals, where accommodative attitudes hold in both groups, where cultural diversity is held within

---

27. Hayes, "Hong Kong: Tale of Two Cities," 4–7.
28. Tsang, *A Modern History of Hong Kong*, 64.
29. Smith, *Chinese Christians*, 139.

tolerable limits and prevented from spilling over into the political arena, where coercion is not the most important means to maintain social and political order, and where nationalist feelings do not loom large.[30]

In other words, according to Lau, racial discrimination and coercion were not significant factors in the Hong Kong colonial model over the past century and a half. Instead, the driving forces of economic prosperity and political stability are keys to the city's success—past, present, and future. And both the British and the Chinese were savvy enough not to mess with a winning formula.

While it is debatable whether this "winning formula" resulted in genuine social harmony, it is clear that the British colonial legacy played an important role in Hong Kong's current status as a global city. Among the most obvious benefits are the wide knowledge of English and the provision of a stable, secure environment for economic flourishing. Nonetheless, according to Tsang, the most significant contributions from British rule were not in the area of economic achievements, which he credits mostly to the Chinese community. Rather, he says

> [T]he most important inheritances the British passed on to the SAR are an independent judiciary and the rule of law. More than any other British legacies, they are not indigenous to the Chinese tradition and are fundamental for the protection and advancement of the rights and dignity of the individual.[31]

Indeed, the protection and advancement of individual rights and human dignity are crucial for the many strangers who continue to arrive in Hong Kong as well as for the ethnic communities that have been present for many generations.[32] From the beginning of the colonial era, Hong Kong was a multicultural society and has remained so ever since, aspiring to join the ranks of other world cities like London and New York as successful spaces of international hospitality. However, the negative experiences of racial minorities (i.e., persons of non-Chinese origin) residing in Hong

---

30. Siu-kai Lau, *Society and Politics in Hong Kong*, 9.

31. Tsang, *A Modern History of Hong Kong*, 274.

32. Other ethnic groups in early colonialism included a) the Eurasian community (typically with Western father and Chinese mother), b) a small, wealthy Parsee community (originally from Persia and settled in India) who were traders and merchants, c) the Indian community recruited by the British to serve in the police force, and d) the Portuguese community who had moved from neighboring Macau to work in government jobs or for foreign firms as clerks and translators. Lethbridge, "Caste, Class and Race in Hong Kong," 52–56.

Kong, whether permanently or temporarily, challenge the city's right to call itself a cosmopolitan society.

Lee says that it is a mistake to assume that the terms globalization and cosmopolitanism mean the same thing. In order to truly become "Asia's world city," Hong Kong must embrace a more genuine cosmopolitanism according to the well-known definition by Hannerz—"an orientation, a willingness to engage with the Other" which requires "a greater involvement with a plurality of contrasting cultures to some degree on their own terms."[33] Lee recognizes that Hong Kong was forced either to engage with the Other or to be viewed as an Other during colonial times, but the postcolonial era raises new issues. The overwhelming dominance of Chinese ethnicity and the Cantonese dialect in Hong Kong makes it difficult to achieve the diversity necessary to be fully cosmopolitan by Hannerz's definition. Yet, interestingly, Lee sees possibilities for a truly cosmopolitan metropolis through the development of genuine local culture. He says

> A strong sense of local cultural tradition can provide a cosmopolitan city with a base and character; otherwise it can only become a superficial hotchpotch. To me the cultural hybridity in a cosmopolitan context is neither 'generic' nor a 'melting pot' but a dynamic mixture of many cultural traditions, local as well as national. In this regard, New York and London are the prime examples. In China, so far none of the major cities is truly cosmopolitan . . .[34]

The quest for a local Hong Kong identity, which began in the mid-twentieth century, has acquired new urgency and vitality in the transition to 1997 and into the postcolonial period. We examine in the next section this phenomenon and its effects on the city's hospitality to strangers, including compatriots from mainland China and racial ethnic minorities.

THE EMERGENCE OF LOCAL HONG KONG CULTURE

The beginning of a distinct Hong Kong identity is often traced to the 1950s and 1960s. This was the period when the colonial government's policy on Chinese immigration began to tighten. Before that time, the border between mainland China and Hong Kong was quite porous, and residents on either side went back and forth with relative ease. The government accepted this

---

33. Hannerz, *Transnational Connections*, 103. Quoted in Leo Lee, "Postscript: Hong Kong," 507.

34. Lee, "Postscript: Hong Kong," 507–8.

freedom of movement as it was assumed that many Chinese would return to the mainland in due course. Besides, the immigrants were of the same ethnicity and able to assimilate into Hong Kong without much problem. Still, there was not yet a large settled Chinese population that considered Hong Kong as their permanent place of residence. That would change as political events over the border led to repeated flows of immigrants seeking safety and stability in the British colony.[35]

Ku persuasively argues that the emergence of a local identity can be understood through the series of immigration measures imposed by the colonial government to protect its own national interests, to address international concerns, and to pacify Hong Kong residents. The shift from the self-professed humanitarian gesture to assist Chinese refugees in the 1950s to a hard-line policy of zero tolerance toward "illegal Chinese immigrants" by the 1980s reflects what Ku calls the politics of local belonging. That is, the birth of a "Hong Kong people" was the result of the British government's decision to control the quantity *and* quality of the Crown colony's residents.

The issue was framed in terms of solving what the government deemed was "the problem of people."[36] It would require successive measures for control, restriction, and planning. The first was the use of the term "settled residence" in the 1960s to designate those who had taken Hong Kong as their permanent home and those who had not. Next was the introduction of the legal category "Hong Kong belonger" in 1971 to distinguish those who had the right to land and reside in the territory from those who did not. Then with the local economy taking off in the late 1970s, the reach-base policy that had allowed any Chinese immigrant who reached the urban areas to stay was abolished in 1980. Thereafter all Chinese arrivals without legal papers could be immediately deported as illegal immigrants.[37]

Ku points out how the Hong Kong identity that was shaped by changing immigration policies was as notable for those that it excluded as much as it was for those that it included. For example, the policy of integration of Chinese immigrants in the 1950s and 1960s was also a means of blurring the difference between refugees and ordinary residents. The British

---

35. "From its earliest colonial days, Hong Kong served as a haven for Chinese refugees: during the Taiping Rebellion (1851–1864), after the republican revolution of 1911 and throughout the turbulent 1920s, after the outbreak of the Sino-Japanese War in 1937, and after the Communist Revolution of 1949." Carroll, *A Concise History of Hong Kong*, 2.

36. "Simply put, the problem was about the consequences of excess population on finance, housing, education, medical services, social welfare, industry, commerce and even political relations and law." Mark, "The 'Problem of People,'" 1146.

37. Ku, "Immigration Policies," 326–60.

government would not need to be entangled in the politics of international refugee resettlement if it could be determined that those coming to Hong Kong in fact wished to make this their home among people they considered to be their own. And while the 1971 category of "Hong Kong belonger" was generally viewed as a positive development, it actually resulted from British nationality acts that in effect denied Hong Kongers the right to live in the United Kingdom.[38] Then, in the late 1970s as Chinese arrivals were increasingly depicted as threats to the quality of life of Hong Kong people, a clear dividing line was drawn between "us" and "them." Colonial Governor MacLehose likely expressed the sentiments of many Hong Kong residents as well as the government's when he said

> Far from being welcomed by our people, the illegal immigrants are now more and more resented as they are seen to be eroding the improvement in standards that the people of Hong Kong have worked so hard to achieve . . . [T]he people of Hong Kong were so alive to the danger that traditional hospitality was creating, that they had to come to accept that it must be abandoned despite the personal trouble and inconvenience entailed.[39]

The traditional hospitality extended by Hong Kong to Chinese immigrants indeed was abandoned as even those who currently arrive with legal status as family dependents, tourists, or investors carry the label of new arrivals, mainlanders, or some derogatory names. Whether habitually poor or nouveau rich, those Chinese coming from outside Hong Kong have frequently been regarded as invaders who neither fit in with nor appreciate what is special about the city—its history, its people, its language and culture, and its success. These special aspects have become all the more precious to Hong Kongers in the postcolonial era as they seek to preserve what makes them different from every other city in China. Thus, resentment is aroused toward those who appear to be exploiting Hong Kong's freedoms and prosperity for their own selfish gain. This is, of course, an oversimplification of the situation as there are great differences between new arrivals from rural China who struggle to find housing, jobs, and schools for their family on the one hand and wealthy mainland Chinese who circulate among Hong Kong's business and political élites on the other hand.

A 2013 government study on new arrivals from mainland China conducted by Policy 21 Limited found that less than 10 percent of the adult new arrivals believed they would be successful in Hong Kong. Financial

38. Ibid., 336–39, 342–44.
39. Hong Kong Government, *Hong Kong Hansard*, 9–10. Quoted in Ku, "Immigration Policies," 350–51.

burden was the top problem for males, while poor living environment was the biggest problem for females. More than 50 percent reported experiencing discrimination in daily life, with another 20 percent indicating sometimes or frequently encountering discrimination. An alarming 17 percent of adult new arrivals had no friends in Hong Kong even after living in the city for more than nine months, while 30 percent had one to three friends.[40] The study lists negative stereotypes of new arrivals prevalent in Hong Kong: "They are being discriminated against and condemned as being the cause of Hong Kong's social and economic problems and are often stigmatized as being poorly educated, impolite, and greedy; having poor personal hygiene; and being unable to tune into Hong Kong . . . "[41] While the government and numerous social service agencies run programs to assist new arrivals, the study makes a cogent point that immigrants should not be the only ones expected to make changes to fit into Hong Kong life. Successful integration is a two-way process that involves effort and change by the receiving community too. The positive outcome is a society that is strong economically and socially and culturally inclusive. But the report warns

> Hong Kong has a history of comparatively successful integration, but the past may not be an entirely reliable guide to the future. The knowledge-based economy and increasingly hostile attitude of locals to new arrivals have changed the situation in Hong Kong in ways that might affect the integration of current and future new arrivals . . . [I]t becomes apparent that Hong Kong's [immigration] policies [during the past three decades] have been characterized by reactive, short-sighted measures with an emphasis on control . . . One of Hong Kong's biggest tests in the years to come will be how it manages immigration and integration.[42]

If new arrivals and mainlanders with Chinese ethnicity are regarded as outsiders in Hong Kong, then what about the racial ethnic minorities in the city? How have they been impacted by the retrocession to Chinese sovereignty? According to Erni, the situation for local racial ethnics on the whole is even more dire than before. With the focus of identity politics on "Hong Kong Chineseness" whether at the local, national, or global level, he asks why racial minorities have been completely left out of the picture and

---

40. Hong Kong SAR Government Central Policy Unit, "A Study on New Arrivals," 3–5.

41. Ibid., 25.

42. Ibid., 105.

forced to fend for themselves. Drawing on the stranger theories of Simmel and Karakayali,[43] Erni analyzes the Hong Kong situation as follows:

> As for the non-European immigrants and sojourners coming into or passing through Hong Kong, they are by a majority South and Southeast Asians, such as Filipinos, Indians, Pakistanis, Indonesians, Nepalese, and Thai . . . They can be circumscribed within Simmel's framework of strangers in mixed and varied ways, for some of these dark-skinned Asians have been in relatively favorable positions as traders, interpreters, judges, and teachers . . . while others have been largely abandoned strangers trapped in a socially isolated, sub-economic existence.[44]

Given that a large proportion of South and Southeast Asians in Hong Kong are in the "abandoned" group, he argues that it is "of paramount importance to *reimagine* the city anew as a particular space of encountering strangers by actively theorizing the problems of race and ethnicity, everyday racism, and ethnocentric forms and practices of 'the local.'"[45]

As is, if the city's ethnic groups are viewed as a pyramid in terms of citizenship rights and social status, says Sautman, Hong Kong Chinese (particularly Cantonese speakers) are at the top; new arrivals from mainland China, East Asians, and Westerners are the next level down; South Asians below that; and Southeast Asian domestic workers at the very bottom. This ethnic hierarchy not only reflects disdain for the racial other as inferior but even more seriously involves an exclusion from political power and social rights.[46] Law and Lee point out that reported incidents of racial discrimination and social exclusion toward ethnic minorities in Hong Kong have been on the rise since the 1997 handover in basic areas such as employment, housing, education, social services, and government services (including law enforcement).[47] Although the Hong Kong Government enacted the Race Discrimination Ordinance in 2008 (after lobbying from local NGOs and criticism from international bodies such as the United Nations Human Rights Committee), over 30 percent of ethnic minorities expressed little confidence in the Ordinance's effectiveness.[48] To tackle this unjust situation, Law and Lee recommend a combination of changes in: a) government policy to help integrate ethnic minorities into the Hong Kong mainstream,

43. Simmel, "The Stranger," 143–49; Karakayali, "The Uses of the Stranger," 312–30.
44. Erni, "Who Needs Strangers?," 81.
45. Ibid., 79.
46. Sautman, "Hong Kong as a Semi-Ethnocracy," 116.
47. Law and Lee, "Socio-Political Embeddings," 998–99.
48. Ibid., 985.

b) societal reception in which Hong Kong Chinese acknowledge their own prejudicial attitudes and also the contributions of ethnic minorities to the good of society, and c) co-ethnic community practices whereby different ethnic sub-communities unite to fight discrimination in a pan-South-Asian movement.[49]

It remains to be seen whether the Hong Kong Chinese, who comprise the majority, are willing or able to make the changes that would improve the livelihood and well-being of a small minority who remain strangers in the wider society. Whether it be policies on ethnic minorities, new arrivals from the mainland, or foreign domestic workers, the support and goodwill from the local Chinese population are critical to lasting solutions to societal harmony. Hong Kong has historically thrived on its openness as a "space of flow" for people, funds, goods, communication, ideas, and cultural practices.[50] The issue of hospitality in postcolonial Hong Kong raises the same hard questions posed by Pun and Wu that must be addressed to avoid a looming social crisis: *Whose city is it? Who has the right to stay in Hong Kong? And for whom does the city develop?*[51]

THE HONG KONG CHURCH AND HOSPITALITY

Introduction to the Hong Kong church

The presence of Christianity in Hong Kong is the legacy of Western missionary endeavors that accompanied the arrival of British colonialism. Before the British army landed in January 1841, there were no Christians among the 5,450 residents, who all were following various Chinese religions.[52] Western missionaries, many who had been working in Chinese communities in Southeast Asia and Macau, came to Hong Kong soon after the British arrival. Some were eagerly waiting to enter mainland China after the Treaty of Nanking of 1842, which opened five ports for foreign residence and ceded Hong Kong Island to the British. Among the nineteenth century Protestant missionaries who settled in Hong Kong were those from the Baptist Mission (1842), London Missionary Society (1843), Anglican Church (1843), Basel Missionary Society (1847), Rhenish Missionary Society (1847), Wesleyan Methodists (1851), and the American Congregational Church (1883).[53]

49. Ibid., 1005.
50. Sinn, "Lessons in Openness," 13–43.
51. Pun and Wu, "Lived Citizenship," 128.
52. Lo, "Taiwan, Hong Kong, Macau," 185.
53. Smith, *Chinese Christians*, 2–7.

The Anglican Cathedral of St. John the Evangelist was erected in 1849 to host an English congregation.

The Roman Catholic Church in Hong Kong was established in April 1841 as a prefecture apostolic, or missionary area, initially to provide spiritual care for British soldiers (Irish Catholic) stationed in the new colony. In 1843, the blessing of the first Catholic church in Hong Kong took place on Wellington Street. Catholic priests and sisters from Spain, Switzerland, Italy, and France were among the earliest mission workers in the territory. Organizations represented included the Franciscans, Paris Foreign Missions Society, St. Paul de Chartres Sisters, Milan Mission Seminary (later PIME), Canossian Sisters, Dominican Fathers, St. Vincent de Paul Society, and La Salle Christian Brothers.[54]

While the early missionaries may have had misgivings about the events that brought them to Hong Kong, they nonetheless used the opportunity to further the spread of Christianity in China. Kwong observes

> Despite the fact that they deplored the Opium War and doubted the wisdom of the Treaty of Nanking, the missionaries believed it was by divine providence that China was forced to open herself up to the Gospel. They were prepared to take advantage of the privileges accorded to traders in the treaty to advance their work. As a result, the territorial boundary for Christian mission was extended to the whole of China. The notion that Hong Kong was part of this vast mission field became apparent and its Church was part of the Church in China.[55]

Hong Kong was regarded as a safe haven for missionaries going to and from China, a stepping stone for missionary activity in the mainland. At the same time, the colony was seen as a place where mission work could be carried out among the local population. Both Catholic and Protestant missionaries soon dedicated themselves not only to evangelical work in building churches and seminaries in Hong Kong, but also to the establishment of schools, hospitals, and social welfare work to serve the pressing needs of residents.

The ultimate goal of the foreign missionary endeavors was to convert Hong Kong natives as part of the establishment of a strong Chinese

---

54. Hong Kong Catholic Church, *Hong Kong Catholic Church Directory 2015*, 622–23.

55. Kwong, *Identity in Community*, 83. See also Neill, *A History of Christian Missions*, 282. Neill comments, "This manifestation of western aggressiveness was bitterly resented at the time by the Chinese, and the feelings which it aroused have never quite died away. That Christian work seemed so plainly to enter in the wake of gunboats and artillery was to be a permanent handicap to it in China" (282–83).

Christian church. This goal was met despite the fact that churches in mainland China were cut off from their sister churches in Hong Kong after the Communist government came to power in 1949. Since contact with Christians in China came to a halt, denominations and church bodies were forced to establish independent bases in Hong Kong, for the political divide made it next to impossible to continue their structural unity.[56] Nonetheless, if current statistics are a reliable indicator, a strong Chinese Christian church did take root in Hong Kong. As of 2015, there were over 800,000 Christians in the city, roughly 10 percent of the population. Protestants churches had 500,000 members in their 1,500 Protestant congregations (representing seventy denominations), while the fifty-one Roman Catholic parishes in the Diocese of Hong Kong had 374,000 members.[57] Major Protestant denominations include Baptist, Christian and Missionary Alliance, Church of Christ in China (Presbyterian/Congregational), Evangelical Free, Lutheran, Methodist, Tsung Tsin Mission, Pentecostal, Anglican, and the Salvation Army, along with independent churches as well as indigenous ones such as the True Jesus Church and the Little Flock.[58] Additionally, there are three Orthodox Christian churches in the city, recorded to have a few hundred members attending worship.[59] Currently, more than 450 missionaries from Hong Kong are serving in foreign countries. Other world faiths present in Hong Kong include Buddhism, Taoism, Confucianism, Islam, Hinduism, Sikhism, and Judaism. After the city's retrocession to Chinese sovereignty in 1997, Hong Kong's religious freedom as a fundamental right is protected by the Basic Law and other relevant legislation.[60]

Although Christians are a minority in Hong Kong, their influence is widely felt in the society through their work in education and social welfare.

---

56. Kwong gives examples from the history of the Chinese Anglican Church and the Church of Christ in China. *Identity in Community*, 83–85. For a concise overview of the development of Christianity in China, see Ying, "Mainland China," 149–70.

57. Hong Kong SAR Government Information Services, *Hong Kong 2015*, "Religion and Custom." It should be noted that church membership statistics in the Hong Kong Government fact sheet are based on self-reporting by church bodies such as the Hong Kong Christian Council and the Hong Kong Catholic Diocese. The *Report on 2014 Hong Kong Church Survey* conducted by Hong Kong Church Renewal Movement (HKCRM) listed official membership of Protestant churches as 560,547, with 327,112 present in Hong Kong and 305,097 on average in weekly worship (Hong Kong Church Renewal Movement, *Report on 2014 Hong Kong Church Survey*, 25).

58. Ibid.

59. St. Luke's Orthodox Cathedral (Greek), St. Thomas Coptic Orthodox Church, and SS. Peter & Paul Parish (Russian Orthodox).

60. Hong Kong SAR Government Information Services, *Hong Kong 2015*, "Religion and Custom."

As one of the city's largest sponsors of schools (from kindergarten to post-secondary), hospitals, and social services, the church has involved itself in humanitarian and charity endeavors throughout its history in Hong Kong. In the past, this was carried out with financial support from the British colonial government and overseas Western churches. Most of the funding is now provided by the Hong Kong SAR Government. Prior to the switch in funding, this social ministry of the churches was especially critical during the post-war years in the 1940s and 1950s. During this time, Hong Kong sought to recover from the Japanese occupation (1941–1945) and to cope with the waves of Chinese refugees crossing into Hong Kong during periods of unrest in mainland China, especially after 1949. With the expulsion of all foreign missionaries from China soon after the Communist takeover, many of these missionaries relocated to Hong Kong and were involved in the church's outreach to the grassroots people by providing medical, housing, and educational services.

Besides carrying out evangelical work and social ministry, the church in Hong Kong advocated for social justice on various issues according to the most pressing needs of the time. Among the public concerns were hygiene (1894), sale of opium (early twentieth century), female child-servants or *mui-tsai* (1921–1938), Chinese refugees (1950s and 1960s), workers' rights and trade unions (late 1960s), Vietnamese refugees (1970s to 1980s), and political reform and democracy (from 1980s onwards).[61] While this advocacy comprised a significant part of the Christian witness in Hong Kong, the church was silent about social concern during some periods, such as during the Japanese occupation in World War II and the early years of the Chinese refugee influx in the 1950s. The relationship between church and state in Hong Kong which began under British colonialism continues to evolve post-1997 in the Hong Kong Special Administrative Region. Lo concludes, "Christians and the churches of Hong Kong have developed their own pattern of social concern in response to different situations at different critical times."[62]

---

61. Lo, "Taiwan, Hong Kong, Macau," 188–89. See Smith, *A Sense of History*, 240–65, 276–82.

62. Ibid., 189. For other perspectives on Christian participation in social movements, see Ka-wai Chan, "Hong Kong's Protestant Social Movement," 109–16; Yuen, "Hong Kong Catholics' Recent Participation in Social Movements," 117–32; Leung and Chan, *Changing Church and State Relations*.

Hospitality as mission in the Hong Kong church

While the Hong Kong church in the twenty-first century is clearly a Chinese church in terms of membership, language, leadership, and support, there has never been a time when it was not required to deal with strangers. From its beginning with the arrival of Western missionaries, it could be characterized as a "church of the strangers" that both sought welcome and offered welcome in the name of religion.[63] Of course, among the earliest tasks of the church was the spiritual care of European residents and soldiers. However, as the mission expanded to include the indigenous population, Chinese Christians at times found themselves strangers in their own community. This situation was partly due to the Western English education they received in the church's mission schools. While this training prepared them to act as middlemen between the British and Chinese for government, trade, and evangelistic purposes, the results of their educational efforts were not what they had planned. "They created a man who stood between two cultures," says Smith, "a man who was not altogether at home in either. He was not wholly in the Chinese model, nor was he altogether Western."[64]

The opportunities afforded to those who took advantage of Western-style education and subsequently converted to Christianity created an élite class among the Hong Kong Chinese. They were seen by the British government as superior to the rest of the local population and were given special privileges such as lighter punishment for criminal infractions and burial rights in the Colonial Cemetery. Smith points out, "This reinforced their marginality and made it easier for them to become Anglo-Chinese."[65] More distance was created between the Chinese Christians and the community as the church required converts to break with some traditional Chinese family practices such as ancestor veneration, concubinage, and women's subservient position; but in the atypical setting of colonial Hong Kong, the society responded to these changes with typical Chinese pragmatism.[66]

As the Christian church grew in numbers and influence in Hong Kong, it realized its calling to welcome and care for the many strangers who continued to immigrate into the territory. With a dual mission of evangelism and service, the church has offered hospitality to various marginalized or disadvantaged groups over the years. These include refugees and asylum seekers, migrant workers from the Philippines, Indonesia, and other Asian

---

63. For contemporary theological perspectives on the role of the missionary as guest and stranger, see Brandner, "Hosts and Guests," 94–102.

64. Smith, *Chinese Christians*, 10.

65. Ibid., 188.

66. Ibid., 195–209.

countries, and new arrival families from mainland China. Nonetheless, Christians are not the only ones to reach out to newcomers and outsiders. Other religions also express concern through spiritual and practical care, especially to those of the same faith. Still, given the church's Western missionary roots and its unavoidable association with British colonial history, Christianity in Hong Kong has perhaps the most multinational, multicultural representation among the religions in the city. While the vast majority of Christian churches use Chinese language (predominantly Cantonese but also Putonghua and other dialects) as the medium of communication, other languages such as English, Tagalog, Korean, French, German, Spanish, Japanese, Indonesian, Thai, and Nepalese are used in other services or congregations. The partnership of Hong Kong Chinese Christians with non-Chinese or "international" Christians in mission is carried out not only with overseas churches or mission boards but also at the local level. International or non-Chinese congregations in Hong Kong possess a particular ministry of hospitality which could be viewed as a noteworthy example of the biblical motif of strangers welcoming strangers. We now turn to the ministry of international congregations for our final discussion.

International congregations and the ministry of hospitality

The term "international congregation" can have multiple meanings. In this book, the following definition is operative: "a multi-cultured, multi-denominational fellowship of expatriate people who are united in Christian belief and who share an identity as foreigners with a common language distinct from the majority in the host country."[67]

The word "international" as used here has a specific meaning to describe those who are expatriates in the context of Hong Kong and who use another language besides or in addition to Chinese for communication in the city. Even if the majority of the congregation members come from the same foreign country, the congregation would still be considered an "international church" because the membership is assumed to be predominantly expatriates, though it often includes some local Hong Kong Chinese who for various reasons choose to worship in a non-Chinese-speaking church. The terms international congregation and international church are used interchangeably as they have similar meaning in Protestant ecclesiology. It must be acknowledged, however, that worldwide Christian bodies and denominations call their church "international" because of global membership and

67. Based on definitions from Pederson, *Expatriate Ministry*, 33, and Klassen, "Exploring the Missional Potential of International Churches," 1.

activity. Thus, the use of the terms international congregation and international church here will be used to refer to individual non-Chinese-speaking local congregations.

By virtue of their most obvious role "to take care of the foreigners" in Hong Kong, international congregations deal daily with a multinational, multicultural population of diverse social backgrounds and needs. This includes groups as varied as expatriate professionals, Filipino domestic workers, African asylum seekers, Nepalese descendants of Gurkhas, and Hong Kong citizens returning from years of work or study overseas. By extending Christian hospitality to these strangers and aliens who may find themselves outside the mainstream of Hong Kong society, international congregations are actively engaged in evangelism, social ministry, justice concerns, and church growth. Though they comprise a small percentage of Hong Kong's churches, they reveal alternative perspectives for a contextualized mission through their ministry to people in transition.

In a comprehensive study of international churches around the world, Pederson's 1999 book *Expatriate Ministry: Inside the Church of the Outsiders* makes two important contributions to understanding the missional nature of international congregations. First, he states that the sociological basis of the international congregation is a movement of people who qualify in missiological terms as a "people movement" due to their distinct status as foreigners in the dominant culture and their use of a common language, e.g., English.[68] He defends his use of McGavran's "homogeneous principle"[69] in this setting, noting that expatriates are not unlike Christians in the early church of the Roman Empire who were "drawn into one homogeneous unit by a force far greater than race, nationality, or family ties. They were foreigners, living far away from their native home."[70] Thus, international churches have significant missional value in evangelizing expatriates as a people movement, especially in major cities around the world.

Secondly, Pederson observes that most international churches face a dual tension concerning identity and mission. Is their role primarily to be an oasis for expatriates in a foreign environment or do they have a wider mission in their host country? Pederson argues that the mission of international churches must go beyond being an oasis. In fact, he believes that they can be potential launching pads for evangelization of the local population ("indigenous community"). He builds his case on the missionary ministry of St. Paul, who was an expatriate himself, having come from Tarsus, and on

---

68. Pederson, *Expatriate Ministry*, 33, 35; See McGavran, *The Bridges of God*, 8–13.
69. McGavran, *Understanding Church Growth*, 69–71.
70. Pederson, *Expatriate Ministry*, 59.

the establishment of an "international congregation" at Antioch composed of Jewish Christians in the Diaspora and of Gentile converts.⁷¹

While there may be some validity in viewing expatriates as a variation of a missiological "people movement," it is questionable whether the primary mission of international congregations is to serve as launching pads for evangelizing local citizens of the host country. Nonetheless, the rich missional potential of Christian hospitality as the gift of international congregations involves more than simply being an oasis for lonely foreigners. Church bodies such as the National Council of Churches USA and the Evangelical Lutheran Church in America have recognized the role of international congregations as companions in mission with indigenous churches in the countries where they are located. Art Bauer, who for many years headed the National Council of Churches USA's unit relating to expatriate American congregations, encouraged international congregations to "seek ways of connecting to local churches, of witnessing to an inter-cultural reality, of being part of a trans-cultural faith."⁷² In agreement with this sentiment, international congregations in Hong Kong are generally eager to be companions in mission with Chinese churches, seeking ways to transcend the language and cultural differences to witness together for Jesus Christ in the city, as part of the nation, and across the region.

CONCLUSION

Hong Kong's long history with strangers reveals a dynamic, ambiguous relationship with the many outsiders and foreigners who arrived on its shores, whether by water, land, or air. Traditionally a haven for those seeking refuge during times of conflict in mainland China, the city demonstrated a remarkable capacity to absorb newcomers and adapt to ever-changing circumstances. With an ethnic composition that has always been predominantly Chinese in number and character, Hong Kong opened or was forced to open its doors to strangers from every corner of the globe for the sake of diplomacy, trade, labor, economic growth, humanitarian causes, or sheer survival. The century-and-a half of British colonial rule set Hong Kong on a path that would distinguish it from every other city in China, for better or worse. While protected from some of the worst political calamities that befell their compatriots in the mainland, Hong Kong wrestled with its colonial past, transitioned to the postcolonial present, and continues to negotiate for a brighter future under Chinese sovereignty. Its current status as a global

71. Ibid., 13–22, 63–66.
72. Ibid., 61.

city is undeniable; its claim to be a truly cosmopolitan one is challenged due to claims of racism and discrimination against ethnic minorities and non-Hong Kong Chinese.

Welcoming the stranger has also been a vital part of the Hong Kong church's mission and ministry of hospitality, even if the earliest episodes involved colonialists looking after their own people or Christian missionaries arriving in the colony as strangers themselves. As part of the spoils extracted from China in the Treaty of Nanking, Hong Kong was viewed by the church as a providential gateway to the mainland as well as a protected port for church workers traveling to and from China. Roman Catholic mission orders and Protestant mission agencies of all backgrounds eventually founded local churches and established schools, social welfare organizations, and hospitals that were sorely lacking in Hong Kong. While Christians are still a minority in the HKSAR at little more than 10 percent of the population, the church's historic influence continues as it still provides educational, social, and medical services to a large segment of the Hong Kong public, in partnership with the government. Outreach in evangelism and charitable endeavors put Christians in direct contact with strangers, more recently with a fresh group of asylum seekers, foreign domestic workers, and new arrivals from mainland China. As part of the worldwide body of Christ, churches in Hong Kong maintain their global connections through official and unofficial church channels, mission work in other countries, and the presence of international congregations made up of Christians from many nationalities and cultures who have made Hong Kong their home.

Chapter 6

Refugees and Asylum Seekers
The Hong Kong Situation

As we have seen, Hong Kong is no stranger to refugee and asylum seeker issues. The history of Hong Kong is also a history of different waves of refugees, and the church has consistently been a part of those who offered service and care. While the focus of this book is refugee and asylum seeker ministry from 2000 to 2014, an understanding of the background of earlier refugee influxes provides us with a context in which to place the situation of the more recent arrivals. The sections on Chinese refugees (1945–1954) and Vietnamese refugees (1975–2000) are brief by comparison since there is already ample research published on both groups. We outline the general situation of the earlier periods followed by a description of the Christian response. After that synopsis, we devote the bulk of the chapter to the current group of refugees and asylum seekers in Hong Kong. We look at who they are, what happened to them, what changed over the years, and how Hong Kong responded. As we shall discover, this latest group of strangers faced many of the same challenges that persons seeking asylum did in the past. Yet, in other ways, they were confronted with special challenges upon arriving after the close of the Vietnamese refugee saga and during the postcolonial era of Hong Kong.

REFUGEES FROM CHINA (1945–1954)

During times of unrest in mainland China, refugees came back and forth to Hong Kong, which had been under British colonial rule since the mid-nineteenth century. Many residents today were refugees or children of refugees who fled mainland China either in the period after World War II (1945–1947) or following the civil unrest after the Communist takeover in 1949. Hundreds of thousands of people from the mainland entered Hong Kong between 1949 and the spring of 1950. According to a survey mission report by the United Nations in 1954, almost 30 percent of Hong Kong's population at the time could be broadly classified as refugees.[1]

However, the British government did not view these new arrivals as refugees. Many were expected to return to the mainland when conditions stabilized across the border. They were able to move about freely and integrate into Hong Kong society without much discrimination among the indigenous poor in the colony. In the global political arena, though, the situation was much more complex. The UK recognized the People's Republic of China as the official government of China, while the United Nations recognized the Republic of China government in Taiwan until 1971. The refugees were nominally protected by the Taiwan Nationalist government; however, to recognize them as refugees under the UN Convention might strain British diplomatic relations with the People's Republic of China. Thus, the Chinese refugee situation in Hong Kong was a multifaceted political matter involving the foreign relations and immigration policies of the governments of Hong Kong, UK, China, Taiwan, and even the USA, each hoping to gain political advantage from the crisis.[2]

The population of Hong Kong, which due to the war had fallen to 600,000 by August 1945, rose to 1.8 million by 1947, and grew to 2.2 million by the mid-1950s. Approximately 885,000 people immigrated to Hong Kong from China between August 1945 and June 1954. Of this number, 667,000 were designated as refugees who were not willing to return to the mainland due to political reasons.[3] In light of serious problems with overcrowding and the lack of social services to match the increased population,

---

1. United Nations High Commissioner for Refugees, *The State of the World's Refugees 2000*, 33.

2. Gatrell, *Free World?*, 59. For an extended discussion on the international politics of the Chinese refugee situation, see Mark, "The 'Problem of People,'" 1145–81. USA intervention in the Hong Kong refugee crisis was due to the fact that the American government recognized the Republic of China as the official government of China until 1979.

3. Hambro, *The Problem of Chinese Refugees*, 27.

the British consulted with the Beijing government in efforts to control the number of mainland Chinese entering Hong Kong. To solve the humanitarian and political crises, the colonial government implemented immigration control measures and eventually allowed refugees and other illegal entrants to settle permanently in Hong Kong. Nevertheless, the "problem of people," as the Hong Kong government labeled the situation, demanded action in a concerted effort to provide housing, employment, social welfare, education, and medical care for the huge numbers who were living in poverty or destitution.

Christian response

With the Hong Kong government, the Republic of China government based in Taiwan, and the United Nations taking the lead in Chinese refugee relief work, there were also a number of private groups, including Catholic and Protestant organizations, which made significant contributions. Among the church bodies were the National Catholic Welfare Conference (USA), Lutheran World Refugee Service, World Council of Churches, Catholic Relief Service, and Church World Service, all working in partnership with various missionary societies, local parishes, and congregations. Their services included free medical care, clothing, food parcels, milk powder, and the setting up of roof-top schools and recreation centers, as well as visitation for psychological and educational support. Housing needs were tackled in a combined effort between churches and the government to build thousands of cement or stone cottages. These low-cost homes were given rent-free and could also be used for cottage industries. The Methodist Church, among others, partnered with the Resettlement Department to build factories, schools, and social welfare centers while a number of church bodies sponsored handicraft workshops to produce refugee-made goods sold abroad to earn income.[4]

Refugees were not the only beneficiaries of church and government relief work. "The position of the government has always been that the indigenous poor and the refugees are not to be distinguished but are to be considered as the same social problem," notes Yueh.[5] Churches followed this principle as well, giving aid and support without discrimination to whoever was most in need.

---

4. Donders, "The Forced Migration," 266–71; Ying, *Yuan ni de guo jianglin*, 155–59; Yiu-chung Wong, "The Policies of the Hong Kong Government," 182–83.

5. Yueh, "The Problem of the Hong Kong Refugees," 32.

For churches, relief work involved an added happy task of welcoming newcomers to the Christian faith. R. Donders, a Catholic missionary, assessed the situation in relation to refugee converts to the Catholic Church in Hong Kong. She reported the situation as follows:

> The bulk of the new converts come from the refugee people, but not, as might be supposed, from the most destitute, the most hopeless, the most unlettered amongst them. Torn from their old life, moved to deep questioning by their own suffering, and by the suffering of those around them, struck by the practical and all-embracing charity of the Church, and by her sure, untroubled and fearless stand in the face of persecution and death, moved by the Grace of God, always seemingly more visible at times such as this, they come in their hundreds, people of every age and social standing, to find a home in the Catholic Church.[6]

Undeniably, other churches in Hong Kong had similar experiences of refugees converting to Christianity and joining their fellowship through the sacrificial witness and service of its members. Ralph Lee, a minister and past president of the Methodist Church Hong Kong, arrived in the city with his family as refugees in 1949. He recalls how churches from overseas poured themselves out day after day to meet the daily needs of refugees in Hong Kong. Their service was a self-giving of kindness and charity, coming from their hearts and minds with no strings attached. Reflecting on the possibility that some joined the church in order to get material goods, he says

> Although many who came to the church were called 'rice Christians,' but among so many, it would be unavoidable. I would think many were touched by the good deeds of the church and also, a church that opened its door for the needy. Fifty years later now, I have met many of the second generation of early Christians (Methodist), always they are grateful for the faith that has built them up to what they are today.[7]

Donders's lyrical description and Lee's more straightforward testimony bring to mind the descriptions of converts to the church in the first centuries seeking care, community, and meaning during chaotic times in the Roman Empire. Undoubtedly, the church grew in numbers and vitality in both eras through the service that was rendered and the new members who were welcomed.

---

6. Donders, "The Forced Migration," 270.
7. Ralph Lee, email correspondence to the author, February 28, 2015.

REFUGEES FROM VIETNAM (1975-2000)

More recently, from 1975 to 1998, Hong Kong was a port of first asylum for Vietnamese refugees, receiving more than 200,000 people from Vietnam during the period. Vietnam's waves of refugee outflow occurred due to political and socio-economic changes in the country following the communist victory over South Vietnam in 1975, the Sino-Vietnamese war in 1979, and the exit of economic migrants in the late 1980s. Eventually, 143,000 refugees in Hong Kong were settled in other countries, 72,000 were repatriated to Vietnam, and 1,400 were allowed to remain in the city.[8]

Given the desperate situation of the huge numbers of refugees and asylum seekers from Vietnam, the Hong Kong government mobilized resources from every department and sector of society as well as from overseas. Personnel from social welfare, the medical professions, and uniformed services were deployed. The United Nations High Commissioner for Refugees was asked to provide more material aid and to speed up the refugee resettlement process. International and local NGOs and charities donated funds and supplies and rendered essential aid, working hand-in-hand with countless volunteers. Among the many agencies and organizations that were active on behalf of the Vietnamese refugees were the International Social Service (ISS), the British Red Cross, Community and Family Services International, Caritas-Hong Kong, and Save the Children Fund.[9]

For the first few years of the Vietnamese refugee crisis, the response from the Hong Kong government and public was largely one of humanitarian concern and sympathy. Many of the early arrivals from Vietnam were ethnic Chinese who reportedly had been pushed out by the Vietnamese government. Their refugee status generally was not questioned, and Western countries such as USA, Canada, Australia, and UK were willing to accept refugees for resettlement. However, the number of new arrivals continued to swell in Hong Kong, reaching a peak of 68,748 in 1979.[10] Evidence of a lucrative black market trade in selling passage out of Vietnam and into ports of first asylum added to the dilemma.

Refugees were initially housed in open centers which allowed them to move freely around Hong Kong and to take up employment. This practice was overturned in 1982 when the government instituted a "humane

---

8. Hong Kong SAR Government Information Services, *Hong Kong 2003*, "Vietnamese Refugees and Migrants."

9. Hansen, "Thanh loc," 88. Hansen notes that these organizations had a permanent presence in the camps although there were many other agencies and NGOs that were involved.

10. Kwok-bun Chan, "The Vietnamese Boat People in Hong Kong," 380.

deterrence" policy, placing all new arrivals in closed centers to be detained indefinitely until resettled overseas. During the late 1980s, there was growing suspicion that many of those arriving were not genuine refugees but instead economic migrants or persons fleeing for other reasons. Unlike their earlier counterparts, many of these later arrivals were from North Vietnam. Public opinion shifted from sympathy to hostility. In 1988, the government instituted a new policy whereby all new arrivals from Vietnam were classified as illegal immigrants and kept in detention centers until their claim for asylum was processed.[11]

One reason for the public's resentment was the perception that the Vietnamese boat people were given better treatment than mainland Chinese people received. Illegal immigrants from China who were apprehended were immediately sent back over the border, so why were Chinese-Vietnamese and Vietnamese allowed to stay when mainland Chinese were not?[12] Local resentment toward Vietnamese also increased in the run-up to 1997 when the British colony would revert to the sovereignty of the People's Republic of China, a time when many anxious Hong Kongers were seeking ways to emigrate to another country. Writing in the early 1990s, Chan noted, "In the eyes of these people, rightly or wrongly, the chances for the Vietnamese to leave Hong Kong are higher than theirs since the Vietnamese are still on the agenda of international discussion and deliberations."[13]

Soon the Hong Kong government was under pressure from all sides over its handling of the situation. The closed refugee camps with their prison-like conditions brought international condemnation, and the screening procedure was criticized by human rights lawyers and refugee advocates. Public opinion about the Vietnamese was overwhelmingly negative, with many complaining that the government policy was not too harsh but rather too lenient. However, the Hong Kong wider community itself was divided on the issue.

> Social debates about the treatment of refugees had split society during the late 1980s and 1990s. Views were especially divided between expatriates and Hong Kong Chinese. A mainstream local Chinese perspective was to see Vietnamese as troublemakers and inauthentic refugees, while the Western media sympathized with the boat people. Many local Chinese also worried about the unending demand on taxpayers due to the expense needed to host the Vietnamese . . . Those who criticized

---

11. Ibid., 380–81.
12. Yuk-wah Chan, "Revisiting the Vietnamese Refugee Era," 9.
13. Chan, "The Vietnamese Boat People in Hong Kong," 380.

the treatment of the Vietnamese in the local English-language press were mostly expatriates.[14]

Hong Kong's port of first asylum policy for the Vietnamese ended on January 9, 1998. As of that date, new arrivals were treated as illegal immigrants to be repatriated as soon as possible. In February 2000, the government announced a resettlement scheme that allowed the remaining 1,400 Vietnamese refugees and migrants who could not be resettled or repatriated to apply to settle in Hong Kong. The last refugee center was shut down in June 2000.

One piece of unfinished business was the government's contention that the UNHCR still owed HKD 1.162 billion (USD 150 million) to Hong Kong for the costs of taking care of Vietnamese refugees. In 2001, the UNHCR Sub-Office head indicated that repayment was impossible, given the agency's annual shortfall. She said, "We would like the money to be written off. It was recognized as an advance in principle so we don't consider it a debt."[15] The outstanding amount was a sum which the Hong Kong government recognized that it was unlikely to recover despite repeated attempts to secure payment.

Christian response

Religious bodies, Christian charities, and local churches were among those who answered the call for help.[16] Some of the most prominent Christian agencies that served the Vietnamese were Caritas-Hong Kong, Hong Kong Christian Aid to Refugees (later known as Christian Action), and Hong Kong Christian Service. At the beginning, the most urgent needs were food, water, clothing, shelter, and medical care to those arriving after a perilous journey across the seas. Later, aid shifted to longer-term needs for those living in camps, such as translation, accompaniment services, immigration and resettlement assistance, vocational training, job placement services, dental care, education, youth and children's activities, language classes, pastoral care, counseling, and befriending. Both Catholic and Protestant clergy

14. Chan, "Revisiting the Vietnamese Refugee Era," 9. See also Davis, *Hong Kong and the Asylum-Seekers from Vietnam*.
15. Schwartz, "Weighing the Cost of Boat People."
16. It should be noted that the Buddhists were involved in serving the Vietnamese refugees, as it was estimated that 70 percent of the refugee population were Buddhists. Besides some monks who were among the Vietnamese refugee population, there were organizations who visited the refugee centers, brought supplies, and organized Buddhist ministry inside the camps.

and laypersons also regularly conducted worship services and religious education classes for refugees as part of their spiritual care.

We highlight several reports that illustrate different dimensions of the contribution of the Christian sector. The first comes from Caritas-Hong Kong of the Catholic Church, the second from a joint action of the Hong Kong Christian Council and the Hong Kong Catholic Church, and the third being a personal story from a former Vietnamese refugee who later resettled in the United Sates.

a. Caritas-Hong Kong retrospect

Chang summarizes her experience of over twenty-five years of involvement with Vietnamese refugees in the foreword to a book whose title recalls biblical strangers—*They Sojourned in Our Land*. She describes the difficulties of being caught between the lenient, crisis-oriented approach of the UNHCR and the minimalist, standard policies of the Hong Kong government. Chang observed the drastic swing in public sentiment as the economic situation changed. In the late 1970s when the economy was buoyant, the refugees were treated as guests, brothers, sisters, partners, and business customers. Then in the early 1980s during an economic downturn, the public became harsh and unwelcoming. This change greatly affected the agency's morale and funding, even leading to reduction in services due to lack of community support.[17]

In response to skeptical friends who asked what she gained from serving refugees, Chang says she considered the work to be a great privilege. For one, the crisis forced Caritas to look for creative solutions to the unprecedented demands that were encountered, resulting in innovative models of programs and services. It was also during this time that she met many remarkable people of different nationalities who worked together for a common cause, such as government personnel, UN officials, and volunteers. This affirmed for her that Hong Kong truly is a global city. Lastly, she experienced tremendous solidarity through the international Caritas network, especially in Europe, which provided funding, resettlement coordination, and even overseas adoption of seven Vietnamese orphans in Switzerland and the Netherlands.

In the end, she says, the work of Caritas-Hong Kong was a Christian response to the moral issue of migration. She recalls the message of Bishop John Baptist Wu in a Mass conducted for refugees in 1976, during which he spoke of the flight of the Holy Family to Egypt to save their lives. The same

---

17. Chang, "Foreword," xv–xvi.

Gospel text would be used by Pope John Paul II in his message for World Migration Day 2000. Chang says, "In [the Holy Father's] reflections on the mystery of the Incarnation, he said that God came to earth seeking human hospitality. We must ask ourselves the question: How do we receive him in our midst?" She concludes that those serving the refugees and trying to improve their lives, in fact, served Christ who was in their midst.[18]

b. Protestant-Catholic joint action

Besides providing frontline service to refugees, Christians in Hong Kong were compelled to speak out on policy issues affecting the welfare of the Vietnamese boat people. One of the earliest statements was issued after the vessel *S.S. Huey Fong* arrived at the entrance to Hong Kong's harbor on December 19, 1978 with 3,383 refugees on board. The government was faced with a humanitarian and political crisis—"a floating human time bomb"—since accepting the refugees might only encourage even more to come to Hong Kong, but turning the ship away would bring international condemnation. Emergency supplies and medical aid were sent out to the *Huey Fong* but the government was firm on refusing to let the refugees cross into Hong Kong waters.[19]

As the situation deteriorated on board, the Hong Kong Christian Council and the Hong Kong Catholic Church released a joint statement to the press on December 28 in favor of allowing the refugees on the *Huey Fong* to land in Hong Kong. This was a courageous stand that went against popular opinion. The church statement acknowledged the difficulties that such a decision would entail, yet urged a humane response to the suffering of the desperate Vietnamese on board, especially the children and the elderly. These were newly arrived neighbors knocking on Hong Kong's door.

On January 19, 1979, the *SS Huey Fong* sailed into the Hong Kong harbor and the refugees were taken ashore. There were conflicting reports whether the ship had entered with or without government permission. Nonetheless, as the joint statement from Hong Kong Christian Council and the Hong Kong Catholic Church concluded, "In the final analysis, whatever the decision, the people and the churches of Hong Kong are involved in the plight of these refugees. World opinion and our beliefs and conscience make this involvement inevitable and imperative."[20]

---

18. Ibid., xviii.
19. Davis, *Hong Kong and the Asylum-Seekers from Vietnam*, 4–6.
20. Hong Kong Christian Council, *News and Views* (March 1979), 14.

c. Memories from a Vietnamese-American

Nguyen tells a refugee's story of life in North Vietnam, the war, and eventual escape to Hong Kong where he and his brother lived in open camps before permanent resettlement in the USA. Looking back on the experience in Hong Kong, he recalls encounters with two Christian groups who ministered among the refugees. One was a Baptist church near the Jubilee Camp where they were first housed. The church offered English classes taught by Western volunteers, two from the UK and one American. Nguyen speaks with great affection for the teachers, who impressed him with their energy and enthusiasm in every lesson and who also organized picnics and other outdoor activities. He remarks how he wished his English had been better at the time so he could talk more with his teachers about their lives and perspectives.[21]

The second Christian group that Nguyen interacted with was a Roman Catholic ministry. Being from a Catholic background, he traveled to Kai Tak East Camp every Sunday to join Mass with friends. He later discovered a small Catholic church in the area where Mass was celebrated in the Vietnamese language by Fr. Minh. Nguyen and the priest often engaged in deep conversation about life—spiritual and otherwise. Minh once gave him a piece of advice which Nguyen says he never forgot: "Living in America, you all should be careful, otherwise you could lose your own faith!" These words were startling to the refugees who assumed that religious freedom was a cherished right in the USA. The priest explained how the opportunities for earning money and advancing one's career would be much greater in the new country compared to North Vietnam. Temptations such as these could easily take priority over church activities until slowly but surely, one's spiritual life had withered. "It is hard to eliminate the faith of someone by external force; however, faith can easily be changed internally," said Minh.[22]

As Nguyen looks back at the refugee days, he expresses gratitude for the Christian churches and individuals who made themselves available during a most vulnerable period. He writes

> [M]any of us were tortured by the nostalgia from time to time. I was young at the time and often felt homesick and powerless. For that, sometimes I felt like I had to do something harmful to myself. I needed some advice from mature adults to guide me with my immature thoughts.[23]

---

21. Nguyen, *My Adventure to the New World*, 300–301.
22. Ibid., 307–12.
23. Ibid., 310.

Through the Christian witness and friendship of churches, many refugees were able to better cope with their lives as strangers in Hong Kong and to prepare for a hopeful future in another land.

REFUGEES AND ASYLUM SEEKERS IN HONG KONG (2000–2014)

Just as the Vietnamese refugee era was coming to a close, a new group of asylum seekers were arriving in Hong Kong. The significant numbers of South Asian and African asylum seekers in the city are a recent phenomenon, starting around the early 2000s. They usually came as individuals rather than en masse as refugees did in the past. According to Mathews, Hong Kong is unusual among developed countries in maintaining a largely open border and liberal visa policy. That means visitors can enter Hong Kong easily, making it a popular tourist spot as well as a potential destination for asylum seekers. He quotes one Somali man who, when asked why he came to the city to seek asylum, answered: "Why did I come to Hong Kong? Because I knew they would let me in!"[24] Another possible reason for the asylum seeker influx was the tightening of visa policies in other countries in the aftermath of the September 11, 2001 terrorist attacks in the USA.[25]

An estimated 10,000 persons seeking asylum were present in Hong Kong as of early 2015. Some entered Hong Kong on tourist or business visas while others entered surreptitiously via mainland China. Although the People's Republic of China is a signatory to the Refugee Convention, it is not possible to apply for the asylum right to settle in mainland China. Overall, the asylum claimants in Hong Kong as of 2015 were primarily from South or Southeast Asian countries such as Pakistan, India, Bangladesh, Sri Lanka, Vietnam, Indonesia, and the Philippines, with a smaller percentage from African countries, and a tiny percentage from other countries such as Egypt, Palestine, Afghanistan, and Iran.[26]

The United Nations High Commissioner for Refugees (UNHCR), which had been present in Hong Kong since 1952, established a permanent office in 1979 to assist with the large numbers of Vietnamese refugees. The agency also founded an office in mainland China in Beijing in 1980 to respond to the Vietnamese refugee influx from the 1979–1980

24. Gordon Mathews, *Ghetto*, 79.

25. Ibid., 172.

26. Refugee number according to the UNHCR. Data on countries of origin as of the end of March 2015, Hong Kong Government Press Releases *LCQ16: "Unified screening mechanism"*—published April 29, 2015.

Sino-Vietnamese conflict. After Hong Kong's return to the sovereignty of the People's Republic of China in 1997, the UNHCR office in Beijing became a Regional Office for mainland China, while the Hong Kong branch was designated as a sub-office for asylum-seeking arrivals in the city.

Until March 2014, the UNHCR Sub-Office Hong Kong carried the main responsibility for Refugee Status Determination (RSD) and assistance to any asylum-seekers and refugees in the city. This situation was due to the fact that the Refugee Convention was not extended to the Hong Kong Special Administrative Region. The Hong Kong government allowed asylum seekers to stay in the city until their cases were resolved, but gave them no legal status.

Once persons seeking asylum landed in Hong Kong, they needed to wait until their visa or permission to stay expired before they could surrender themselves to the Hong Kong Immigration Department. After emerging from detention, they registered with the UNHCR office for asylum. The asylum seeker's first interview at UNHCR may have been scheduled for a date as far away as one year later, and many cases took years to be resolved. According to Hong Kong's immigration policy, protection claimants were almost never allowed to settle permanently in the city. They must be resettled in a third country.

Besides the UNHCR asylum process, there was another avenue to apply for protection in Hong Kong. The other method of the "dual-track" protection system was to file a claim under the United Nations Convention Against Torture (CAT), which was extended to Hong Kong in 1992. Some asylum seekers who registered with the UNHCR also registered simultaneously or subsequently as a CAT claimant through the Hong Kong Immigration Department. In 2004, the Hong Kong court ruled that the government's policy in compliance with the Torture Convention on non-refoulement did not meet the necessary standards of procedural fairness. Thus, the Secretary for Security was required to make an assessment of torture claims that was independent of the UNHCR's refugee status determination decision. A torture screening mechanism was put in place with the establishment of the Immigration Department's Torture Claim Assessment Division.

Three other Hong Kong court decisions had a major impact on the Immigration Department's handling of protection claimant cases. In 2008, a court judgment declared that the department's policy of denying publicly-funded legal aid to torture claimants was unlawful. Screening was suspended and a backlog of over 6,000 torture claims accumulated. The screening policy was revised to include publicly-funded legal assistance, but the backlog continued to be a problem. Next, a court decision in 2012 ruled that protection against "cruel, inhuman or degrading treatment or punishment"

(CIDTP) was guaranteed in the Hong Kong Bill of Rights. This required the Immigration Department to screen claimants on the grounds of both CIDTP and torture. Finally, in a landmark judgment in 2013, the Court of Final Appeal ruled that the Hong Kong government could no longer rely solely on the UNHCR to carry out refugee status determination. The Director of Immigration had the responsibility to ensure that decisions to deport refugee claimants were based on high standards of fairness and subject to judicial review. The Unified Screening Mechanism whereby all asylum claimants, CIDTP claimants, and torture claimants would be screened by the Hong Kong Immigration Department came into effect on March 3, 2014. Thus, the Hong Kong government's responsibility for protection claimants in the city had greatly expanded, despite its best efforts to do exactly the opposite.

LIVES OF REFUGEES AND ASYLUM SEEKERS

The living situation of asylum seekers and refugees in Hong Kong was particularly dire in the years leading up to 2008. "Dogs and cats are in a better position than refugees in Hong Kong," said Mark Daly, a Canadian lawyer who had represented refugees in Hong Kong since the mid-1990s. He pointed out the existence of the Dogs and Cats Ordinance, a statute which provided an independent board for appeals and provisions on detention of animals. In contrast, there was no existing legislation in Hong Kong specifically dealing with asylum seekers at that time.[27]

Asylum seekers and refugees who arrived in the early 2000s reported that there was little assistance from agencies or awareness of their plight by the public. They were forced to sleep on the streets, often at the Star Ferry Pier. With no kitchen for storage or cooking, they hauled around useless food such as uncooked bags of rice that had been donated by charities. They were harassed when seeking medical care at public hospitals and clinics because they lacked money to pay the bill. Those in detention could be held indefinitely and conditions varied.

In a meeting before the Legislative Council in 2006, the Society for Community Organization together with other organizations submitted their views on the situation of asylum seekers, refugees, and claimants against torture. The submission outlined problems resulting from the lack of a coherent asylum policy: no legal aid, no valid identity papers, arbitrary detention, poor detention conditions, unreported violence and rape, threats of deportation, inadequate provision of housing and food, no automatic right to education for children, no support to unaccompanied minors, risk

---

27. Gentle, "Pets Better Served Than Refugees."

of detention when approaching hospitals, and impractical waiver system for medical care.[28]

Subsequently, due to policy changes, the situation improved somewhat for persons seeking asylum. A series of judicial reviews on the Hong Kong government's legal obligation of preventing destitution of protection claimants brought changes to the welfare system. In 2006, the Social Welfare Department commissioned the International Social Service-Hong Kong Branch (ISS-HK) to provide in-kind assistance on the basis of humanitarian grounds. The level of assistance was designed "to provide support which is considered sufficient to prevent them from becoming destitute while at the same time not creating a magnet effect which could have serious implications on the sustainability of our current support system and on our immigration control."[29]

Arbitrary detention of asylum seekers and torture claimants was subject to judicial review in several court cases. In 2009, the court ruled that the government must pay damages to four torture claimants who were unlawfully detained according to the Hong Kong Bill of Rights. The judgment criticized the government's lack of a published detention policy and its arbitrary and capricious detention practice. The four were awarded a total of HKD 510,000 (USD 66,233).[30] The Security Bureau later amended its detention policy.

In 2012, the Security Bureau reported that the number of former foreign domestic workers in Hong Kong who lodged torture claims had clearly increased. In 2010 and 2011, foreign domestic workers comprised roughly 30 percent of the new torture claimants. In response, the Immigration Department revised the visa application form for new domestic workers, requiring applicants to declare there were no circumstances in their home country that would prevent them from returning there after completion of their contract. According to an article in *Asia Times Online*, foreign domestic workers from the Philippines were reportedly applying as torture claimants or asylum claimants in order to extend their stay in Hong Kong and work illegally. Some were said to be living with male African or South Asian asylum seekers, and those who got pregnant were sent back to the Philippines.[31]

---

28. Society for Community Organization et al., "Denial of Asylum Seekers' Rights."

29. Hong Kong SAR Government Security Bureau and Social Welfare Department, "Humanitarian Assistance for Torture Claimants."

30. Tsui, "Asylum Seekers Who Filed Torture Claims Get Damages for Time in Jail."

31. Jimenez, "Abuse Me Please, Sir." See also Constable, *Born Out of Place*, 183–215.

In his research on Muslims in Hong Kong, O'Connor heard various explanations as to why Indonesian domestic workers claimed asylum. One reason was that the woman became pregnant by a boyfriend who encouraged her to apply for asylum. A boyfriend may also have been an asylum seeker working illegally and persuaded the girlfriend to leave her job to work with him. Another situation involved domestic workers who terminated their contract and claimed asylum to work as sex workers. The purpose was to make money to clear debts. A third possibility was that Indonesian women who became lesbian couples chose to quit their jobs, claim asylum, and live off the money that they received as torture claimants.[32]

O'Connor's analysis of the phenomenon among Indonesian women could be applied to other foreign domestic workers in similar circumstances.

> The whole process of claiming asylum as foreign domestic workers is fraught with contradiction and questionable ethics. Many of these women claim that they cannot return home because of violence, maybe because they have had a child out of wedlock, or that they are in debt. Nevertheless, it is clear that these women arrived in Hong Kong in order to work, not to flee dangers in Indonesia. At the same time, the social circumstances . . . do suggest that there are particular hardships and risks that make Indonesian foreign domestic workers vulnerable.[33]

Although the number of foreign domestic workers applying for asylum decreased after the new immigration contract rules, their involvement with male asylum seekers continued, raising questions of "gendered entrapment" whereby the women pay a high price to survive financially and emotionally while living in Hong Kong.[34]

REFUGEE AND ASYLUM SEEKER CONCERNS

a. Extended waiting period for resolution of cases

Various explanations were given as to why the process of refugee status or torture claimant determination took so long, sometimes stretched out for years. Among the most common explanations were: i) lack of manpower

---

32. O'Connor, *Islam in Hong Kong*, 53.

33. Ibid. According to O'Connor's findings, "the whole process of migration for many of the women has been quite traumatic . . . Indonesian foreign domestic workers are actually quite vulnerable to physical and sexual abuse, exploitation, debt, imprisonment, and deportation" (47).

34. Vecchio and Gerard, "Surviving the Politics of Illegality," 188.

and resources in the UNHCR Sub-Office Hong Kong, ii) the Hong Kong government's refusal to implement a unified screening mechanism, and iii) asylum seekers and torture claimants intentionally delaying the process to take advantage of the system to stay in Hong Kong to work illegally.

i. United Nations High Commissioner for Refugees

According to Philip Karani, head of the UNHCR in Hong Kong and Macau in 2013, his office had a severe funding shortage. Hong Kong was not a high priority for UNHCR funding compared to other troubled areas in the world, largely due to Hong Kong's comparatively low number of refugees and the perception that the city was wealthy and secure.[35] While Karani expressed appreciation for the financial assistance provided by the Hong Kong government to refugees and its recognition of the principle of non-refoulement, he was concerned that basic rights such as right to employment and access to education for children could not be guaranteed. "It's not enough to ensure protection, but you have to put forth durable solutions and that is not possible in Hong Kong because they don't have the right for local integration, to settle in Hong Kong."[36] The length of time for resettlement of recognized refugees was not determined by the UNHCR, he said, but rather by the availability of third countries to receive them.

Less than 10 percent of those who applied for asylum in Hong Kong could meet the criteria for being a refugee as defined by the Refugee Convention. According to Karani, many of the people who came to UNHCR in Hong Kong had a personal fear of persecution but that was not sufficient grounds to give refugee status. However, critics complained that the UNHCR's screening process was not transparent and its decisions were not subject to judicial scrutiny. While there was speculation that the Hong Kong sub-office would close or shrink in importance after the Unified Screening Mechanism was implemented, the agency indicated that its role would change but that there were no plans to close its office.

ii. Hong Kong Government

Since the end of the Vietnamese refugee era in Hong Kong, the government made clear that it had no intention to take up responsibility for refugees or asylum seekers in the territory in the future. As the Security Bureau stated in

---

35. Chiu, "Refugees at Their Wits' End."
36. Philip Karani, interview with the author, July 17, 2013.

a 2006 briefing before the Legislative Council, the Refugee Convention did not apply to Hong Kong and the government was justified in its decision.

> Hong Kong is small in size and has a dense population. Our unique situation, set against the backdrop of our relative economic prosperity in the region and our liberal visa regime, makes us vulnerable to possible abuses if the 1951 UN Convention were to be extended to Hong Kong. We thus have a firm policy of not granting asylum and do not have any obligation to admit individuals seeking refugee status under the 1951 UN Convention.[37]

Barbara Harrell-Bond, a world expert on refugee rights, visited the city in 2008 to lend support for legal aid for asylum seekers. She said, "Even if the government wants to keep refugees out, unfortunately it can't. Refugees will still come to Hong Kong. The answer is to find a fair and effective way to solve [the problem], otherwise the outcome will be more tragedy."[38]

iii. Asylum seekers and torture claimants

As far as the accusation that asylum seekers and torture claimants themselves were the reason that cases are stretched out for years, the Hong Kong Immigration Department cited examples of procedural abuse: "claimants deploying delaying tactics by spreading out submission of evidence over a long period of time, repeated absence from interviews, reopening of claims after withdrawal, making subsequent new claims before removal, making false representations, etc."[39]

Such "delaying tactics" may indeed have occurred, though it would be difficult to prove the reasons behind them. As a researcher and friend of asylum seekers in Hong Kong, Mathews witnessed both sides of the situation. On the one hand, he heard stories first-hand from asylum seekers whom he could only conclude were "flamboyantly lying." UNHCR personnel also told him they had to suppress their laughter after hearing an oft-told story from applicants from Africa about being the son of a tribal king and having to flee because of refusal to follow pagan rituals like eating the father's heart after his death.[40] On the other hand, Mathews recounted his

37. Hong Kong SAR Government Security Bureau et al., "Situation of Refugees, Asylum Seekers and Torture Claimants."
38. Tsang, "Refugees Need Legal Framework."
39. Hong Kong SAR Government Immigration Department, *Annual Report 2011*, chapter 4.
40. Mathews, *Ghetto*, 174–75.

experience helping an asylum seeker whose UNHCR case had been rejected several times. After Mathews personally got involved in the case by getting the necessary evidence from Africa on his behalf, the asylum seeker was given refugee status after seven years in Hong Kong and resettled in Canada. Without this intervention, Mathews doubted that the case would ever have been resolved successfully.[41]

b. In-kind assistance and living expenses

Since refugees and asylum seekers in Hong Kong are not allowed by law to work in either a paid or unpaid capacity, they were expected to rely on meager social welfare benefits provided by the government through International Social Service (ISS). The in-kind assistance provided a small rent allowance of HKD 1,500 (USD 195) a month paid directly to the landlord as well as HKD 1,200 (USD 156) a month in food coupons, an allowance for clothing and toiletries, and cash reimbursement for transportation. Protection claimants said they desperately struggled to pay expenses for daily necessities and had resorted to becoming "refugee beggars." Under such conditions, many would seek additional assistance through charities or religious bodies.

c. Educational opportunities

While protection claimants under eighteen years of age in the city were allowed to enroll in school and granted a tuition waiver, there were still a number of problems that affected successful access to education. For one, the financial assistance for students did not cover uniforms, school supplies, or fees for school activities. Secondly, transportation allowance was limited to student travel with none provided for parents or adults to accompany the children. Thirdly, language and cultural differences were often barriers to communication between teachers and parents as well as to integration of children into a foreign school.

d. Health care

Until 2006, the UNHCR funded the Caritas Medical Centre to provide outpatient services to asylum seekers. After this funding ended, access to emergency medical care was available through a medical waiver system

---

41. Gordon Mathews, interview with the author, May 6, 2013.

on a case-by-case basis at public hospitals or outpatient clinics. However, appointments were often scheduled with a long wait time, particularly for specialist units. In addition, some staff in the public health system were unfamiliar with the procedure and documents for protection claimants, leading staff to demand to see Hong Kong identity cards, which refugees and asylum seekers were not eligible to have. Dental care was another health issue where affordable treatment was problematic. Some asylum seekers and torture claimants who were refused medical waivers sought treatment at hospital emergency rooms instead. Often, they were unable to settle the bill afterwards and reported being repeatedly contacted by the hospital collection agency for payment.

e. Employment

Although some countries such as Canada and the UK have a policy that allows refugees to take up employment while they await resettlement or the resolution of their cases, the Hong Kong government does not. Any protection claimant who is caught taking up employment without permission—whether paid or unpaid—could be liable on conviction of a fine of up to HKD 50,000 (USD 6,494) and a prison term of up to three years.

Mathews concludes that the great tragedy in the current asylum system is that it rewards people who are least deserving and punishes people who are most deserving. Those who are least deserving, in his opinion, were suspected economic migrants, many from Southeast Asia, who used the asylum system to work illegally in Hong Kong. Those who were most deserving were those who fled their homeland seeking safety for any number of reasons. They were afraid to work because it was against the law, but they consequently suffered financially as well as psychologically. The result was ironic and contradictory as "almost as a rule the asylum seekers who break the rules and work are far happier than those who follow the rules and do not work."[42]

Alternatively, Francesco Vecchio takes another perspective on the income-generating activities of protection claimants. From his extensive research on asylum seeker livelihood and survival strategies, he observes that asylum seekers are easily exploited by ethnic businesses as cheap labor with the requisite language skills. Those employed could be found working in two industries in particular: recycling in the New Territories rural towns and trading in the Kowloon urban area. He argues that asylum seekers do make a contribution to the "local informal economy," although this is not

---

42. Mathews, *Ghetto*, 194.

acknowledged by the government. Vecchio says that contrary to the widespread view of asylum seekers as illegal immigrants exploiting the system to make easy money, his research indicates that asylum seekers were forced by Hong Kong's refugee policy to seek unauthorized work in dangerous, irregular, or low-paid jobs that actually benefited the resident population of the city.[43]

f. Acceptance in Hong Kong society

The issue of refugees and asylum seekers in Hong Kong is one in which residents were often found to be misinformed or to express negative sentiments. There were suspicions that most of those seeking asylum were bogus and involved in illicit activities and crime. Asylum seekers themselves said that they had three "strikes" against them: they are dark-skinned foreigners, they have no legal status in Hong Kong, and they may have been held in detention, which people equate with being a criminal.[44]

Biases against asylum seekers and torture claimants were reinforced by reports in some media outlets. In an opinion column for *China Daily*, a university lecturer warned against signing the Refugee Convention. Otherwise, he claimed, the floodgates would open and the city would be swamped and drowned by economic refugees.[45] *Next Magazine*, a Chinese weekly, featured an article claiming asylum seekers were selling their food coupons and earning money by lining up for others to buy the latest iPhone.[46] In the English-language newspaper *The Standard*, the editor warned that government action on bogus asylum seekers, particularly those of South Asian origin, was urgently needed to defuse a "ticking time bomb."[47]

In order to open better communication, refugees and asylum seekers established their own website called "Seeking Refuge." It was described as a "community website where asylum seekers in Hong Kong can make their voice heard, and a place where the general public can learn first-hand about the experience and lives of asylum seekers residing in Hong Kong."[48] While postings were minimal, this outlet represented efforts by protection

---

43. Vecchio, *Asylum Seeking and the Global City*, 164–89.

44. Refugee A (Africa), interview with the author, May 3, 2012.

45. Fung, "Opening a Floodgate to Refugees."

46. As reported on RTHK, "Asylum Seekers in Hong Kong," *The Pulse*, December 2, 2011.

47. Ma, "Ticking Time Bomb."

48. The website www.seekingrefuge.hk was moved to Facebook under the screen name "seeking refuge hk" in 2013.

claimants to connect with the Hong Kong Chinese population through new media technology.

One potential indicator of change in Hong Kong's attitudes toward protection claimants was what appeared to be an increasing number of marriages between male asylum seekers and Hong Kong Chinese women. Though the numbers were not believed to be large, churches and agencies reported that some male asylum seekers known to them had officially married Hong Kong wives. After marriage to a permanent resident, asylum seekers cannot be deported. They are also eligible to apply for a Hong Kong identity card, which would give them right of residence and right to work. However, receiving the identity card after marriage was not automatic and was considered on a case-to-case basis by the Immigration Department. Some former asylum seekers reportedly had waited up to two years after their wedding and had still not received a Hong Kong identity card. This created a hardship for men who needed to support their families. Others who married received their identity card after a shorter waiting period. According to informal information from church sources, there were success stories as well as failures in asylum seeker marriages in Hong Kong. As might be expected, it depended on the individuals involved, their personal circumstances, and the support that they received from family, friends, and community.[49]

REFUGEE AND ASYLUM SEEKER VOICES

However complex and diverse the reasons for persons to end up in Hong Kong while seeking protection, the fact remains that many refugees, asylum seekers, and torture claimants lived a bleak existence. They were stranded in the city indefinitely, unable to travel outside Hong Kong, and awaiting a favorable decision from the UNHCR or Hong Kong Immigration that would let them move on with their lives. As Mathews notes, "The standing joke among many asylum seekers is that Hong Kong is a very strange place, because it's so easy to get in and so hard to get out (unless the asylum seeker agrees to return to his home country)."[50]

---

49. See also Vecchio, *Asylum Seeking and the Global City*, 144–48. It should be noted that some asylum seeker women from Vietnam had married lower class, older Hong Kong men and settled in the city as a means of survival. Chan, "Revisiting the Vietnamese Refugee Era," 11–12.

50. Mathews, *Ghetto*, 178.

Asylum seekers described their lives in Hong Kong in personal interviews. "Hannah" from the Middle East spoke of her family's struggles after they arrived in Hong Kong in 2011.

> Of course, we feel very upset. Very depressed. Just to stay home. No work. No money. No study. No friends. No relatives. No English. Strange food. Strange country. It's not easy for *anyone* to leave their country . . . You know I sit down on the bus and three seats beside me are empty, but no one sits down beside me or in front of me. I ask myself why. Do I smell? I think my smell is OK . . . but it is happening and it is still happening. And neighbors don't say hello or good morning. They just slam the door. I sense the people here are very tough, serious. No smiling. I didn't expect to find people like this in Hong Kong.[51]

"Prakash" from South Asia lived in a shelter and expressed hopelessness after eight years in Hong Kong.

> I came here by myself for political reasons. My life was in danger. I had no idea about Hong Kong. I applied for asylum in 2006, and until now no decision. If I am refused, they say 'Go back.' I cannot. If I could, I would go back tomorrow. After eight years here, I got nothing. I don't have a criminal record. Only wait, wait . . . my friends helped me. Outside groups cannot. No one helps us. I got no place of my own or my belongings. All I got is a bunk bed space. I go out at 10 AM and come back at 7 PM. No money, just walk, walk, walk. My dream? My dream is finished already.[52]

"Fred" from Africa reflected on an asylum seeker's dilemma.

> Not all asylum seekers come for political reasons. I had a family dispute and was tortured for three days. I'd be happy to go back if it was safe at home. Not all refugees and asylum seekers are bad. We are not allowed to work. We have to wait and beg. How far can you do that? You have to control yourself first. Love yourself before you can love someone else. You have to be careful or you become someone you don't want to be. Some get involved in criminal stuff. It's understandable because you are so low, you have nothing to lose. If you have a family, you risk your life to support them. If you go to jail, there's no way to help

---

51. Asylum Seeker M (Middle East), interview with the author, August 18, 2013.
52. Asylum Seeker A (South Asia), interview with the author, August 31, 2012.

them. A man can't stand his family to suffer like this. He must work if he can, even if it's illegal![53]

"John" from South Asia described the fears and tragedies he faced in Hong Kong.

> Well, the first fear we have is we will be rejected and they will ask us to leave. It's the first shock to us, the first *mental* torture. Every time we hear something bad from Immigration, oh, they are going to change the rules or something, you know, it's already a torture to us. And when we are rejected by Immigration, the rejection letter, it's another torture. And then I can tell you I have lost several friends in Hong Kong. They were waiting for, they were depending on Immigration but they lost their lives, in some kind of accident. One got burned and he died, you know Fa Yuen Gai [Fa Yuen Street]? There was big fire and the guy from Pakistan died. He was eating with me the night before. And very next day, we could not find him. Just gone . . . Then there was a friend who died in a vehicle accident, there was a tree that fell on him in the truck and he passed away. And there was a friend from India. He was found dead in his apartment. And several others they lost their lives in Hong Kong. They were just waiting for the mercy from Immigration, but couldn't find it. Immigration doesn't know that. But if someone died, [Immigration says], "We did not kill him." See, they are responsible.[54]

Some asylum seekers composed rap music to express their feelings. "Dixon" performed a song entitled "Where is My Future?" on an independently released album "Naked Backs."

> O God we need your help
> We stuck in da land of HK
> Which is da land we can't make our future
> So I check myself
> Pinch myself
> I gotta nothing
> Still seeking your world help
> I don't know how my future will be
> And where my future will end
> It turns to a burden in my heart
> I can't sleep
> Cause I'm thinking deep

---

53. Asylum Seeker C (Africa), interview with the author, August 31, 2012.
54. Asylum Seeker F (South Asia), interview with the author, June 16, 2013.

> I feel like I can't breathe
> Cause there is a lot of heat coming off me
> I don't know where is my future
> I don't know where is my life
> I came from my old place
> Only to survive.[55]

AGENCIES AND ORGANIZATIONS SERVING REFUGEES AND ASYLUM SEEKERS

The following are presented in roughly chronological order of entry into the network of organizations and agencies that served the refugee and asylum seeker population. Other groups from the Christian sector will be discussed separately in chapter 7 to give more space for discussion on how churches and Christians NGOs worked together within the overall network. Some of the same agencies and persons who had worked for Vietnamese refugees were again active in helping the current group of asylum seekers, although to smaller numbers of claimants from different nationalities in a changed political situation.

Legal Sector

The firm of Barnes & Daly Solicitors was prominent in representing protection claimants *pro bono* in Hong Kong's courts. Barnes & Daly was established in 1999 by Australian Peter Barnes and Canadian Mark Daly. Both began working in Hong Kong in 1995 and were trained in the area of human rights law under Pam Baker & Company. Baker was a British lawyer who had set up her own law firm in Hong Kong to advocate for the Vietnamese boat people. In 2013, Daly & Associates was established to continue the work of Barnes & Daly. The Law Society of Hong Kong and the Hong Kong Bar Association are also among professional groups advocating for reform in refugee, asylum seeker, and torture claimant laws.

Christian Action

Christian Action began operating in 1985 to help the poor and disadvantaged in Hong Kong and has also been assisting the needy in mainland

---

55. "Where is My Future?," written and performed by Dixon and Alladin, with Amy, *Naked Backs*, Hong Kong, n.p., 2008.

China since 1997. The agency, formerly known as Hong Kong Christian Aid to Refugees, has a history dating back to the early 1950s helping Russian and Vietnamese refugees. It opened the first refugee service center in Chungking Mansions in 2004 in response to a request from the UNHCR. Christian Action provides refugees and asylum seekers with hot meals, clothing, baby supplies, emergency shelter, counseling and mental health support, educational grants and classes, and outreach work in the community. The legal assistance services eventually branched off into a separate organization with the blessing and support of the agency.

Society for Community Organization

The Society for Community Organization (SoCO) is a non-profit NGO formed in 1972 to work for equal rights and opportunities among the grassroots population in Hong Kong. Christians were among those who helped start SoCO along with funding from overseas bodies, the Community Chest, and individuals. SoCO sought to help protection claimants on several levels including direct services, home visits, and advocacy. The organization regularly held meetings with protection claimants to discuss policy issues and learn what kinds of changes they wanted. Refugees and asylum seekers were trained how to talk to the media and to hold press conferences as a means of empowerment in the community. In its advocacy work, SoCO submitted letters to the United Nations, recommendations to the Hong Kong government, and papers to the Legislative Council to push for better welfare provision and legal protection for refugees and asylum seekers.

International Social Service-Hong Kong Branch (ISS-HK)

International Social Service is an NGO that facilitates social services for needy families and individuals who require intercountry cooperation. ISS-HK had worked with refugees and asylum seekers since 1969, first serving refugees from mainland China and later from Vietnam. The agency was contracted to implement the "Assistance in-kind to Asylum-Seekers and Torture Claimants Project" of the Social Welfare Department in 2006. ISS provides in-kind services for temporary accommodation, food, clothing, and other basic necessities and allowances.

Hong Kong Justice Centre

Hong Kong Justice Centre was established in 2007 as a non-profit human rights organization to provide free legal advice and support to refugees and asylum seekers applying for protection under the United Nations High Commissioner for Refugees. The Centre had its beginnings as the Refugee Advice Unit of the agency Christian Action. Due to the growing demand for its services, the Refugee Advice Unit became an independent organization with transitional support and funding from Christian Action. The Centre partners with law firms in Hong Kong who commit funds and provide *pro bono* hours to refugee and asylum seeker clients. The Justice Centre also partners with university law faculties and other law firms.

Vision First

Vision First started in 2009 with an exclusive focus on service to refugees and asylum seekers in Hong Kong. The NGO relies on an all-volunteer staff and donations to run its humanitarian programs. Besides giving direct assistance, the organization also carries out advocacy campaigns to promote the rights and welfare of protection claimants. These include organizing public demonstrations ("March for Protection"), monitoring agencies that serve the refugee population, conducting research on refugee policy debates and service provision, and educating the public through social media and community events.

Refugee Concern Network

Refugee Concern is an informal network of organizations and agencies in Hong Kong that meets regularly to share information and coordinate support for protection claimants. Two networks co-exist, one being a larger circle including lawyers, agencies, NGOs and Christian groups, the other a smaller circle of Christian organizations and churches. Hans Lutz, a long-time Swiss missionary in Hong Kong from Basel Mission/Mission 21, was instrumental in organizing the Refugee Ministry Group.

Others serving refugees and asylum seekers

Numerous groups and individuals in Hong Kong are involved in supporting refugees, asylum seekers, and torture claimants in various capacities. These include organizations such as Amnesty International, CEDAR Fund, Civic Exchange, *Médecins Sans Frontières*, and Crossroads International, as well as university groups, charities, religious organizations, and service centers, some partnering with agencies serving protection claimants. Hong Kong legislators Fernando Cheung and Emily Lau were among those publicly working to improve the situation of asylum seekers and refugees. NGOs and refugee advocates consulted with the two lawmakers, who are known for their efforts in social welfare and human rights concerns.

Imam Muhammed Arshad of the Kowloon Mosque and Islamic Centre said that he had been approached by some Muslim asylum seekers asking for assistance. The Mosque could offer a small amount of financial help on a case-by-case basis from its charity collection, but there was no organized service specifically for this group. He estimated that four to five asylum seekers were helped each month, with perhaps one hundred persons given assistance in a year. Refugees and asylum seekers could come to the mosque for prayers and stay for the dinner served every evening during Ramadan. The Imam expressed concern that some asylum seekers got involved in "unhealthy activities" in Hong Kong and warned them that their lives would be bleak here without valid papers to live and work. He saw no problem with other religions offering charitable service to refugees and asylum seekers, but said that there should be no link between giving service and teaching faith. The help should be given on a humanitarian basis, not as an invitation to join another religion. As for the welfare of protection claimants, Arshad expressed confidence in the Hong Kong government to handle the situation properly.[56]

CONCLUSION

With the first two waves of Chinese refugees and Vietnamese refugees, Hong Kong did indeed extend hospitality to those fleeing from unrest, danger, or poverty in the mainland and after the Vietnam War. The political sensitivities surrounding the issue of mainland refugees settling in British Hong Kong were dealt with by viewing the matter as a social problem rather than a refugee crisis to be solved. Nonetheless, as the numbers swelled, the colonial government sought to reduce the inflow from across the border through strict immigration measures. The "problem of people" was then tackled to provide basic services and livelihood for refugees, illegal migrants, and the indigenous poor all together. Chinese refugees eventually became the working force that helped develop Hong Kong into a modern

56. Imam Muhammed Arshad, interview with the author, August 29, 2012.

entrepreneurial society. In terms of the Vietnamese influx, Hong Kong was initially sympathetic to the plight of ethnic Chinese who were subjected to discrimination and pushed out of Vietnam in the aftermath of war. As the numbers swelled and resettlement to third countries slowed, however, the city began to withdraw its welcome. This was especially true regarding later arrivals who were ethnically Vietnamese and under suspicion of being economic migrants or coming from criminal backgrounds. During both refugee eras, Christians were on the front lines providing service, funding, and advocacy. The contribution of overseas church bodies to refugee ministry in Hong Kong was substantial through strong cooperation and coordination with local Christians as well as the government and international NGOs.

Memories of the Vietnamese refugees were still fresh on the minds of the government and public when the current wave of persons seeking asylum began arriving around the year 2000. It was understandable if Hong Kongers were experiencing "compassion fatigue" and were resistant to any effort to take care of more refugees in the future. The average Hong Kong person could easily hold the view that this small, crowded city had done more than its fair share of looking after refugees, had done a good job despite all the problems, and in the end was left with a huge unpaid bill by the UNHCR.

The new group of asylum seekers began trickling in one at a time by land or air, often indistinguishable from ethnic minorities, tourists, or foreign businesspeople in Hong Kong. As their situation became known through contact with law enforcement, immigration, charities, religious groups, human rights advocates and individuals, a system emerged for claiming non-refoulement protection under the UN Refugee Convention or the Convention Against Torture. Despite the Hong Kong government's persistent efforts to avoid any responsibility for asylum seekers except for deportation, it was forced to assess torture and CIDTP claims and provide minimal social welfare assistance after legal challenges were lodged by human rights lawyers on behalf of their clients. The dual-track system whereby the UNHCR handled asylum claims and the Immigration Department handled torture claims was deemed a violation of the Hong Kong Bill of Rights in a 2012 court ruling. In 2014, the Unified Screening Mechanism was implemented with the Hong Kong Immigration Department taking responsibility to assess all non-refoulement claims. With a population of concern of over 10,000—including UN recognized refugees, protection claimants, and those whose cases had been unsuccessful but were still residing in the city—Christians were once again challenged to offer hospitality to the "least of these" not only from a biblical understanding, but also in the face of skepticism from the local community. Let us now turn to the ministry and mission of the church in Hong Kong with refugees and asylum seekers in the twenty-first century.

Chapter 7

Refugee Ministry in Twenty-First-Century Hong Kong

BEGINNING IN THE NEW millennium as more and more refugees and asylums seekers showed up at the door of the church, Hong Kong Christians knew that they must respond to this new wave of needy strangers in the city. Who were these congregations and organizations and what kinds of service did they provide? How did Christian ministry evolve in caring for this population? What were the impacts on both hosts and guests in the quest for Christian hospitality?

Christian groups that interacted with refugees and asylum seekers in Hong Kong include Christian churches and fellowships, Christian non-governmental organizations (NGOs), and social service charities with Christian background. We explore their situations and ministries to get a picture of the variety and commonalities of their outreach. The aim is to provide an in-depth rather than an exhaustive examination of Christian groups who welcomed asylum seekers, refugees, and torture claimants into their midst. In the process, we see how international churches and overseas Christians in Hong Kong partnered with Chinese churches and organizations in a classic East meets West model, yet go beyond it with global dimensions of mission and ministry in the local context.

MAJOR REFUGEE MINISTRY PROGRAMS

Since most local churches in Hong Kong use Chinese language for communication, asylum seekers and refugees turned primarily to English-speaking international congregations. On any given Sunday, one could find refugees and asylum seekers in many different churches—Protestant, Catholic, and Orthodox—all over the city. Some individuals related to more than one church or pastor. This was understandable given how long some had lived in Hong Kong and the diversity of the population. Asylum seekers may have had contact with churches from many backgrounds and language groups, often attending the programs of several churches and organizations at different times during the week.

For the purposes of this book, we examine churches and agencies that had a special focus on asylum seekers and refugees. We look at two international churches and one Christian charity with noteworthy programs: a) Kowloon Union Church, b) The Vine, and c) Christian Action. Then we survey other churches and organizations that were involved in this ministry to get a wider picture of how Christians came together to serve the "least of these" in Hong Kong.

Kowloon Union Church

Founded in 1927, Kowloon Union Church (KUC) is an independent Protestant church with historic links to the work of the London Missionary Society. With the motto "Where All Are One," the church strives to be an inclusive community of the Christian faith and is known for its commitment to social justice and ecumenism.

Background of refugee and asylum seeker ministry

A minister and longtime member of KUC, Maggie Mathieson recalled

> When I came to Hong Kong in 1996, there had always been refugees and asylum seekers from different countries in Kowloon Union Church. They were from South Asia, like Pakistan, Bangladesh, India, and Nepal. The whole situation was different as the numbers [of refugees and asylum seekers in Hong Kong] were not as huge as now. Back then, there was no organized approach at KUC to helping, just helping on a weekly basis. We always made sure there was food on Sundays after church because agencies giving food didn't open on Sundays. The government organizations were not as efficient as they are now.[1]

---

1. Maggie Mathieson, interview with the author, April 25, 2012.

The church got involved in caring for refugees and asylum seekers on a case-by-case basis, providing basic necessities such as food packages and vouchers, rental assistance, and donated goods through KUC's mission committee. Friendship and pastoral care were vital as refugees and asylum seekers navigated the rocky road with UNHCR, Hong Kong Immigration Department, landlords, detention centers, doctors, hospitals, psychiatric wards, and social services. From time to time, the church or individual members paid for air tickets on behalf of asylum seekers whose cases were rejected and who chose to return home voluntarily rather than be deported. KUC's commitment to serving refugees and asylum seekers was formed from this experience among those from South Asia. Later, other persons seeking asylum from Africa and other parts of the world started to attend.

After joining Kowloon Union Church, refugees and asylum seekers participated in worship and Bible study and served the church in various capacities. They formed a choir called "African Voices" (later renamed "Voices of Peace") that performed singing and drumming every second Sunday of the month during the worship service. This reciprocal arrangement worked well, said Mathieson: "The one thing the 'brothers' have is *time* and the one thing people in church don't have is *time*." Outside the church, several asylum seekers were able to study in Bible colleges, seminaries, and universities in Hong Kong or Asia to further their education. Admission and fee sponsorship were arranged through friends and agencies in the Christian community.

Mathieson observed growth and change in the congregation's attitude over the years. Speaking frankly, she said

> A lot of members were very racist, very suspicious. They would very easily point a finger—'The black ones did it.' That was the real situation and the [African] brothers felt it and shared with me how embarrassed and sad they were. They knew within the church that they had 'sisters and brothers.' But they knew when they saw the [church member] in the street, and the person crossed over the other side to avoid contact, that not all was what it seems. There were still underlying issues.[2]

Later there was more acceptance from the congregation as members began to know them as individuals with names, not as just one big group. The church reached the point where the brothers could serve as worship leaders, Sunday School teachers, and church council members. A growing number of women asylum seekers also joined the church. Some were mothers of young children, so their time was more restricted.

2. Ibid.

One Christian family who fled their home country due to religious persecution found refuge at Kowloon Union Church. Although the family faced many hardships to survive in Hong Kong, they were grateful for the day that they walked by the church, saw the cross on the building, and decided to go in to pray. The wife and mother of the family said

> Many times I ask my children and husband, and then my husband asks me the same, 'If we didn't go to KUC, if we didn't go to this church, what will happen in our lives?' Of course maybe we would be destroyed. Because really this church is very helpful, very supportive, very much cared for my children, cared for me. We have fellowship with my family, my friends, every Sunday, we came and prayed. My children come every Saturday for programs, [the minister] is very kind to my children. So really the church changed our life. They reduced our difficulties in Hong Kong.[3]

One of the great joys of the ministry was celebrating with those who obtained refugee status and were resettled overseas to Australia, USA, or Canada. Mathieson had knowledge of eight refugees or refugee families from the church who had gotten resettled in the past ten years. She related their amazing stories of overcoming adversity and their will to survive. Several still wrote to her at holiday time and shared family news with the church.

Peacemaking Program

One of the unique ministries that the church developed for refugees and asylum seekers was the Peacemaking Program. Phyllis Wong, KUC Minister-in-charge since 2008, said the ministry started as a way to go beyond simply giving tangible service.

> I could see that they had different kinds of needs. During Bible study or individual counseling or conversation, these needs come up. They had different struggles—to face an uncertain future, they can't work, racial discrimination. As a pastor, I could see giving tangibles was not enough. Everyone has been given positive gifts from God to help and serve others. It's being empowered. From faith and pastoral perspectives, I asked, 'What are their talents?' Obviously drumming, dancing. Let them lead

---

3. Asylum Seeker M (Middle East), interview with the author, August 18, 2013.

sessions to teach in the congregation. It helps them to feel good to share with others, it makes them feel appreciated.[4]

Wong said that since many had faced threats to their lives in their own country, the issues of peace and security were so important. Thus, as they shared their struggles and stories with Hong Kong people, they could become "Ambassadors of Peace." She wanted the Hong Kong Chinese community to become more aware of this group as they were also God's people, neighbors who needed care and love. "To do that," she said, "you must *know* them." As a social worker before entering ministry, Wong utilized her own network in the Chinese community to arrange the peacemaking team to visit local schools, churches, service organizations, and community centers. The team members were heartened to receive a warm welcome, especially among school-aged and university students. Programs might include talks, music, games, drumming lessons, and French classes, as many African asylum seekers spoke French. On several occasions, the peacemaking ministry invited groups that they had visited to come to Kowloon Union Church, where the team could host the gathering and reciprocate with hospitality in their own "home."

Wong emphasized that the main purpose of the program was to benefit the asylum seekers and refugees who participated. By helping them to develop positive relationships in the community and allowing them to share their talents and cultures, KUC strived to lessen their loneliness and stress and to give them a sense of purpose while living in Hong Kong. The program expanded in partnership with other community groups and NGOs, with a social worker and ministry assistants serving as coordinators. The success of the group's outreach was reflected in the church's annual report.

> Through our peacemaking programs we were able to serve people of different religious backgrounds, such as Muslims and Buddhists, to promote KUC spirit of ecumenism, justice, and peace. The peacemaking team shares the gospel of peace, love, hope, joy, friendship, respect for human dignity, harmonious society, and the love of Jesus Christ. Through sharing Bible stories, personal stories, drumming, singing, dancing, and praying, we are able to pass this message of love to the people of different age groups, genders, social status, and background that we met.[5]

Each Thursday, the peacemaking ministry ran an afternoon fellowship. The initial aim was to allow time for team building and planning for

---

4. Phyllis Wong, interview with the author, April 19, 2012.
5. Kowloon Union Church, *Annual Report 2012*, 35.

the outreach activities. Over the years, the fellowship time included interest classes, workshops, guest speakers, Bible study, and choir practice. Besides sharing the love of God and helping the community to understand the situation of marginalized people, the program impacted the lives of the asylum seekers and refugees in positive ways.

> All the brothers and sisters find this ministry meaningful in that it helps them get out of a stressful zone into a serving zone, from a thinking zone into a thanking zone, from a crying zone into a comforting zone. The love we shared from our fellowship, the songs, dances, the stories, and meal gave each one of us the sense of belonging in a family that cares for each other.[6]

This sense of family included sharing joys and sorrows in major life passages. There were parties to celebrate marriages, and baby showers to welcome a newborn. When members received sad news of the death of a loved one overseas, the church arranged a memorial service at KUC so the community could mourn with the bereaved who could not attend their loved one's funeral abroad. In September 2011, the church was shocked to receive news of the death of one of the members, Abraham Orume, who had returned to Cameroon after his asylum-seeking claim was rejected. A memorial service was held in the sanctuary. During the service, a moving video of his life in Hong Kong was shown. The documentary had been produced earlier by a group of university students as a school project.

Each year, the Peacemaking Program took charge of one Sunday service to celebrate World Refugee Day (June 20). The worship included prayers, testimonies, music, drumming, and a sermon, all led by the members. The team also performed for special occasions throughout the year such as the Christmas Eve service and the World Refugee Day events of other agencies.

Roy Njuabe, former Ministry Assistant at KUC, emphasized the importance of refugees and asylum seekers being welcomed in Hong Kong. He said, "When people reject you, it's difficult. We want to empower asylum seekers to feel a part of the community through this ministry." He cited the case of an asylum seeker who was afraid of going outside his apartment in Kowloon. For three years, he mingled only with other Africans. However, once he became involved in the peacemaking team, the young man reported, "Now I know I am in Hong Kong society where I can be inside and people are nice."[7]

---

6. Kowloon Union Church, *Annual Report 2013*, 24.
7. Roy Njuabe, interview with the author, June 1, 2012.

A female asylum seeker described how she came to Kowloon Union Church through the peacemaking ministry.

> The very first time I came here was to participate in a drama [in the role of Mary in a nativity play]. That first time I came here, I felt it was my pattern to be here. I need to be here. I think that is when I started to come to church. I decided I will come here . . . I am *home*. Even when I miss church, I don't feel good, because I feel I am missing this family. I need to be there.[8]

She joined the peacemaking team and found that it not only alleviated her loneliness and boredom, but it gave her a chance to have friendly interaction with Hong Kong people from all walks of life.

Another asylum seeker, who later received refugee status, was a core member of the Peacemaking Program. He described his experience.

> In Hong Kong society, there is a lot of discrimination. People don't like foreigners, black people. What this ministry does is create awareness of the life of refugees, to show we are human beings and promote acceptance. The refugee situation can happen to anyone. There's a lot of ignorance about Africa. Some young person asked me, 'Do you sleep with lions?' I told the kid I've never seen a lion in my life! A Hong Kong teenager asked me, 'Is your blood black?' I said no, it's red just like yours . . . But I can see the changes, the impact on Hong Kong society. It's changing the minds of Hong Kong people. They would hold their nose if they sat next to you. Now we can see African brothers getting married to Chinese . . . Where I live when I step out my house, someone always says, 'Hello!' The village people even help me take groceries up the stairs. At Lunar New Year, they brought me gifts . . . This experience as an asylum seeker has strengthened my faith and my wife [in Africa] encourages me. I seek a life where I am safe, I can eat, I have a place to sleep. What is my dream? To go home.[9]

The church recognized that women asylum seekers and refugees had special needs. Some were single mothers raising young children without the traditional support of family and community. Others were separated from their children who remained behind in their home country or refugee camps. Some were victims of violence. In order to minister to these women, KUC was sensitive to the need for extra support for female asylum seekers and refugees. Wong encouraged the mothers to bring their children to

---

8. Asylum Seeker N (Africa), interview with the author, September 1, 2013.
9. Refugee A (Africa), interview with the author, May 3, 2012.

church programs. She knew that it was a long journey for some, but she told the mothers that the church could not help them if they did not make an effort. Besides, when the children were baptized, the congregation made a pledge to nurture and care for them in the community of faith. Special programs for mothers and babies were started at the church with plans for training classes in parenting and childcare.

Since most asylum seekers and refugees were in Hong Kong only temporarily, Njuabe asked how as Christians they could make an impact. He believed that their mission was to take love into the community, to share love with those who are different because love transcended national identity and languages. In terms of personal relationships, he added, "Maybe one day [Hong Kong people] will remember there was a black boy who came and played African drums, and remember and keep the bond. Maybe that person will react toward black friends differently later in life." In terms of social change, he saw a very good future for the Peacemaking Program as they increased their platform, showed they were not beggars, made them feel courageous, and helped them to stand up in the community.[10]

Hong Kong Chinese perspectives

Leslie Chow, a Hong Kong Christian, worked with the Peacemaking Program from September 2011 to March 2013. His involvement came about through a partnership between Kowloon Union Church and an NGO for youth called A-generation. Chow arranged and accompanied the team on many of the community visits as they served as peace ambassadors of their own countries. He said, "Peace is not just talking, communicating. Peace is symbolized by action, eating African food with our hands, playing games, singing, and drumming. There are many good things in African culture. Not all of the asylum seekers left the country because of war or political situation. Some left for religious reasons."[11] When the team visited Christian groups, it provided valuable opportunities for Hong Kong residents to have fellowship with believers from different countries.

Chow expressed that working with the peacemaking ministry was a learning experience for him as well. One challenge revolved around the concept of time. He discovered that "African time" often meant that the brothers would come one hour later than the appointed time. As one member told him, "In African culture, there is no past, no future, just present 'now.'" Another explained, "In African time, you eat the fruit and throw the

---

10. Roy Njuabe, interview, June 1, 2012.
11. Leslie Chow, interview with the author, May 7, 2012.

seed to the ground, a tree will grow. Don't think in small segments of time, think of seasons." Chow said he had to adjust. He also learned to ask them to arrive one hour earlier than the actual scheduled time.

Another insight was that building relationships of trust between Hong Kongers and Africans was a gradual process. It was not easy for some of the asylum seekers to talk publicly about the circumstances that led them to leave their country or to share about their difficulties in Hong Kong. Chow trained the team to use a story-telling form of drama called "Playback Theatre." He said, "From these stories the audience figures out during the refugees' stay in Hong Kong, what they need most is not material assistance but the community's acceptance and inclusion."[12]

In order to build up their positive identity and self-image, he preferred to arrange settings with small-group sharing rather than large audiences in a big hall. He observed that students in big groups tended to ask silly questions, but they shared more in-depth in small groups. Also, it was better for asylum seekers if they focused on topics that allowed them to speak freely, such as comparing political systems in their country with Hong Kong's. For example, one team member observed that in Ghana, citizens can vote for the president while citizens in Hong Kong cannot. It was a challenge to the view that Africa was "uncivilized," which the member attributed to Hong Kong media bias in reporting on Africa.

Besides going out as peace ambassadors, the ministry organized leisure activities for the asylum seekers and refugees to mix with Hong Kong people. These included playing football, swimming, visiting country parks, and sightseeing. Recreational activities provided an outlet for them to relax and enjoy themselves and to feel happy and normal, even if only for short periods of time. Chow stressed the importance of appreciation and respect for these men and women whose lives in Hong Kong were tough to maintain and unnaturally passive. He was confident that the Peacemaking Program would continue to be effective even after he gave up the post to continue his social work studies.

Hong Kong Chinese churches

What about the Chinese churches that the peacemaking ministry visited? What was their response? The author interviewed staff of two churches that had an extended program with the Peacemaking Program.

---

12. Chow Tze [Leslie], "Being Peace Makers."

a. Tsing Yi Chuen Yuen Church

Tsing Yi Chuen Yuen Church is located in the campus of Yenching College, a junior-senior high school in Tsing Yi, New Territories. Both church and school are sponsored by the same denominational body, the Hong Kong Council of the Church of Christ in China (HKCCCC). The minister of the church, Wong Wai-cheong, also served as the school chaplain. He did not have a prior connection with Kowloon Union Church, but he was a seminary classmate of Phyllis Wong. It was God's blessing, he said, that allowed the two churches to come together through their ministerial friendship. The first meeting with the Chuen Yuen Church was a sharing talk by the peacemaking ministry with the youth group in 2008. Wong Wai-cheong described the encounter.

> Phyllis [Wong] came here with Roy [Njuabe] and some asylum seekers to visit the youth fellowship, praying with the youths, singing African songs, playing drums. Even though Hong Kong is a so-called international city but we seldom have a chance to communicate with others, even use English, so [the youths] were very happy and excited. The brothers talked about their history and background, the reasons why they came to Hong Kong. Different countries have different cultures. Even they came from the same region, Africa, but they are not all from the same country. They explained what is the difference. [For example] some of them their mother tongue is English, others the mother tongue is French. It was very special for us, even for me! Afterwards, I tried to have a contact again with them. I said, hey, can we have another gathering or even some programs where we join together?[13]

The following summers in 2009 and 2010, the peacemaking ministry visited the church in a more intensive program. The team taught the youth how to play African drums and cook African food, taking advantage of the large kitchen facilities of the school. The program also involved outings to go hiking or to the beach. At the church's twentieth anniversary event, the peacemaking team and church youths gave a drum and dancing show on stage before an audience that included the school principal, teachers, parents, students, church members, and others from the community.

For Wong Wai-cheong, the program was an invaluable opportunity to expose the youths to other cultures and peoples. However, he needed to find adults from the church to serve as translators, which was not an easy task.

---

13. Wong Wai-cheong, interview with the author, August 12, 2013.

Still, he emphasized to KUC that he expected the young people to be pushed to speak English as much as possible. Most of the youths did not have many chances to interact with people from other countries and were afraid to talk in English. He said, "We claim we love everyone. But we seldom have contact with people of different color, especially Africans. Maybe most of us fear to have contact with them."

After the program, he noticed a marked difference in the youths' confidence to interact with strangers and their openness to learn about other cultures. In subsequent exposure trips to mainland China arranged through NGOs, the youths were not scared to speak in English to some NGO staff who were foreigners. Even now, years after the program, the students often mentioned their exciting time together with the African friends. He said for everyone involved, "It was a very, very special experience." Chuen Yuen Church felt encouraged to continue such exposure programs with other groups in Hong Kong to help the young people to grow in faith and to broaden their worldview.

b. The Church of St. John the Baptist

The Church of St. John the Baptist is an Anglican church (Sheng Kung Hui) in Tseung Kwan O, New Territories. The Peacemaking Program's involvement there included drumming lessons for elementary school students and the elderly. It ran from 2011 to 2013. One of the ministers, Leung Siu-chun, was a seminary classmate of Phyllis Wong. She welcomed the idea of having the African brothers come to the church for cultural exchange and a music program. Another staff member, Angela Kwong, was asked to be in charge since she was a church musician and fluent in English, having studied at a university in the UK.[14]

The students and senior citizens were recruited from the community as part of the church's ministry. The classes involved drumming lessons, singing, and games. The session would start with a prayer led by the peacemaking team and included the sharing of African culture and Christian faith. After the course was completed, the children were given a chance to perform at the church's annual fundraising program, while the elderly performed for a large evangelistic program at Easter. On each occasion, the peacemaking team would perform together with their students. The staff reported a positive response from the audience and the congregation.

---

14. Information and quotes taken from interview with Leung Siu-chun and Angela Kwong by the author, July 25, 2013.

Similar to Cheun Yuen Church, one of the challenges of running the program was language. Kwong recalled the situation:

> Most of the Hong Kong children were shy. They don't talk a lot especially in English. But they can understand, even if I don't translate. But the African brothers are friendly, always smiling, and always saying something funny. After a few lessons, the children feel very comfortable to talk to them.

The elderly participants required more patience and assistance. Most were sixty to eighty years old and did not understand English, so they needed translation. They also needed to go more slowly in learning the drums and preferred some notes or writing on the board to follow. Nonetheless, according to Kwong, the elderly were very happy to be with them. Though they could not communicate in English, they could catch the meaning through body language. Both children and elderly understood that even though they did not speak the same language or have the same culture as the African brothers, they could still communicate by playing the same music.

When asked about the value of the program, Leung said, "We try to let our elderly and children have contact to understand African brothers and sisters and learn from them. In our culture generally many persons dislike black persons. So we try to build a bridge between them." She felt that the peacemaking team was sensitive to the cultural gap and used humor in addressing stereotypes and fears. For example, one member put out his hand and talked about how people might think that black skin was dirty and not want to shake hands with him. He showed them his hands were very clean. He explained how dark skin color protected them from sun damage in African climate. This helped the children to understand that though they had differences in many things, including appearance, that each one is a special creation of God.

Like Chow from A-generation, the church discovered that another difference revolved around issues of time and schedule. On the one hand, the church admired the spontaneity and flexibility demonstrated by the peacemaking team. They were able to change plans quickly to improvise in any situation, whether it was in a lesson or during a performance. On the other hand, there were anxious moments as the church was left waiting for the team to arrive for scheduled meetings. Kwong remarked that strict punctuality and detailed planning did not appear to be as important in African culture as it was in Hong Kong culture. These issues were eventually resolved through better communication between the church and Peacemaking Program leaders in terms of expectations and needs.

The church regarded the program as a great success for all participants. This approach was a soft way to change lives through the medium of music education. Building friendships over time required direct, personal contact. Just talking would not be enough. Leung expressed sympathy for the situation of refugees and asylum seekers in Hong Kong. She said, "Their financial situation is not good, they cannot work. In Hong Kong everything is expensive. Kowloon Union Church tries to help them live better and to help Hong Kong people understand them more."

THE VINE CHURCH

The Vine is an English-speaking evangelical church that grew out of the international church Repulse Bay Baptist Church in the 1980s. After several changes of meeting venues and leadership, the church was established under the name of The Vine in 2002. The name was taken from Jesus' words in John 15:5 ("I am the vine"). The church moved into a new state-of-the-art Vine 2 Centre in Wanchai in 2011. According to their website, "The Vine is a dynamic community of faith called to creatively build the family of God, transforming lives, cities, and society by the intimate presence of Jesus Christ."[15]

The Vine and social justice

In terms of church mission, The Vine has become increasingly involved in social justice ministry. Outreach to refugees and asylum seekers was the start of a new and challenging course for the church.

> Right at the beginning when God brought to us refugees who needed help and fellowship we sensed an awakening of purpose in this direction. As the church has grown there have been new opportunities to reach out and be involved in the community. Social justice is now becoming a significant driver in our understanding of an appropriate Christian response to the issues faced by society today.[16]

The church explained the significance of social justice for The Vine as a church in the following four statements:

---

15. The Vine, http://www.thevine.org.hk.
16. Ibid.

1. Social Justice is at the very heart of the gospel. We see social justice as an expression of God's heart to save the world He loves.

2. The gospel is at the very heart of social justice. We are unashamedly Christian and evangelistic in the work that we do.

3. The grace of God will transform lives and bring justice. Our purpose is the transformation and influence of communities, societies, and nations for the glory of God.

4. The church should be a voice for justice. We should be active in society to speak up for those who are denied justice.[17]

Background of refugee and asylum seeker ministry

The Vine had the largest ministry to refugees and asylum seekers among churches in the city. About 250 refugees/asylum seekers received assistance with shelter, food, medical care, transportation, a small monthly cash allowance, counseling, and pastoral care in a comprehensive program that included Christian fellowship and spiritual instruction. The decision to give a monthly cash allowance of a few hundred Hong Kong dollars was controversial and counter to the policy of most agencies such as International Social Service and the Social Welfare Department. These agencies provided direct payment to landlords for rent and distributed vouchers for food, transportation, and medical care. The church acknowledged that giving cash was a risky move. Yet, The Vine felt these persons needed some measure of dignity and choice in their everyday spending. The church tried its best to keep the spiritual and material aid together, believing that both were required according to the teachings of Christ. The staff also spent time to accompany asylum seekers and refugees in receiving medical treatment and dealing with legal and social problems.

When asked how this ministry started, Vine Founding Pastor Tony Read said it began with a letter sent to the church office around 2003. The letter was from an Indian national being detained at nearby Victoria Prison with a plea for a pastor to visit him. Read made a visit to the prisoner who was an asylum seeker detained for overstaying his tourist visa. To the pastor's surprise, there was a whole group of asylum seekers of different nationalities in the prison, living under deplorable conditions. With nothing else

17. Ibid.

to do, the group met for prayer and Bible study twice a day in the prison. After the asylum seekers were released, some began coming to The Vine.

> They turned up at the church, and we thought, 'Oh, we'd better do something with them.' Of course we did what we're supposed to as Christians. Some we helped financially, some we had fellowship with them. Then their friends were released and then their friends started coming. And it just suddenly started growing and growing and growing from that. Nothing we could calculate on at all. But of course the interesting thing is for international churches that their common language is English. Although it's [the asylum seekers'] second language, they are in an English-speaking church and at least they can begin to understand and make sense of what is happening around them and you can begin to feed into that. So that is the reason why the English-speaking churches are involved in refugee ministry and refugee work.[18]

As the numbers increased, The Vine became aware of other agencies and churches working with refugees and asylum seekers. The Vine initially channeled its donations through the charity organization Christian Action to support its service center in Chungking Mansions. With the growing caseload and urgent needs of refugees and asylum seekers, the church believed it was being called to set up its own program to provide spiritual care and additional material support. Read was convinced that this was The Vine's specific calling, their heart, though not exclusively theirs. It was to be shared with other churches and agencies. He described their initial efforts.

> We've had to work it out as we went along. We've made mistakes. At one stage, we decided that we would try to help, to give money to anyone who came to the church. And you can imagine what happened! [laughs] So then we started to say things like, 'Well, you really need to come to our [worship] services, you need to be a part of the community in some way' and then of course they kept saying yes, yes, we are, so then we had to monitor, we had to start taking attendance for those who were coming. And then we started refugee fellowships. That was when John Mac [Macpherson] really then became a pastor to work specifically with them. He had been doing it before voluntarily. Then he was taken on to do that work. Then they started to grow spiritually.

---

18. Information and quotes taken from interviews with Tony Read by the author on December 8, 2010 and May 29, 2013.

The ministry expanded into two weekly fellowships at The Vine for refugees and asylum seekers under the guidance of a full-time social worker, John Macpherson, who was hired as community minister in 2007.

Weekly fellowships

The Vine established two mid-day fellowships to cater to the needs of refugees and asylum seekers, one on Tuesday for Africans and another on Wednesday for South Asians. Macpherson recalled when the church decided to reach out to asylum seekers, some church members did not agree with getting involved in social concern. When the decision was made to start the fellowships, some Vine leaders were skeptical, saying it would not work, that these asylum seekers would not become Christians. His response was, "It doesn't matter. They are still people who need help."[19]

There were around one hundred persons from twenty nations attending the African fellowship, which was conducted in English and French. They came from countries such as Ghana, Cameroon, Somalia, Uganda, DR Congo, and Togo. Approximately sixty persons attended the South Asian fellowship conducted in English with small groups in various Asian and Middle Eastern languages (Hindi, Pakistani, Urdu, Sinhalese, Tamil, Indonesian, and Arabic). The church monitored the numbers with attendance sheets due to the need to provide transportation allowance. A separate Nepalese fellowship reached the point of being self-run by leaders and met in homes with Christian study materials in Nepalese provided by the church. The Nepalese community was a combination of those with Hong Kong residency and those who were refugees and asylum seekers. A number of church members regularly participated in the fellowships to lend support and guidance. The author also observed several visitors with special interest in the ministry who joined the meeting each time she attended.

The weekly fellowships included a time of worship, sharing, and Bible study followed by a simple buffet-style meal. Both groups were predominantly men, though there were some women and a few children in attendance. The African fellowship was lively with an abundance of praise music, drums, testimonies, and prayer. Macpherson said the group was largely able to organize the fellowship themselves since many were Christian. In June 2013, the African Fellowship staged a musical extravaganza called "Telema—An Authentic African Musical" at The Vine for World Refugee Day. The production featured African music, drama, dance, and Christian

---

19. Information and quotes taken from interviews with John Macpherson by the author on December 8, 2010, December 14, 2010, and May 9, 2012.

testimonies to share the stories of refugees and asylum seekers in Hong Kong. The South Asian fellowship was a smaller, less organized group with many who were not Christian but seeking to know more about the faith. The fellowship time started with singing praise songs selected by the participants. A small band led the music with different persons leading prayers and guiding the worship, either the staff or a member of the church. Bible readings were given in representative South Asian languages followed by a short teaching from the pastor. After the group assembly, the meeting broke into small discussion groups according to language.

Macpherson said, "One of the greatest needs for this vulnerable group of people is a safe place where there is trust and acceptance. There are few rules in the fellowship meetings except respect and kindness for one another." He shared that it had been a difficult process that had taken several years to reach a point of smooth operation. For example, the African fellowship was initially filled with conflict carried over from national tensions in their own countries. Finally, it was made clear that all these political differences had to be "checked at the door." They had to cooperate and get along in the spirit of Christian love. Similarly for the South Asian fellowship, there remained the stigma of caste among some cultures. It was decreed that caste was not operative at The Vine and everyone was equal in the eyes of God.

The Vine had a strong emphasis on evangelism and spiritual growth in their refugee outreach. As stated earlier, their social justice work is unashamedly Christian and evangelistic—what Read describes as "incarnational justice" that is personal and embodies the spirit of Jesus. This evangelical spirit was a natural extension of what the church desired for everyone who walked through its door—to equip every person to lead a life worthy of the calling of Christ. The Vine taught that the church is a fellowship of believers in which everyone is a minister, accountable to and capable of serving others. The church intentionally put refugees in charge of their own fellowships to build up leadership as well as a sense of ownership.

About 70 percent of those who attended the fellowship groups also worshipped at The Vine on Sundays. Others were known to attend different churches. Macpherson said they were always welcome to join any of the church's Christian discipleship courses. He noted as well that the church found out they are the best in service, and he commended their faithfulness to the congregation. He said, "We are teaching them practical skills that will go with them wherever they are, make them employable, like how to lead small groups, how to be accountable, show up on time, and work hard. They are not able to work, so it's not good for a mature man in his prime to not have anything to do."

The Vine wanted asylum seekers and refugees to have opportunities to do something for others and lessen their sense of isolation in Hong Kong. For instance, some of the Africans were involved in visitation to the Chinese elderly through the church's partnership with a local charity, St. James Settlement. A Chinese-speaking person accompanied them to translate, and feedback was positive on both sides. The African fellowship managed to raise HKD 2,000 (USD 260) one year toward the church's gift-giving to the elderly for Christmas visitation. Macpherson hoped that there could be more exchanges with Chinese churches, but none of The Vine pastors at the time spoke fluent Cantonese, so there were few contacts that allowed them to do so. Read expressed appreciation for the partnerships with Chinese churches that Kowloon Union Church was able to establish through the Peacemaking Program.

In September 2010, the Hong Kong Council of Social Service conducted a survey of The Vine's refugee work via interviews with the service users. In the published report from the Centre for Social Impact, the Council gave The Vine high marks for quality service, especially in the areas of improving refugees' psychological stability, financial condition, and sense of worth.[20] This report was a confirmation to the church that their refugee ministry was making a significant difference in the lives of people seeking asylum in Hong Kong.

Evangelism in a multi-faith setting

The issue of evangelistic efforts among asylum seekers and refugees who were adherents of other faiths was raised by the author. What was the church's position on evangelizing persons, for example, who were Muslims, Buddhists, or Hindus attending the fellowship groups? Macpherson responded, "I don't ask them to unlearn what they know. I just try to teach what is really important, what makes God pleased. I never comment on their religion." The fellowship group meetings always included the reading aloud of Bible passages in different languages, which he felt made a big impact. He recalled an asylum seeker approaching him after hearing the story of Jesus healing a blind man. The asylum seeker had a disabled son and said this was the first time that he had hope. In Macpherson's experience, just reading the Bible aloud was so powerful when people could hear the "word of God" in their

---

20. Hong Kong Council of Social Service, *Centre for Social Impact Newsletter*, September 28, 2010.

own language. He acknowledged that understanding Christian faith took time, and besides, "You can't rush belief."

Read shared the case of a Nepalese refugee who converted from Hinduism to Christianity after contact with the church. The refugee had lived in Hong Kong for about seven years. During that time, he demonstrated his natural ability as an evangelist, bringing hundreds of his compatriots to different Christian small groups that he oversaw. Now resettled overseas in the USA, he continued his evangelistic work among refugees in his new country. He even asked permission to use the name "The Vine" for his new church. Read visited him overseas at the church and was impressed with the ministry and social service that were being provided and recognized in the community.

When asked his position on refugees' changing their faith, Read answered

> I would say the key phrase is you don't try to change them in order for them to receive your help. You give them help and in that process, you believe they will begin to see the truth and reality of the gospel for what it is, because you don't hide that from them. The fact is these people need people to welcome them, they need family. And one of the things we try to do well at The Vine is to be welcoming and family to people. And that is always their testimony after they've been here four or five years, when they've been at the church for a long time. They say, 'This is my family, you were my family when I didn't have family, you looked after me.' It's not so much the fact that we give them money, the amount of money we give them is actually small really, but the fact that we trust them. You have to restore their dignity basically. They are not trusted. They are not loved so it's quite a long sort of process you have to go through.

The church also witnessed Muslims who asked to receive Christian baptism. According to Read, many had said to him, "I had a vision of Jesus." Then they proceeded to describe the vision in detail. At times, he wondered if they were saying this to impress him. But it happened often enough, that he believed these were genuine conversions, stressing that he never pressed them. However, he added, "There is one little thing we have to be careful about. We don't push this but some of them feel that if they become Christian, this will increase their chance of having refugee status. Because they feel they wouldn't be welcome back if they go back home." All candidates for baptism at The Vine went through a process of examination and instruction.

When the process was satisfactorily completed, the person was baptized. In one case, an asylum seeker family of parents and children were baptized at the same time.

Asylum seeker voices at The Vine

Four male asylum seekers from a South Asian country volunteered to be interviewed after a Wednesday morning fellowship meeting. Three were converts to Christianity while the fourth remained an adherent of another faith. They told their stories and perspectives.

"Michael"

Michael entered a church for the first time in Hong Kong, as he was not allowed to do so in his country. He was in contact with different churches, including one Chinese church whose pastor helped him to get a Bible in his own language. Eventually he came to The Vine.

> Since 1999, I have been very interested to be close to the world of Jesus Christ. But I did not understand much English. God helped me to be close. He wants me, so I follow, follow, follow him. From 1998 to 2009, that long period, I really want to know who God is and what is your relationship with God and me and my family. Finally I found God, I got close to God. God is with me in my heart so I got baptism in 2009. In The Vine Church, all the pastors, all the brothers and sisters, they really have heart to feel what kind of situation I am living here. God bless them, this is a blessing from God in The Vine Church, sharing, caring. This is the way I am surviving in Hong Kong right now. I am the longest [one from my country] in the church, I brought eight to ten persons into this church. They are really strong believers. I am very happy. I follow God. And he is my way and my life. My life is bright. That's all.[21]

"Samuel"

Samuel had been in Hong Kong for a little over a year. He attended the fellowship meetings at The Vine when he had free time, usually after getting a phone call from his friends. He was not a Christian, but said he came for

21. Asylum Seeker I (South Asia), interview with the author, June 26, 2013.

information. "I come here because these people are my friends. I like this church. Love my friends. See with your eyes, observe your humanity, what we need is love from the pastor."

He received financial support from his family back in his home country, so he declined offers for rent or transportation subsidies from the church. "When I have money in my pocket, I come here. Many times I have come here. I don't waste my time. I learn something. Thank God. If I have any problem, I pray to God, God helps me." On other occasions, he visited the Sikh temple and the Thai Buddhist temple in Hong Kong at the invitation of friends, as well as visiting the mosque.[22]

"Henry"

Henry came to The Vine in 2007 and received baptism in the church a few years ago. When he informed his family back in his home country about his religious conversion, he said they rejected him and cut off contact. His life was difficult and he had been waiting over two years for a decision from the UNHCR on his asylum application. He indicated that he had attempted suicide numerous times (this was demonstrated in the interview by gestures of strangling himself with a rope). Henry was taken to the hospital where the doctor gave him medicine for depression. He continued to take pills at night, otherwise he could not sleep. He wanted to study so he could tell others about Christ.

> I come to church every Wednesday, every Sunday for the past four years. [He attended another international church before]. Before, I don't understand. I study, study. Go to school. Then I go outside with friends. But I don't understand. Then one time I was crying with Jesus, you sacrificed yourself. I accept you, Father. Why don't you give me a chance to study? I was crying, crying. Do you believe that, God? Now I understand, later, later. 75 percent, 80 percent understand. Really, really I too must believe. I told the guys, fine, one hundred years I cannot die, my life is in God's hands. But I believe in Jesus. In Matthew 28, Jesus says go, you go, give back the mercy of God to other people.[23]

He said that he was unable to return to his own country since he converted to Christianity because his life would be in danger. He asked many

---

22. Asylum Seeker J (South Asia), interview with the author, June 26, 2013.
23. Asylum Seeker K (South Asia), interview with the author, June 26, 2013.

pastors if they would help his family move to Hong Kong, but no one would guide or help him.

> Because Jesus asked me, this is part of the body of Jesus. Are you part of the body of Jesus? I think you should help me, open any gate, because if they allowed working, then no problem. I can earn money, support my family. One year, two years, I can survive. But I spent seven years here, and no hope. If you [the author] have any power, maybe you can discuss the problem.

"Stephen"

Stephen was a convert to Christianity. After inquiring about the author's identity, he said he had a message to the Christian community about the situation of asylum seekers like himself and Henry.

> The people coming here are facing a lot of problems. Like me, like this brother, somehow the Lord chose us to be a Christian. And today we are facing more troubles than before. Before we go where we want, whatever we do, we don't realize. But today we have one shepherd, the sheep of the shepherd whose name is Jesus Christ. And he gave us such a beautiful way to live in this world. But we didn't still get any right to stay [in Hong Kong]. We are still facing many problems like [Henry's] family, he needs to get his family from [home country] to here. But the Christian community, there are missionaries working with many other countries, there is a lot of money going to the missionaries, but why are they not able to give funding for one family to get out from that country? That is my question. Why do they use a million dollars to go to many [other] countries to share God's love, but they are getting nothing [no results in new converts]. But if they bring his family here, if they think about this way, they have five members that are going to be saved, to become Christian. If someone is able to understand this problem, I have shared with a few people this problem, but there is no answer.[24]

For Stephen, the answer would be for churches to take concrete action to help asylum seekers, especially those who joined the body of Christ. He was angry that some Christians were reluctant to help people in need in their own church, even doubting the genuineness of their conversion. It

---

24. Information and quotations taken from interview with Asylum Seeker L (South Asia) by the author, June 26, 2013.

appeared that some Christians believed that most asylum seekers were liars and "putting on a drama" in order to get money and help. He challenged the comfortable lifestyles and material wealth that he observed among Hong Kong Christians.

> So how about one person in front of you says, I am Christian. And please help me. You are my church, you are the body of Christ. I'm coming to you and you don't listen to me? That's painful. I accept your community, I come into your community, living in your community, coming in front of you. Even if he didn't ask you for help, but God gave you to feel his problem. 'I have very beautiful clothes. Why don't you have? I have many clothes in my home, why I cannot help? I have a lot of bank balance, why I cannot give him monthly some support?'
>
> The Lord says in the Bible, Matthew [7]: Many people are coming to me and they said we are doing many things in your name, but the Lord said, 'I don't know you. Go away.' Why? Because the time is coming already. [knocks on the table for emphasis] They are nominal Christians. They call themselves Christians, they want to be big headlines in the newspaper, they want to get approval for themselves, they are proud. They have egos, they are pastors, they are hearing many people, but they have nothing to do with their people in their own country. You are responsible here to your community, for your country.

Stephen acknowledged that there might be some asylum seekers who were lying or living immorally. However, he resented that all asylum seekers were viewed in this negative way. Due to his conversion to Christianity, he said he would face the death penalty back home. "I want to stay here. I want to work. I have no future in my country. So what do you need from me? What do you want from me? It's painful."

Pastoral postscript

When asked about the challenges of this ministry, Read shared what he had learned over the past ten years about serving asylum seekers.

> Of course you get your disappointments. I always say to people who want to work with refugees, particularly pastors in churches. Someone is going to rip you off somewhere. You cannot expect to do this work without someone 'taking you for a ride.'

And if you want to be in the work of compassion and helping refugees, you cannot go into that, [demanding that] whatever you give them, whatever or however much you help them, that it is all genuine, you know. So you have to be ready for that. Because some churches take the view that we're giving this money, this money is from the congregation and we have to be wise with God's gifts, to know where it is going, we have to monitor it and make sure it's being used properly. You know what? They can't do it. You know? Because they can't. They get taken for a ride once, and they say, these people are here just for the money. You have to get rid of that attitude, otherwise you'll never help anyone. And you've got to believe that the money is going to be used for good purposes, you have to give it with a genuine giving heart. And release it. Otherwise you can't do it with a good heart, you're always suspicious in your mind. So that was another interesting sort of revelation along the way for us. How it affects your heart of compassion and heart of giving.[25]

CHRISTIAN ACTION

Christian Action, which had worked with refugees in Hong Kong since the 1950s, began winding up its refugee services in the late 1990s as the Vietnamese boat people situation reached its conclusion. In 2004, Executive Director Cheung-Ang Siew Mei was approached by the UNHCR who asked Christian Action to assist in providing services to the latest group of refugees and asylum seekers. The work was restarted and appeals were made to Christians and churches to support opening the Centre for Refugees in Chungking Mansions, where many asylum seekers often congregated. Financial support for running the Centre was given by churches and Christian organizations including Hong Kong Christian Council, Tsung Tsin Mission, and the Council for World Mission Nethersole Fund.[26]

The mission of the Centre for Refugees is to provide a holistic support system to refugees and asylum seekers in Hong Kong that increases social, financial, cultural, mental, and spiritual well-being. Newly arrived asylum seekers with no access to any services often made their first stop at the Centre for emergency housing and supplies. Besides running a drop-in center, the agency distributed basic necessities such as food, clothes, baby formula, diapers, and toiletries. Multilingual staff (fluent in Chinese, English, Urdu,

25. Tony Read, interview, May 29, 2013.
26. Cheung-Ang Siew Mei, interview with the author, May 11, 2012.

Nepalese, Hindi, French, Arabic, or Tagalog) provided case work, advice, and referrals to partner organizations along with assistance with education for children, and support to unaccompanied minors. Adult classes for computer and language study along with workshops for women and men sought to empower clients. Each month, the agency served six hundred families in a comprehensive program of care and development. In addition, outreach activities with local/international schools, universities, companies, and community groups helped to spread awareness and provide platforms for the resident population to engage with refugees.

Religious groups in Hong Kong were among Christian Action's strong supporters. These included international churches, Hong Kong Chinese churches, Christian NGOs, and a Jewish synagogue. The relationships often came through personal contact from a staff or volunteer. Christian Action also partnered with a wide network of companies, professional mental health and medical groups, organizations, schools, and NGOs in its programs. Julee Allen, Manager of the Centre for Refugees from 2012 to 2014, said that Christian Action shared the love of God through *action* and demonstrated the love of God through selfless service. Since the clientele came from multi-religious backgrounds with the majority not being Christian, it was important to respect the different faiths of those coming for assistance. A Christian pastor might come to offer a weekly Bible study, but attendance was strictly voluntary as were all the programs. She commended the dedication of the small core of churches and religious organizations that faithfully supported the Centre's programs year after year through their donations, volunteers, and hosting of events.[27]

Still, there were challenges. Fundraising was one of the most pressing. As is the case in many charities, donors were more likely to give to particular programs rather than to general operating costs. Yet operational costs were essential for maintaining the Centre, and some charitable foundations would only fund programs whose beneficiaries were residents holding Hong Kong identity cards. Since refugees and asylum seekers were not eligible to receive Hong Kong identity cards, the agency had to raise its own budget as well as rely on community contributions and in-kind donations of goods and services. Another issue was how to raise awareness in the community about refugees and asylum seekers while respecting their requirement for protection and privacy. The public wanted to hear stories and see evidence of the Centre's impact, but the agency had to be sensitive about how it shared this information. Lastly, it was a challenge at times to meet the expectations of diverse Christian groups in terms of how the Centre for Refugees should

27. Julee Allen, interview with the author, March 27, 2013.

operate. As for Cheung-Ang, a member of the Anglican Church, the bottom line was clear. She emphasized, "As Christians, we have to care about social justice issues. That's why I am doing this job, where I place my energy. If we see people suffering, don't wait for government funding. The church needs to wake up and get moving."[28]

OTHER CHURCHES AND ORGANIZATIONS

Numerous other churches and organizations reached out to this vulnerable population as awareness of the need became evident. Some congregations got involved due to their proximity to places where asylum seekers and refugees gathered or lived. Others became active through contacts with Christians NGOs that they already supported in mission. A few churches reached out through the natural connection of shared language and culture with those seeking asylum. We examine them below.

a. St. Andrew's Church

St. Andrew's Church is an evangelical, international Anglican church in the Tsimshatsui district near Chungking Mansions. The church was frequently visited by asylum seekers and refugees, who asked for help with accommodation and food. According to the mission director Shirley Cheng, the church helped where it could, but the needs were greater than St. Andrew's could handle. The congregation was happy to partner with Christian Action so those in need could get basic assistance and legal help.

Most of the asylum seekers and refugees worshipping at St. Andrew's were African men, some with Anglican background. When asked how the refugee ministry in the church developed, Cheng recalled that it started with a Sunday dinner program featuring a simple meal. She discovered that most people came because they wanted to meet and have fellowship with one another rather than coming just for food. She conducted a questionnaire to follow up and concluded that the hunger of refugees and asylum seekers who came to St. Andrew's was more spiritual than physical. A midweek Refugee Fellowship was started with Bible study and prayer. Around ten persons attended regularly, half from St. Andrew's, the other half from other churches. The church encouraged each asylum seeker to have a "home church" to ensure pastoral care and supervision of their spiritual growth. All asylum seekers from any church were welcome to join the programs at St.

---

28. Cheung-Ang Siew Mei, interview with the author, May 11, 2012.

Andrew's, including online theological training courses from Moore College in Australia. Asylum seekers who wanted to take the course were given financial help to cover the fees.

As a church, it became important to involve the whole congregation in the ministry. Cheng said

> The best way is for the community to care for them. So we stopped the Refugee Fellowship several months ago since other churches [were doing something similar already]. We changed the fellowship to put them into local fellowships. We asked each asylum seeker to be a part of one small group at St. Andrew's, so the group can learn how to care for them. We really try to get them to become a member, to participate as regular church members. The group leaders are to care for them, and the [asylum seekers] are supported spiritually and financially by their own group. The group leaders can always come back to church for help or advice.[29]

Recognizing that the majority of asylum seekers in Hong Kong were not Christian, the church started a program to teach English as a way to serve non-Christian asylum seekers. A number of Muslims were coming to the church to learn English, which would be useful for communicating in Hong Kong as well as in a third country when they were resettled. This could also be an opportunity to expose them to Christianity for the first time.

Cheng welcomed the opportunity to cooperate with other English-speaking churches and agencies through the Refugee Ministry Group. She found the group to be an effective means of advocacy for fairer and more humane policies.

> It's a hard issue but I still think that Hong Kong is an international city. We benefit from the world, all the international trade. We bear certain responsibility to the world to some suffering countries. Yes, it might be a big number, but even if we can take in a small number, it would be a great help to the world and encouraging other countries to do the same.[30]

b. SS. Peter and Paul Church

Saints Peter and Paul Church is a Catholic parish located in Yuen Long, New Territories. The church's ministry to refugees and asylum seekers had been

29. Shirley Cheng, interview with the author, June 5, 2013.
30. Ibid.

operating for over ten years through the parish's St. Vincent de Paul Society. According to parish priest Gervais Baudry and society member Minnie Siu, the church assisted over sixty refugee and asylum seeker families in Yuen Long and nearby Kam Tin. This area, far from the city center of Hong Kong, was home to many refugees and asylum seekers due to the lower cost of housing. The program focused on filling in the gaps where government funding fell short, such as materials needs, transportation fees, school uniform and book fees, and rental costs. Families came to the church once a month to collect goods and receive cash. Home visits to each family were conducted every three months to see what was needed and to help refugees and asylum seekers fight for their rights.[31]

The program was run by volunteers and funded through donations from the churches. Due to high demand, priority was given to families or single women with children. It was felt that single men had other means to supplement their income, but families carried special burdens. They needed larger living spaces than the government allowance could provide. Mothers could not go out freely as they needed to care for young children. Fathers could not risk involvement in activities that might lead to arrest and detention. Siu recalled times that the Society received phone calls from panicked families when one of the family members "disappeared." Assistance was provided to track down the missing person who had been picked up by the police and put in detention. The church also supported refugee families in their dealings with immigration, police, lawyers, government departments, landlords, hospitals, and doctors.

Most of the families that were served came from South Asian countries such as Pakistan, Sri Lanka, and Indonesia. Only two or three families over the years were from a Catholic background. Most were adherents of other faiths. At the end of home visits, Siu said that Society members would have a short prayer with the family and take leave with "God bless you." She reported that the families expressed appreciation for the church's concern and help, such as one who remarked, "Wow, Catholics are really good!" Baudry emphasized that the service was given as a Christian witness but was not for evangelization purposes. The parish wanted to do more to help refugees and asylum seekers and was exploring other programs that could serve them and get more volunteers involved.

Siu had seen many members of refugee families suffering from depression and loss of self-confidence. This was especially evident in the men, who legally were not allowed to work. In some of the home visits, she only saw

---

31. Gervais Baudry and Minnie Siu, interview with the author, September 11, 2013.

the mother and children. When she inquired about the father, he reluctantly would come out from another room and stay only briefly. It appeared there was a sense of shame in not being able to provide financially for the family. The church sought to send a message of love through building friendships with refugees and asylum seekers and serving their daily, practical needs.

c. Love and Peace Ministry

Love and Peace Ministry was started in 1995 by Syed Kamran Hashmi ("Pastor Kamran"), a Baptist minister from Pakistan. He and his family joined the International Baptist Church of Hong Kong and started outreach to ethnic minorities from South Asia and the Middle East. Eventually a home Bible study fellowship was begun for Indians and Pakistanis who were from Hindu and Muslim backgrounds. This became the Indo-Pak Chapel of International Baptist Church. The ministry held Sunday worship, Bible studies, and discipleship classes at facilities in Mongkok belonging to the Baptist Convention of Hong Kong. The emphasis was on interfaith friendship, evangelism training, and programs for South Asian children and youth.

By 2005, Victor Joseph, a Pakistani Christian, joined the ministerial team focusing on prison ministry and asylum seekers. Some asylum seekers who attended Love and Peace Ministry had been visited by Brother Victor while in prison. For asylum seekers and refugees, Pastor Kamran stressed that Love and Peace Ministry could not do anything beyond giving spiritual help. Financial and practical assistance were being provided at other churches. He especially commended Pastor John Macpherson at The Vine who "really gives his heart and soul for the asylum seekers." Pastor Jacqueline Chan, a Hong Kong Chinese staff of the Love and Peace Ministry, reflected on the church's role in the lives of asylum seekers that they had touched. "We see them come for [many] reasons but when they find Christ, God has a purpose for them in coming to Hong Kong."[32]

d. Inner City Ministries

Inner City Ministries (ICM) was established in 1994 as an evangelistic mission to minister and proclaim the gospel in Chungking Mansions. The population of the complex at the time was primarily South Asian, residing and working in the heart of the inner city. While many legitimate businesses

---

32. Syed Kamran Hashmi and Jacqueline Chan, interview with the author, June 16, 2013.

operated out of Chungking Mansions, the high-rise was also known as a place where drug addicts, sex workers, asylum seekers, and others conducted questionable or illicit activities.

The impetus for the ministry came from a group of young people, many from St. Andrew's Church. The group started "prayerwalking"[33] around Chungking Mansions and believed it to be completely unreached in terms of Christianity, despite being within the church's parish boundary. Christian groups, however, were already meeting in Chungking Mansions, although they were not so formally organized. St. Andrew's leased an apartment on the fourth floor in the complex to start a mission under the name of Inner City Ministries. ICM was governed by a group of English-speaking churches and organizations including St. Andrew's, Union Church Hong Kong, International Baptist Church, Youth With A Mission, and Evangelical Community Church. The ministry expanded and acquired a second apartment in the same building, one for males and one for females.[34]

A variety of ministries were offered at ICM, but it was primarily set up as a Christian drop-in center. Anyone was welcome to drop by, whether for worship, prayer, Bible study, respite, food, or medical assistance. For several years, fellowship groups were under the oversight of Missionary Pastor Alem Meren and his family, including daughter Naro Keitzer, who developed the Women's Ministry. According to Keitzer, the first asylum seekers to show up at ICM were a family from Ethiopia. The wife was pregnant and the family was in desperate need. ICM and churches helped the family with medical care and daily necessities. They joined the fellowship and soon attracted other asylum seekers to attend. For Keitzer, the most important thing that was offered to asylum seekers was the family of faith, a caring fellowship for those who were alone, in need and far away from home. The ministry brought asylum seekers together with others facing similar trials and gave them a place where they could share their burdens and be encouraged.[35]

Martin Radford, the Executive Director of ICM since 2011, first got involved around 2004 when he came to preach once or twice a week at the mid-day worship. Worship was held at 12 noon, followed by lunch. He said

> The lunchtime was rather a focus. We were feeding fifty people a day. Worship was great. They'd become passionate about it.

---

33. "Prayerwalking" is a Christian practice of intercessory prayer conducted while walking street by street in a city or neighborhood. Hawthorne and Kendrick define prayerwalking as *"praying on-site with insight."* See Hawthorne and Kendrick, *Prayerwalking*, 12.

34. Martin Radford, interview with the author, August 12, 2013; Inner City Ministries, http://www.innercityministries.org/about/index.html.

35. Naro Keitzer, phone interview with the author, August 25, 2013.

But a lot of people were dropping in, collecting lunch, and leave. And many of them were from different faiths but the outreach side was not good. This was beginning to disturb me and to disturb Ian [the Executive Director, Ian Ashby] and couple of other staff. [Some of them] were heavily involved in cooking meals and their heart was for evangelism.[36]

As the demography of Chungking Mansions changed, the ministry became more and more dominated by asylum seekers, many from Africa. In terms of giving assistance, the staff found it increasingly difficult to distinguish between those who had escaped serious cruelty and abuse and those who were simply "overstayers." ICM often ended up serving more as a soup kitchen, feeding them, and then sending them upstairs to the sixteenth floor where Christian Action had established a refugee and asylum seeker service center in 2004.

According to Radford, the original mission of Inner City Ministries was to deal with the more resident South Asian ethnic minority community that was as yet unreached in terms of the Christian gospel. In 2007, ICM decided to close its Chungking Mansions center and move to another district to concentrate on ministry among South Asians. However, one staff member, Samuel Dhavale, was keen to continue the ministry in Chungking Mansions. Union Church Hong Kong agreed to take over the lease of one flat, and Chung King Ministry was established with Dhavale as supervising pastor.

While ICM's target population was South Asian residents, two or three recognized refugees were among those invited to enroll each time for "Taste of Grace," a three-month commercial cooking course offered free-of-charge since 2011. Radford said, "It's a real success story and blessing in training those with refugee status. It's given them something to do during the long wait. It's been well accepted that the course has been useful. We've trained eight refugees who have now all left Hong Kong."

e. Chung King Ministry

Chung King Ministry is an evangelical mission sharing the gospel in the heart of Chungking Mansions. It was established in 2007 to continue the ministry that was previously carried out under Inner City Ministries. The center remained a drop-in center to serve the needy such as refugees, the homeless, the unemployed, drug addicts, alcoholics, and sex workers—those who for whatever reason found themselves at the "bottom of the

---

36. Martin Radford, interview, August 12, 2013.

heap." The mission was supported by various evangelical churches including those worshipping in English, Chinese, and Korean. Pastor Samuel Dhavale, former staff of Inner City Ministries, was supervisor of Chung King Ministry along with his wife Shlivya Dhavale. The center offered a daily worship service at noon followed by lunch and dinner meal two nights a week. There were other meetings during the week such as a Ladies' prayer meeting, Tea Time Evangelism meeting, and Friday night intercessory prayer and testimony meeting. Additional services included pastoral care, hospital and prison visitation, counseling, and helping people deal with the authorities. Chung King Ministry also ran two shelters for refugees.[37]

Volunteers from churches helped to lead services and Bible studies. Refugees and asylum seekers shared in the worship ministry. In this author's visit to the Friday night meeting, there were approximately thirty persons in attendance. Asylum seekers were in charge of music (electric piano and drums), gave testimonies, and voiced intercessory prayers.[38] From time to time, the Chung King Ministry Worship Team was invited to speak at Christian churches and events in the community.

Vitalis N.M., a Cameroonian asylum seeker, came to Hong Kong via Beijing in 2004. After a few months sleeping on the streets, he stayed in the mission's shelter and became part of the fellowship. He was taught how to play the guitar and joined the worship ministry team. In 2009, he received a scholarship to study in Hansei University in Korea with the assistance of churches and Christians in Hong Kong. Before he left, he wrote

> I came to HK alone and with nothing except with an uncertain future. But now I have a large loving and caring family, thanks be to God who led me to Chung King Ministry and surrounded me with wonderful people. And I will be leaving with satisfactory experiences and with great hope in the Will of God concerning my life.[39]

f. Hong Kong Christian Institute

Hong Kong Christian Institute (HKCI) was started in 1988 as an ecumenical Christian NGO with emphasis on social concerns such as human rights, democracy, and justice. Davy Wong, HKCI Project Secretary, became aware of the issue of asylum seekers in Hong Kong around 2006 through contact

---

37. Chung King Ministry, organization brochure and *Newsletter—Summer 2013*.
38. Visit to Chung King Ministry by the author, September 6, 2013.
39. Chung King Ministry, *Newsletter—October 2009*.

with a member of Kowloon Union Church.[40] The organization included asylum seekers and refugees among its concerns in a solidarity night event later that year. Another project was the Green Christmas Campaign promoting simple holiday celebrations in December 2006, co-sponsored with the Catholic Diocesan Justice and Peace Commission. The charitable donations to the campaign were given to the refugee and asylum seeker program of Christian Action in Chungking Mansions.

In 2007, the Asylum Seeker Concern Group was formed with participation from different Hong Kong Chinese churches and organizations. Among the churches were Shum Oi Church, Cheung Chau Church, Christian and Missionary Alliance Tai Wai Church, and Blessed Ministry Community Church. The Hong Kong Christian Council, Hong Kong Women Christian Council, and Student Christian Movement were organizations that also partnered with HKCI in this initiative.

The Group sponsored a signature campaign among Christians in March 2007 that successfully petitioned the Immigration Department to release a seventeen-year-old African unaccompanied minor asylum seeker being held in detention. Then, for World Refugee Day in June 2007, a program called "One Church, One Family" was held to educate churches about the difficult situation of refugees and asylum seekers in Hong Kong. Bible passages such as Jesus' flight as a refugee from King Herod's persecution in Matthew 2 and Jesus' teaching to care for the stranger in Matthew 25 were among the scripture verses used to connect the Christian story with concrete stories of refugees suffering in the society.

Contrary to the perception that Hong Kong Chinese Christians did not care about refugees and asylum seekers, Wong discovered that there was empathy among church members. She recalled speaking to a women's group in a church which had a number of women from mainland China. Their initial response was surprise. "Hong Kong still has refugees?" they asked. Yet, the mainland Chinese women were very understanding and sympathetic about refugees' lives since they were migrants themselves. Churches generously responded by giving donations of toys, food, and goods to be passed to charities for asylum seekers and refugees. However, it was a challenge to sustain long-term action as churches were so busy with their own programs and other mission projects.

Since 2011, HKCI supported asylum seekers and refugees through its partnership with other organizations including A-generation and special events for the annual World Refugee Day. Refugees were also among the international human rights concerns in HKCI's Interfaith Dialogue program.

---

40. Davy Wong, interview with the author, August 30, 2013.

g. Caritas–Hong Kong

Caritas–Hong Kong was founded in 1953 as the official social welfare bureau of the Hong Kong Catholic Church. The agency was involved in assisting refugees from Russia, mainland China, and Vietnam for many decades. An implementing partner with the UNHCR since the 1970s, Caritas–Hong Kong launched a joint project with the UNHCR in 2000 to provide protection and essential assistance to UN recognized refugees. Services included financial aid, housing, medical care, counseling, visitation, community liaison work, education, training programs, and leisure activities. According to Betty Mok, who was project officer in charge, "Caritas is a local NGO with Christian belief. All human beings regardless of their gender, age, nationality, status, religious beliefs . . . are entitled to basic needs according to basic human rights such as food, shelter, medical care and education."[41] Funding was almost solely from the UNHCR with additional charitable donations from sources such as the Operation Santa Claus campaign in 2008. The project ceased in March 2010 due to changes in the UNHCR's welfare assistance program.

CONCLUSION

Christian ministry to refugees and asylum seekers in Hong Kong from 2000 to 2014 was impacted by the same factors that distinguished this group of protection claimants from those of the past. The smaller numbers arriving individually plus their racial/ethnic diversity resulted in the international congregations playing a more prominent role as refugees and asylum seekers sought out English-speaking and other non-Chinese language churches for help and worship. Case studies of two international congregations—Kowloon Union Church and The Vine—demonstrate different approaches to ministry with refugees and asylum seekers. While both offered pastoral care and social welfare assistance, Kowloon Union Church developed a program whereby small teams of refugees and asylum seekers were sent out into the community as ambassadors for peace through cultural sharing and testimonies. The overall tenor of openness to other cultures, backgrounds, and religions reflected Kowloon Union's history as an ecumenical church. The opportunities to connect the peacemaking team with the Chinese community were made possible through the efforts of Hong Kong Chinese staff members. At The Vine Church, programs centered around two weekly Christian fellowships, one for Africans and another for South Asians. An

---

41. Benitez, "Australian Group's Donation Helps Refugees."

emphasis on worship, Bible study, discipleship training, and evangelism reflected The Vine's roots as an evangelical church. The presence of a full-time social worker who was a church member to oversee the fellowships was a key to the ministry's growth and integration into The Vine Church as a whole. From the author's interviews and observations of the ministry at both churches, it was evident that refugee and asylum seeker ministry in Hong Kong required substantial commitment from the staff and congregation to sustain the programs. Yet both churches were clearly proud of what had been achieved and hoped that their efforts would encourage more churches and community groups to care for the marginalized in the society. Indeed, other churches and Christian NGOs did make their contributions according to their particular mission.

Charities with Christian backgrounds such as Christian Action and Caritas provided a vital link to larger agencies to coordinate and improve social services for refugees and asylum seekers. Given the rapidly increasing caseload, the limited funding available, and lengthy protection claim process, it was inevitable that meeting the needs and demands of this population would be a challenge. There were no easy answers since there was no central coordinating authority to assign a role to each agency or service provider as there had been with the Government Security Bureau during the Vietnamese refugee era in the camps. Thus, there was the possibility with the latest group of refugees and asylum seekers that programs were duplicated or there might be competition among NGOs for funding and volunteers. This could create confusion in the minds of the refugees and asylum seekers themselves as to who was looking after their best interests. Thankfully, however, conflicts appeared to be minimal. Overall, those serving this population in the Christian community were committed to working together to maximize the resources and manpower for the well-being of the refugee and asylum seeker community. The Refugee Concern network of agencies, NGOs, and churches was a concrete example of this concerted effort.

In the final chapter, we will summarize our findings on Christian hospitality to refugees and asylum seekers as a form of mission in the Hong Kong church. We will discuss significant issues that have arisen in our research, evaluate Christian response, and draw conclusions about possible ways forward for the common good of the wider society.

Chapter 8

Putting It All Together

WE HAVE TRAVELED ON a long journey in our study of Christian hospitality from the ancient Near East all the way to Hong Kong in the twenty-first century. What have we discovered along the way about welcoming the stranger? What have we learned about the lives of refugees and asylum seekers and how to care for them? What do we know now that we did not know before about mission in the Hong Kong church? This chapter answers those questions along the same three lines of enquiry, namely:

- The nature and meaning of Christian hospitality to strangers
- The distinct situation of refugees and asylum seekers that calls for hospitality, and
- The witness and service of Hong Kong churches through Christian hospitality to displaced persons and the wider community.

Let us summarize our findings to put it all together for the reader.

a. The nature and meaning of Christian hospitality

Ancient roots

In the study of hospitality's ancient origins, we saw how the initial motivation to offer hospitality to strangers was self-protection. In fact, the rituals of hospitality evolved for the mutual protection of travelers far away from home and of the households and communities that they sought to enter temporarily. This element of danger existed on both sides. While hosts may believe that they carry the greater risk in allowing the entry of an unknown visitor, the guests are also vulnerable because they are subject to the authority and will of others who are likewise strangers to them. Hospitality provided one means of alleviating this danger and the fear that naturally accompanied it. In both the Semitic culture of the ancient Near East and the Greco-Roman culture of the Mediterranean, the established customs for welcoming the stranger developed into an honorable tradition based on exchange and reciprocity. The practice of hospitality as an exchange of gifts and honor may well be universal.

Another aspect of ancient hospitality was the belief in the religious nature of the encounter between hosts and guests. The worldview of many peoples in antiquity was thoroughly religious with no clear separation between matters of the sacred and profane. Belief in the divine protection of strangers provided a strong motivation for hosts to treat guests well in order to avoid punishment by the gods. Another belief widespread in antiquity was the possibility that a stranger could also be a god in disguise. This phenomenon of divine visitation was often depicted in ancient folklore and literature, with the story of Abraham entertaining three divine guests in Genesis 18 as a hallmark text of ancient Near Eastern hospitality. In Greco-Roman literary texts, the appearance of gods in disguise in order to test the hospitality of mortals is a recurring motif in Homer's *Odyssey* and other stories. Reverence for the gods along with subsequent moral and ethical sanctions from society all contributed to an unwritten law of hospitality that governed civilized behavior between hosts and guests.

Despite fixed rules of conduct and the compelling association with the divine, hospitality to strangers was never guaranteed. According to protocol, the host was the master of his or her domain as well as ruler over the fate of the guest. That meant that the guest must invariably assume a subordinate and submissive role. The structure of hospitality thus reveals inherent tensions concerning identity, power, and control. This asymmetrical relationship would normally be balanced in future encounters when the roles were reversed. However, hospitality was always shadowed by its linguistic twin—hostility—which sprang forth when hosts or guests refused to follow their assigned roles. Rebellion, betrayal, or upheaval were violations of the code of conduct and as a result could turn strangers into enemies rather than guests or friends. While these transgressions by either party were disastrous to the relationship, they did reveal how hospitality depended on the suppression of any underlying conflicts and the possibility of inequities built into the system.

Biblical and historical witness

The Hebrew tradition of caring for the stranger was based on the memory of God's provision when the Israelites were aliens in the land of Egypt and sojourners in the wilderness in search of a homeland. With the understanding that God was their host and they were God's perpetual guests, the Israelites established a new society with special attention to those who lived among them in need of protection and livelihood, namely the poor, widows, orphans, and aliens. This concern for the welfare of the vulnerable was a sign of God's justice and love for all humanity. As people in a covenant relationship with a holy God, the Jews were also called to be holy. They fulfilled this command by setting themselves apart to maintain spiritual purity, following the Law, and performing deeds of lovingkindness in imitation of the divine *hesed*. In keeping with their primary mission of "hallowing the name of God," Jewish hospitality in the first century CE was mostly extended to fellow Jews—the needy and travelers as well as teachers of the Torah and their pupils—and possibly to those seeking to convert to the faith.

The ministry of Jesus as recorded in the New Testament testifies to a radical reinterpretation of the relationship between hospitality and holiness. Rather than separation from those who did not share the same faith or even separation from Jews who were ritually unclean, Jesus used table fellowship to break down religious and social barriers. In particular, he reached out to those who were marginalized in Jewish society and welcomed them as honored guests in the kingdom of God. His teachings, such as the parable of the Good Samaritan, pointed to his own embodiment of divine hospitality that was poured out to those in need from any religion, race, or culture. His identification with humanity, who were all sinners in need of grace, culminated with his sacrifice on the cross. Through his death and resurrection, all creation was reconciled with a Holy God and invited to partake in the heavenly banquet where persons from east and west and north and south would sit together at the table of the Lord.

The belief in the possibility of divine visitation continued to inspire the church throughout the centuries to welcome the stranger as a manifestation of Jesus Christ himself among them. His appearance in the form of a needy guest was a crucial test of their generosity and hospitality. Those he called the "least of these"—the hungry, thirsty, stranger, naked, sick, the prisoner—were not only the most destitute and abandoned in society, but they were also the ones with whom he chose to identify himself on earth. While similar acts of mercy could be found in Jewish and Greco-Roman cultures, the church's teaching that connected service to the needy with service to Jesus himself carried the added weight of eternal consequences. Thus, in perhaps an act of divine mercy, Christians had already received fair warning that the needy stranger who appeared at their doorstep was in actuality their Lord and Savior in disguise. There were to be no more excuses for inhospitality. On the Day of Judgment, actions taken would speak louder than words.

Contemporary theological contributions

Twenty-first-century Christians are reminded that a contemporary theology of hospitality should always begin with worship. First and foremost, hospitality is our participation in the triune life of God through the liturgy and sacraments of the church. The language of worship is overflowing with gracious words such as invitation, welcome, table, bread, wine, rest, and refreshment. It is in worship that Christians learn what it means to be guests and hosts in the kingdom of God. As recipients of the divine hospitality of the One who is at once "Host, Guest, and Home," the church responds in gratitude with words of praise, the giving of offerings, and sharing of the good news with others. Through steady spiritual nourishment and formation in the house of the Lord, churches are thus equipped to practice Christian hospitality in all its dimensions—first to God, then to one another, and finally to strangers.

In offering hospitality to strangers, churches should be alert to how the roles of host and guest are carried out. The philosophical categories of Self and Other are helpful in conceptualizing what is taking place in the host-guest encounter and whether it contributes to an honest welcome of the stranger. Those who assume the position of host traditionally define the terms upon which hospitality will be offered. Thus, the host's perspective as Self becomes the standard of truth and the norm for all behavior. That means that the guest becomes an Other whose being and behavior are by default judged as different, strange, exotic, and possibly offensive. Christian theologians and ethicists advocate a number of alternatives: a de-centering of perspective from host to guest; a total rejection of the category "Other" in favor of "riotous difference" as a gift of the Holy Spirit at Pentecost; a solidarity with strangers; and even a solidarity *of* others whereby all are subjects, none are objects, and all are equally responsible to one another. Whatever approach is used, it is clear that the ministry of Christian hospitality requires a journey to the margins to find God's guests and our place as hosts in society.

To carry out this ministry of hospitality with strangers, churches must come to terms with limits and boundaries. These are not necessarily negative but rather an indication of our own human finiteness. Limits ensure that certain conditions are present in order for Christian hospitality to take place, such as the provision of safe spaces and adequate resources to be generous, attentive hosts. Boundaries need not become barriers if they are put in place nonviolently with the capacity to expand or adapt to changing circumstances. Furthermore, a spirit of hospitality always seeks to communicate the love of God. In order for Christians to embody this gracious spirit day after day, they must not neglect to draw upon classic spiritual disciplines such as scripture study, prayer, solitude, fasting, and confession on a regular basis. Hospitable places require hospitable people with spacious hearts. After all, Christian hospitality is more than simply welcoming a stranger into one's church or household. There is the greater call of Christ to welcome the stranger into the home of one's heart so that host and guest may meet God there and both be transformed.

Finally, it is acknowledged that the theoretical frameworks of most contemporary theologies of Christian hospitality originate from the West. Nonetheless, even though they rely primarily on Western concepts and experience, the hospitality writings of scholars such as Henri Nouwen, Miroslav Volf, and Christine Pohl are appreciated in other regions of the world, including Asia, and are influential in academic circles. In fact, at the Seventh Congress of Asian Theologians in 2012 on the theme of hospitality, the writings of all three were frequently cited as authorities in the field. Still, the need for Asian contributions to the study of hospitality is apparent, perhaps most critically on the subject of interfaith relations. Here, theologians from different parts of Asia have challenged ecclesiocentric, christocentric, or theocentric models in formulating a theology of religions. They demand recognition of the vitality of ancient spiritual traditions such as Buddhism, Hinduism, Confucianism, and Taoism, not only as spiritual and cultural treasures of Asian people, but also as indispensable influences in their own spiritual and cultural identity as Christians. Churches in postcolonial Asia are called to be hospitable places and hospitable people through welcoming opportunities for interfaith friendship so that religious strangers become religious neighbors and even angels unaware.

b. Hospitality to refugees and asylum seekers

Issues in the international community

With its origins as a practice to protect vulnerable strangers, hospitality has an intrinsic connection to the care of refugees and asylum seekers. Providing asylum can be viewed as a form of hospitality that extends welcome, sustenance, and security to persons who are forced to flee their homeland. International law recognizes refugees as a special category of human rights victims who should be granted protection and support.

Given the various legal instruments in force related to the rights of refugees and the global presence of the United Nations High Commissioner for Refugees (UNHCR), it is tragic that refugees and asylum seekers in the twenty-first century have not been received hospitably in some host countries and cities. There are a variety of reasons for this, including i) suspicion that many protection claimants are actually economic migrants who are unfairly taking advantage of the system, ii) fear that entry of refugees and asylum seekers into the community threatens the quality of living for the established population, iii) compassion fatigue in which hosts are overwhelmed by the number of refugees and demands to care for them, and iv) xenophobia in which persons of a different race, ethnicity, culture, or religion are regarded as foreign or strange and unwelcome. Hence, when the political, social, or economic self-interests of a nation are perceived to be under threat, governments may choose not to honor their obligations as signatories to the Refugee Convention. Even some states that do honor their commitments may do so by providing the absolute minimum required and no more. In the face of this culture of rejection, disbelief, and blame surrounding refugees and asylum seekers, there is an urgent need for other sectors of the community to step forward and demonstrate hospitality to strangers who find themselves stranded in hostile territory.

Issues in the Christian community

The need to protect certain categories of persons whose lives are in jeopardy has been recognized as a religious duty since antiquity. In formulating a modern theology of refugee ministry, it is important to distinguish how refugees and asylum seekers differ from other migrants. While the categories of forced versus voluntary migration are not always clear-cut, there is an element of coercion or duress that pushes refugees and asylum seekers to leave their homeland. They are literally people without a place or the protection of their own country. In terms of vulnerability, they can be identified with every needy person that Christians are commanded to look after in Matthew 25: the hungry, thirsty, naked, friendless, sick, and incarcerated. The church's mandate to care for the "least of these" is more than a call to do charitable deeds for the less fortunate. It is a call to confession and repentance over our failure to love God and to love our neighbor. It is a call to serve Jesus Christ who became society's Other so that sinful humanity could be reconciled to a Holy God. It is a call to sacred hospitality by offering a home to the homeless, protection to those in danger, and a new family to those without kin. In so doing, the church welcomes refugees and asylum seekers to participate in both divine and human communities with dignity as beloved children of God.

In reaching out to refugees and asylum seekers, churches should prepare to be stretched in what can be a difficult ministry. Christians face the same dilemmas that governments and other organizations experience when working among this population: compassion fatigue, fear and resentment from within and without, suspicion that their kindness is being abused, and unexamined issues of prejudice and racism. To prevent these from becoming insurmountable problems, churches should put a priority on nurturing relationships that allow refugees and asylum seekers to get to know and be known in the community of faith. That is not to say that churches do not have a vital role in providing material aid and welfare services. However, there are few places left in society where strangers in the city without money or sponsor or reputation are welcome to enter and allowed to belong. One of the greatest gifts that local congregations have to offer then is a public place where displaced persons of any background can find friendship, pastoral care, and spiritual help. Churches should never underestimate the value of God's standing invitation to grace for those in desperate need of a sign of peace and a word of hope.

Another role of churches in this ministry is providing opportunities for refugees and asylum seekers to offer their own gifts in service to God and the community. Christian hospitality involves the giving, receiving, and passing on of God's blessings. Whether blessing congregations or other sectors of the society, these programs are ways for those excluded from the mainstream to build bridges with the wider society and lessen their sense of isolation and fear. It also provides a chance for the established population to have positive personal contacts with refugees and asylum seekers, who are often vilified in the media and shunned by the public.

While local congregations are at the heart of the ministry of the church, much of the day-to-day service for refugees and asylum seekers is carried out by Christian ministries that specialize in working with this population. There is much to be learned from their extensive experience in dealing with large numbers of displaced persons in their communities. One obvious lesson is the need to coordinate services with other NGOs and government departments in order to maximize resources. This is particularly important in serving refugees in urban areas where there may be no central coordinating authority. Some agencies operate as multi-service centers while others choose to focus on one task such as housing, detention visits, or an area where there is a service gap. An agency may target particular sub-groups, for example, refugee and asylum seeker families, while another organization works only with recognized refugees or lawfully-residing asylum seekers. This prioritizing of service is usually necessary due to limited resources or funding restrictions. However, it indicates that Christian organizations also seek assurance that their support is going to the most "deserving" persons, which is largely determined by one's UNHCR or immigration status. The persons who are most vulnerable to exploitation, mental illness, and destitution may well be those classified as failed asylum seekers who fall outside eligible categories for lawful residence, aid, or even sympathy.

Another lesson learned from those working on the front lines is the need to foster independence and responsibility among refugees and asylum seekers. This is a key point as the current legal system for processing asylum cases tends to foster dependency and a sense of helplessness. One international refugee service organization emphasizes that their staff never do things for protection claimants that they can do for themselves. This builds self-reliance and confidence as well as establishing a measure of accountability. That said, some organizations make it standard practice to include refugees and asylum seekers in the planning, delivery, and evaluation of programs. Granting empowerment to the asylum seekers returns agency to protection claimants by giving them a voice on matters that directly affect them and a sense of ownership over projects designed for their benefit. For refugees and asylum seekers who have limited control over decisions about their future, the opportunity to have choices and make changes is a precious gift, if not their human right.

Lastly, the place of faith in the lives of refugees and asylum seekers is an issue that Christian organizations handle in different ways. While almost all agencies offer service to persons of any religious background without discrimination, there are varying approaches to the matter of open discussion of Christianity. One approach is that religion is not discussed with the protection claimants at all. It is considered inappropriate to introduce Christian teaching or practice unless the refugee or asylum seeker specifically asks, and even then staff will take care to emphasize positive aspects that all religions have in common. This neutral stance is welcomed by government departments and secular NGOs in our study and may be official policy for those wishing to have access to claimants, funding, or contracts. It allays concern about favoritism to a particular religious group and also rules out proselytizing among refugees and asylum seekers of other faiths.

In some Christian bodies, however, the purpose of social service among displaced persons is not only to meet humanitarian needs but also to witness openly to God's redeeming love and power in Jesus Christ. An "evangelical" approach would not view sharing the Bible or discussing spiritual matters with persons in crisis as an abuse of power, but rather an essential part of Christian faith and mission. Any accusation of deception or coercion is strongly denied. Even so, it must be acknowledged that there is a huge power differential between refugees and asylum seekers and those organizations that potentially provide them with housing, food, financial aid, and other means of survival. Christian service organizations that seek to operate among this sector should be sensitive to perceptions that they are imposing their beliefs on others, especially with a population that has been forced to leave behind almost everything from their previous life. Religious identity is one cherished asset that they still possess that can provide meaning, strength, and comfort. Surely Christian hospitality would include the rule of not doing to others what we would not want done to ourselves. Finally, Christians should acknowledge that religious conversion may pose real danger to an asylum seeker or refugee who may be disowned by their family and ethnic community or even subject to death threats on the charge of apostasy. A decision to change one's religion is an extremely sensitive issue in many cultures and requires much discernment, time, and prayer.

c. The witness and service of the Hong Kong church to refugees and asylum seekers

The church as first responders

This study of Christian ministry to refugees and asylum seekers reveals a Hong Kong church that needed to rise to the challenge of welcoming thousands upon thousands of displaced persons seeking safety and a better life. As a small city with a big reputation, Hong Kong offered haven to different waves of refugees during the twentieth century including Russians, mainland Chinese, and Vietnamese boat people. In each case, churches and Christian agencies were among the first responders in partnership with overseas bodies to meet the demands for humanitarian aid. Hong Kong Christians took seriously their duty to care for the strangers among them as a witness to God's compassion and justice.

With the most recent wave of refugees and asylum seekers around the beginning of the new millennium, Hong Kong churches were presented with quite a different situation. Coming individually from many different countries, these persons seeking asylum entered Hong Kong almost unnoticed until their desperate living situation was brought to the attention of congregations and charities in the city. Since Hong Kong had no administrative framework to deal with asylum seekers at the time, those who arrived in need of protection depended on the kindness of strangers, compatriots, and their own wits. With a heart for mission and accustomed to welcoming strangers, international congregations were among the first responders when needy persons from South Asia, Africa, and other places appeared on their doorstep. The opening of Christian Action's Chungking Mansions Centre for Refugees in 2004 was a major step forward in coordinating wider Christian response through one professional multi-service agency.

After successful legal challenges headed by expatriate human rights lawyers, the government began to provide basic subsistence allowances and food packages to registered asylum seekers. Still, the support was hardly adequate for such an expensive city like Hong Kong. Some UNHCR cases dragged on for years and even recognized refugees were waiting years for resettlement to a third country. Without the legal right to work or even legal immigration status in the city, protection claimants were effectively given the message that they were unwelcome and unwanted.

To counter this lack of hospitality, international Christians in the city reached out to offer friendship and pastoral care. A number of churches developed specialized ministries for refugees and asylum seekers that incorporated social welfare support with Bible studies, fellowship groups, cultural sharing, and other activities. The different approaches to refugee ministry in Hong Kong reflected not only different theological backgrounds—from mainstream ecumenical to evangelical-charismatic—but also the different resources available including staff, facilities, finance, and networks. Even with these differences, there was a common commitment among all those who served to care for the marginalized and to improve the lives of displaced persons during their time in Hong Kong. Through a growing network of international and Chinese congregations, Christian organizations, and community ministries, the Hong Kong church was blessed with the gifts and service of refugees and asylum seekers and the opportunity to make the city a more inclusive and fair society.

The challenges of refugee and asylum seeker ministry

This book raised some significant issues about refugee and asylum seeker ministry, in particular how Hong Kong churches dealt with the challenges that arose when working among this population. We examine them as follows: i) compassion fatigue, ii) public opposition to protection claimants, and iii) unrealistic expectations and hopes.

i. Compassion fatigue

While churches in Hong Kong encountered only a small portion of the estimated 10,000 protection claimants in the city, individual congregations were often the initial point of contact for asylum seekers known to the Christian community. Local churches could offer assistance to the handful that were part of their fellowship when refugee numbers were small. As the numbers increased, churches quickly discovered that once they helped one asylum seeker or refugee, more would follow. It would be easy to feel overwhelmed since most churches had limited time and emergency funds. Here, churches responded to the dilemma not by shutting the door but by inviting refugees and asylum seekers into the life of the congregation. After all, the church ministers or staff should not be the only persons who related with them. For those protection claimants from a Christian background, this was relatively comfortable even if the members and the style of worship were foreign to them. For protection claimants of other faiths, this presented a bigger dilemma. Would they be required to join Christian activities in order to receive help? Most refugee ministries had a minimum requirement of attendance at worship or church programs in order to receive material assistance. Otherwise, persons would simply show up for a handout or a meal and then leave. Christian ministries are interested in nurturing relationships and becoming a friend to those who are strangers in the society. Some type of reciprocity is needed in order for that to happen. If indeed the greatest needs among refugees and asylum seekers (besides a safe place to live) are acceptance, trust, and love, then the ministry of the church goes beyond just addressing their physical needs. Christian hospitality welcomes guests to become friends with a community of followers of Jesus Christ and to experience God's acceptance and love through them. Not all asylum seekers accepted the invitation, but many who did found a spiritual home with brothers and sisters in faith.

That said, congregations as well as the wider society are keen to have designated agencies that can provide broader services to a larger number of protection claimants. Local churches were happy to support the opening of the Chungking Mansions Centre for Refugees, if only to relieve themselves of having to judge who was "deserving" or "undeserving" of help. However, service agencies could be overwhelmed as well with higher caseloads than expected and lack of funding to meet multiple demands. Service agencies with a Christian background depend on the backing of churches not only for donations and volunteers, but also for prayer and moral support. Nonetheless, agencies such as Christian Action's Centre for Refugees that work with clients who are predominantly of other faiths should not be expected to function as centers for evangelism. Rather, they are places where refugees and asylum seekers are given help with their requests and treated with dignity and respect. That may already be a profound Christian witness to persons who have had no contact with Christianity or had negative experiences in the past. As is with many Christian social service agencies in Hong Kong, staff are hired based on professional qualifications and not necessarily on religious affiliation. Therefore, the Christian witness of the organization comes not only from the service rendered to clients, but also in the way that employees are valued and the manner in which congregations, ministers, and church bodies offer encouragement rather than discouragement in the inevitable times of difficulty.

ii. Public opposition to protection claimants

Another challenge of refugee and asylum seeker ministry in Hong Kong is overcoming resistance from the public to be involved. Hong Kong Chinese in general have little exposure to resident ethnic minorities, much less to asylum seekers from South Asia and Africa. With three "strikes" against them—their dark skin, their lack of legal status, and their "criminal" background having been in detention—refugees and asylum seekers are arguably at the bottom of the pile in Hong Kong. Many citizens would heartily agree with the government that given the city's small size and relative prosperity in the region, it would be a mistake to extend the Refugee Convention to Hong Kong or to give any incentive for asylum seekers to come or to stay. As it is, they say, the city struggles to deal with the thousands that are already here who are assumed to be illegal migrants who have come for economic or other reasons unrelated to persecution or torture.

In terms of changing public opinion about refugees and asylum seekers, churches are strategically positioned to do so with their networks in the Christian community and the wider Chinese community. Direct refugee ministry had been carried out for the most part in non-Chinese congregations in the city. This is logical given their use of English or other languages and the multinational composition of the memberships. However, many of these congregations and ministries have Chinese-speaking members or ministerial staff who are well-connected to the Chinese Christian community. Thus, the traditional partnership in mission between Hong Kong Chinese churches and the global Christian community is carried out on a smaller scale through a ministry of introduction by key bridge people who linked their refugee programs to opportunities for friendship and service with local Chinese congregations and the general public. Of course, in the long run, it was the asylum seekers themselves who made the biggest contribution by sharing their talents, cultures, and stories to open the minds of Hong Kong citizens.

One other crucial way that churches help to change the public image of asylum seekers and refugees is through their participation in wider campaigns for justice and human rights. Human rights lawyers in particular have shown determination to challenge Hong Kong's policies regarding protection claimants that are in violation of Hong Kong's Bill of Rights and international conventions. Through their efforts, which had precedence in the fight for the rights of Vietnamese refugees in Hong Kong, the overall policies have improved since 2000. Churches would do well to keep abreast of legal developments that have a crucial impact on the fate of current and future refugees and asylum seekers. In smaller but no less important ways, churches are part of networks like Refugee Concern that campaign for better policies on basic livelihood issues. By taking joint action to appeal to government bureaus, the Hong Kong Legislative Council, or the public, Christians testify to their belief in God's demand for justice and compassion to the vulnerable and in the inherent worth of every person regardless of their immigration status.

iii. Unrealistic expectations and hopes

Those who serve the refugee and asylum seeker population in Hong Kong are painfully aware that there are limits to what can realistically be done for them as far as their long-term future is concerned. Since the HKSAR shows no intention of signing the Refugee Convention, protection claimants have little hope of being allowed to live and work in the city or to bring their family from overseas. Some dream of being resettled in the West in places such as the USA or Canada. But again, the recognition rate for asylum or torture claimants is exceptionally low in Hong Kong. The UNHCR Sub-Office Hong Kong's recognition rate was reportedly around 10 percent in 2012 (compared to a global rate of 38 percent), while the Convention Against Torture (CAT) recognition rate was less than 1 percent with only twenty-eight successful applicants from 1992 to February 2015.[1] It is debatable whether the overwhelming rejection of most cases is due to a "culture of bias" in the screening process, particularly at the Immigration Department, or whether most cases in fact cannot meet the criteria for approval because they have not presented credible evidence of persecution or torture. This author concludes that both are likely true to some degree. Therefore,

---

1. Man, "Refugees in Hong Kong See Little Improvement."

it is not helpful for churches and Christian agencies to join in sweeping generalizations that paint one side as sinners and the other side as saints. Nonetheless, given the huge power imbalance between the rights of states and the rights of unprotected individuals, there is no doubt that churches are called to accompany refugees and asylum seekers during their sojourn in the land. And in so doing, churches seek to discover how together they all might fulfill God's purpose for them in Hong Kong.

Besides looking to UNHCR and Immigration, refugees and asylum seekers may have high expectations of churches and Christian agencies that show interest in their welfare. Some asylum seekers expressed anger that church members were not doing more to help them resolve their situation. In fact, they questioned why churches in Hong Kong were so eager to spend millions of dollars to engage in mission around the world when there were needy persons right in the congregation or neighborhood. How could genuine Christians enjoy their middle and upper class lifestyles with their families while there were those suffering in the body of Christ in Hong Kong, people far away from home with no means to earn a living? Surely Christian hospitality should impact a believer's attitude about wealth, possessions, and community just as it did in the early church. While the proper solution may not be an immediate transfer of resources from rich to poor, these challenges do indicate the humiliation that some refugees and asylum seekers feel as beggars in the public eye. It is difficult to show gratitude for things that they believe they are entitled to have in the first place.

Most refugees and asylum seekers are living uncertain lives under stressful circumstances. That might explain why some make decisions that disappoint their pastors, case workers, or brothers and sisters in the church, such as engaging in "unhealthy activities" or getting involved in risky relationships. Ultimately, given their limited options, refugees and asylum seekers must be allowed to make their own choices. They also must be allowed to accept responsibility for the consequences. Churches and Christian agencies too must make choices about how to run their ministries responsibly and how to use their resources wisely. Yet, the church should continue to love and pray for refugees and asylum seekers even after they leave the host's zone of obligation. It is worth remembering that the Holy Spirit moves in mysterious ways, and that the God of Law is also the God who surprises both sinners and saints.

Evaluation of refugee and asylum seeker ministry in Hong Kong

This study of refugee and asylum seeker ministry has been conducted through the theological lens of Christian hospitality to strangers. Therefore, in a final evaluation of the response of the Christian community in Hong Kong to unprotected persons since the year 2000, we ask the questions that were raised in chapter 2—*Did we see Christ in them? Did they see Christ in us?*

From our research, it is evident that churches indeed took to heart the biblical command to welcome the stranger as Christ himself in their refugee ministry. International congregations in Hong Kong were strategically positioned to befriend this group not only because of their use of English language, but even more so because of their openness to people of all races, ethnicities, and backgrounds as children of God. International churches that were founded to take care of the foreigners in the days of privilege have evolved into multicultural congregations of all social classes and many nationalities, including a large Asian membership and some local Hong Kong Chinese. This ministry of hospitality is a special gift that they offer to strangers in general and to unwanted sojourners in particular.

Just because refugees and asylum seekers turned up at the threshold of a church did not mean that the minister and congregation automatically knew how to take care of them. The need to provide immediate material help to individual asylum seekers was obvious enough. Attending to their emotional and spiritual needs required more time and commitment. Even if the congregation was happy to view refugees and asylum seekers as members just like everyone else, in fact, their situation was far from ordinary. In response, some churches started specific programs for this population in their own premises with Christian teaching or worship combined with a meal, fellowship, and social assistance. In addition, there were supported ministries by different churches in commercial spaces where South Asians and Africans tended to gather. A number of evangelical ministries provided various inspirational programs throughout the week with lunch or dinner, along with social welfare provisions such as shelters. One might get the impression that asylum seekers were being forced to attend Christian activities in order to eat, but this author observed that most participants appeared to come willingly and welcomed the spiritual help as well as the free food. The opportunity to share their troubles and pray together was comforting. It may be that those who were not willing to follow the schedule simply dropped out of attendance. In any case, this model reflects the essential place of worship, Christian fellowship, and a shared meal in the church's hospitality.

Other churches provided a different model for refugee ministry. One Catholic society focused on providing assistance and home visitation to needy asylum seeker and refugee families who lived in the parish's district. The emphasis was on humanitarian aid and social support for the poor and disadvantaged and not on evangelism. Most of the families who were helped were not from a Christian background, but they expressed appreciation for the church's concern as recalled in the remark, "Wow, Catholics are really good!" The peacemaking ministry of a Protestant church demonstrated another approach that allowed asylum seekers to meet the public and for the public to meet them. This more outward-looking model reflected the church's ecumenical background that sought to build bridges with the society. Interestingly, the peacemaking team freely shared Bible stories, Christian songs, and testimonies as part of their community programs. For many of the African brothers and sisters who came from a charismatic or evangelical background, this was a way of witnessing to the gospel and sharing a faith that is an integral part of their lives. Finally, the prison visitation and spiritual growth programs of an Indo-Pakistani church sought to witness among the South Asian population in Hong Kong, especially to the youth. Asylum seekers were welcomed to all the activities of the church, although social welfare needs were referred to other churches. The church's programs for interfaith dialogue and friendship were a noteworthy expression of Christian hospitality to other religions in the Hong Kong context.

No matter how devout a refugee or asylum seeker might be or become, however, there was need for them to be involved in other activities besides going to church. With many of them being young men in their prime, they were frustrated to be idle and feel their lives were wasting away. In their homeland, they might have been going to school, establishing their careers, taking care of their families, and working for the advancement of their country. Recognizing this need, most ministries and agencies organized various events such as soccer matches, beach outings, boat trips, and visits to theme parks. These leisure activities were thoroughly enjoyed, although occasionally asylum seekers would meet with rude stares and remarks from the public. Then besides recreation and entertainment, many longed to put their energy into activities that would help them in the future. Opportunities for further education for adults were limited due to costs and the need to obtain government permission. Nonetheless, some were able to get sponsorship to study a course in the university, seminary, or Bible school in Hong Kong or even overseas countries such as Korea. The author was inspired by the initiative shown by asylum seekers and refugees to improve their lives and to establish a degree of normalcy in abnormal conditions that stretched out for years.

At the end of the day, protection claimants needed resolution of their cases at the UNHCR and the Immigration Department and a means of supporting themselves and their families while in Hong Kong. This is where Christian social service agencies have been crucial in helping many more refugees and asylum seekers than those who went to churches. Besides launching the Justice Centre for free legal assistance, Christian Action took up the mission to provide a holistic support system to enhance refugee and asylum seeker well-being in Hong Kong. To this end, the agency maintained good working relationships with UNHCR, the Hong Kong government, and a wide network of social service, community, business, and religious groups. Without their support, it would be impossible to serve effectively. Refugee advocates in the Christian community also supported the implementation of the Unified Screening Mechanism and improved policies with hopes for building a compassionate and just asylum seeker and refugee system.

Through their participation in refugee networks and the asylum seeker world up close, Hong Kong Christians gained a new dimension in their understanding of twenty-first-century global issues and the role of social justice in formulating durable solutions. The Vine Church credits their experience with refugees as the catalyst for the congregation's awareness of social justice issues and the integral relationship to Christian faith and witness. As The Vine's community minister concluded about the asylum seekers, "They completely changed the church." At Kowloon Union Church where social justice has long been a central part of its mission, the gradual migration of persons seeking asylum from the back of the church to the front and even to positions of leadership was a means of doing justice in their own household. Indeed, the blessing of seeing Christ in the stranger comes to both hosts and guests who are willing to be transformed by the gift of hospitality. That has been the illuminating experience of the Christian community in Hong Kong when "strangers welcome strangers" as an act of faith, a sign of hope, and a time to love.

Recommendations

We conclude our study on Christian ministry and mission to refugees and asylum seekers in Hong Kong with some recommendations on how churches could serve more effectively to meet the challenges for the future.

Part Two: The Practice of Christian Hospitality

i. More support from churches

One must remember that the actual number of churches and Christian ministries involved with this special population is not large when compared with the over 1,500 Christian churches and Catholic parishes in the city. Those highlighted in this book are among the major ones serving refugees and asylum seekers, although there are certainly more that are not included here due to limitation of space and scope. Nonetheless, one of the hardest issues for the ongoing ministry with refugees and asylum seekers is funding and resources. That is not to say that every church in Hong Kong needs to be involved in refugee ministry. Each congregation, denomination, and church organization must discern for itself what God is calling them to do individually and collectively as the body of Christ. Some churches have the particular calling to carry out refugee and asylum seeker ministry with joy. That is one of the keys for unprotected persons to experience a genuine welcome among Hong Kong Christians. Still, more churches could find a way to include the welfare of refugees and asylum seekers in their mission programs, such as an annual donation to refugee agencies or a one-off project with asylum seeker children and families. Those Christians who are suspicious that they are being conned by shady persons taking advantage of their kindness are probably better off waiting until they commit the matter to prayer and their hearts are in congruence with their hands.

ii. Friendship and public support in the Chinese population

The acceptance and support by the mainstream population is crucial to the mental health and emotional well-being of marginalized foreigners. While Hong Kong Chinese churches may not be leaders in carrying out this ministry, their support has a huge impact on public opinion. I recall a few years ago asking one refugee friend whether I should join a public demonstration for asylum seeker rights. It was not my usual practice to join protest marches. I was surprised by his answer. He said, "Well, yes, because it always helps when there are locals who show support for our situation." I did not consider myself to be a local Hong Kong Chinese but I was willing to pass as one. When we gathered at the ferry pier, there were hundreds of marchers ready to go, surrounded by drums, banners, and some media outlets. But as my friend predicted, there were very few Chinese faces. As we marched from Central to Wanchai, onlookers stood back as we passed. I was aware that their seeing Chinese faces among the demonstrators did send an important message: We care and Hong Kong should care. The march for protection did not require much courage from me. In fact, the refugees and asylum seekers who led the march were really the courageous ones. Yet, every Christian in his or her way can do something to make one's own city a better place—sometimes all it takes is just showing up.

iii. Fighting for a fairer refugee system

In the big picture, what churches can do for refugees and asylum seekers in Hong Kong is both major and minor. It is major in offering hospitality and incarnating God's love in Jesus Christ to persons seeking sanctuary in the city. It is minor in having any actual power to change or speed up the system that will allow them to move on with their lives in a new country. While it is unlikely that Hong Kong will sign the Refugee Convention that would permit refugees to settle in the city, the Christian community can advocate for policy changes that would make a world of difference to some protection claimants. For example, giving all recognized refugees and recognized torture claimants the legal right to work while residing in Hong Kong would allow them to support themselves and their families and give them back a measure of dignity and self-respect. Another area that could be expanded is empowerment of refugees and asylum seekers to give them a voice in the decisions that affect their livelihood and the right to have their actions and opinions count. Authorities are understandably resistant to any move that would recognize that asylum seekers and torture claimants have any rights in Hong Kong. Yet, as the UNHCR has affirmed, "Seeking asylum is lawful and the exercise of a fundamental human right."[2] When churches work to guarantee that refugees and asylum seekers do have human rights in the city, then the human rights protection for all Hong Kong citizens that is enshrined in the Basic Law and its Bill of Rights Ordinance is all the more secure for present and future generations in terms of the law and in daily life.

A final word

In this study of Christian hospitality, we confirm that refugee and asylum seeker ministry has brought a measure of Christian cosmopolitanism to Hong Kong through opening doors and hearts to vulnerable strangers within its gates. The ministry of hospitality provided opportunities for

---

2. United Nations High Commissioner for Refugees, "UNHCR Calls for End to Detention of Asylum-Seekers and Refugees."

international congregations and organizations to contribute to the overall mission of the Hong Kong church as a witness to an inter-cultural reality and as part of a trans-cultural faith. Still, international Christians did not achieve this by themselves. Strategic partnerships with Chinese Christians and the wider community revealed that there were many more hospitable people and hospitable spaces all over the territory. Through their united efforts to welcome refugees and asylum seekers, they demonstrate the desire of people of goodwill throughout the city for a more just and humane approach to people seeking sanctuary in Hong Kong. And in so doing, they seek to reclaim the culture of hospitality that is Hong Kong's proud legacy from its Chinese foundations, its colonial history, its postcolonial development, and its spiritual and religious inheritance. Beyond duty, it is the Christian community's privilege to be a part of a movement that blesses the churches, the persons seeking asylum, and the city with God's plans for prosperity and not for harm, to give everyone a future filled with hope.

Bibliography

Agamben, Giorgio. *Homo Sacer: Sovereign Power and Bare Life*. Translated by Daniel Heller-Roazen. Stanford: Stanford University Press, 1998.
Ager, Alastair, and Joey Ager. "Faith and the Discourse of Secular Humanitarianism." *Journal of Refugee Studies* 24, no. 3 (2011) 456–72.
Akpinar, Snjezana. "Hospitality in Islam." *Religion East and West* 7 (2007) 23–27.
Ali, A. Yusuf. *The Holy Qur'an: Text, Translation and Commentary*. Brentwood, MD: Amana, 1983.
Allard, Silas Webster. "In the Shade of the Oaks of Mamre: Hospitality as a Framework for Political Engagement between Christians and Muslims." *Political Theology* 13, no. 4 (2012) 414–24.
Ariarajah, S. Wesley. "Changing Paradigms of Asian Christian Attitude to Other Religions." In *The Oxford Handbook of Christianity in Asia*, edited by Felix Wilfred, 347–67. New York: Oxford University Press, 2014.
Arias, Mortimer. "Centripetal Mission or Evangelization by Hospitality." *Missiology: An International Review* 10, no. 1 (1982) 69–81.
Arterbury, Andrew. *Entertaining Angels: Early Christian Hospitality in its Mediterranean Setting*. Sheffield, UK: Sheffield Phoenix, 2005.
Baker, Gideon, ed. *Hospitality and World Politics*. Basingstoke, UK: Palgrave Macmillan, 2013.
Bell, Daniel, and Chaibong Hahm, eds. *Confucianism for the Modern World*. Cambridge: Cambridge University Press, 2003.
Ben Jelloun, Tahar. *French Hospitality: Racism and North African Immigrants*. New York: Columbia University Press, 1999.
Benitez, Mary Ann. "Australian Group's Donation Helps Refugees Learn Additional Skills." *South China Morning Post*, December 25, 2008. http://www.scmp.com/article/664933/australian-groups-donation-helps-refugeeslearn-additional-skills.
Benveniste, Émile. *Indo-European Language and Society*. Coral Gables, FL: University of Miami Press, 1973.
Berling, Judith. *A Pilgrim in Chinese Culture: Negotiating Religious Diversity*. Maryknoll, NY: Orbis, 1997.
Béthune, Pierre-Françoise de. "Interreligious Dialogue and Sacred Hospitality." *Religion East and West* 7 (2007) 1–22.
Betts, Alexander, ed. *Global Migration Governance*. Oxford: Oxford University Press, 2011.

Boardman, John, et al., eds. *The Oxford History of the Classical World*. Oxford: Oxford University Press, 1986.

Brandner, Tobias. "Hosts and Guests: Hospitality as an Emerging Paradigm in Mission." *International Review of Mission* 102, no. 1 (2013) 94–102.

Bretherton, Luke. *Christianity and Contemporary Politics: The Conditions and Possibilities of Faithful Witness*. Chichester, UK: Wiley-Blackwell, 2010.

———. *Hospitality as Holiness: Christian Witness Amid Moral Diversity*. Aldershot, UK: Ashgate, 2006.

Browner, Jesse. *The Duchess Who Wouldn't Sit Down: An Informal History of Hospitality*. New York: Bloomsbury, 2003.

Byrne, Brendan. *The Hospitality of God: A Reading of Luke's Gospel*. Collegeville, MN: Liturgical, 2000.

Candea, Matei, and Giovanni da Col. "The Return to Hospitality." *Journal of the Royal Anthropological Institute* 18 (June 2012) S1–S19.

Caritas Hong Kong. "Caritas Social Work Division Annual Report 2009–2010." http://sws.caritas.org.hk/EN/0910annualreportEN.pdf.

———. "Service for Refugees and Asylum Seekers of United Nations High Commissioner for Refugees (UNHCR)." http://www.caritas.org.hk/swsd/os/eng/Refugee/Refugee.html.

Carroll, John M. *A Concise History of Hong Kong*. Hong Kong: Hong Kong University Press, 2007.

Castles, Stephen, et al. *The Age of Migration: International Population Movements in the Modern World*. 5th ed. Basingstoke, UK: Palgrave Macmillan, 2014.

Chan, Joseph. "Giving Priority to the Worst Off: A Confucian Perspective on Social Welfare." In *Confucianism for the Modern World*, edited by Daniel Bell and Chaibong Hahm, 236–53. Cambridge: Cambridge University Press, 2003.

Chan, Ka-wai. "Hong Kong's Protestant Social Movement." In *Hong Kong's Social Movements: Forces from the Margins*, edited by Sophia Woodman, 109–16. Hong Kong: July 1 Link and Hong Kong Women Christian Council, 1997.

Chan, Kwok-bun. "The Vietnamese Boat People in Hong Kong." In *The Cambridge Survey of World Migration*, edited by Robert Cohen, 380–85. Cambridge: Cambridge University Press, 1995.

Chan, Wing-tsit. *A Source Book in Chinese Philosophy*. Princeton: Princeton University Press, 1963.

Chan, Yuk-wah. "Revisiting the Vietnamese Refugee Era: An Asian Perspective from Hong Kong." In *The Chinese/Vietnamese Diaspora: Revisiting the Boat People*, edited by Yuk-wah Chan, 3–19. London: Routledge, 2011.

———, ed. *The Chinese/Vietnamese Diaspora: Revisiting the Boat People*. London: Routledge, 2011.

Chang, Joyce. "Foreword." In *They Sojourned in Our Land: The Vietnamese in Hong Kong 1975–2000*, edited by Joyce Chang et al., xv–xviii. Hong Kong: Social Work Division Caritas, 2003.

Chang, Joyce, et al., eds. *They Sojourned in Our Land: The Vietnamese in Hong Kong 1975–2000*. Hong Kong: Social Work Division Caritas, 2003.

Chiu, Joanna. "Refugees at Their Wits' End Without Status in Hong Kong." *South China Morning Post*, December 2, 2012. http://www.scmp.com/news/hong-kong/article/1095161/refugees-their-wits-end-without-status-hong-kong.

Chiu, Stephen, and Tai-lok Lui. *Hong Kong: Becoming a Chinese Global City.* London: Routledge, 2009.
Chow, Tze [Leslie]. "Being Peace Makers." *Share*, Cedar Fund, May–June 2013. http://cedarfundeng.wordpress.com/2013/05/10/share200e-a4/.
Christian Conference of Asia. *CTC Bulletin* 28, nos. 1–2 (2012).
Chrysostom, St. John. *Homily XLV, Acts 20:32.* Translated by J. Walker, J. Sheppard, and H. Brown. In *NPNF*^{1}, edited by Philip Schaff, 11:272–77. *Christian Classics Ethereal Library.* http://www.ccel.org/ccel/schaff/npnf111.vi.xlv.html.
Confucius. *The Analects.* Translated by D. C. Lau. Hong Kong: Chinese University Press, 1992.
Constable, Nicole. *Born Out of Place: Migrant Mothers and the Politics of International Labor.* Hong Kong: Hong Kong University Press, 2014.
Coton, Jennifer. *Alltogether for Asylum Justice: Asylum Seekers' Conversion to Christianity.* London: Evangelical Alliance, 2007. http://www.eauk.org/current-affairs/publications/upload/alltogether-for-asylum-justice.pdf.
Coulton, Nicholas. "Asylum Injustice." Letter to the Editor. *The Times*, April 30, 2007.
Davis, Leonard. *Hong Kong and the Asylum-Seekers from Vietnam.* Basingstoke, UK: Macmillan, 1991.
De Waal, Esther. *Seeking God: The Way of St. Benedict.* Collegeville, MN: Liturgical, 1984.
Derrida, Jacques. *Acts of Religion.* Edited by Gil Anidjar. New York: Routledge, 2002.
———. "Hostipitality." *Angelaki: Journal of the Theoretical Humanities* 5, no. 3 (2000) 3–18.
Derrida, Jacques, and Anne Dufourmantelle. *Of Hospitality.* Translated by Rachel Bowlby. Stanford: Stanford University Press, 2000.
Donders, R. "The Forced Migration and the Refugee Problem of Hong Kong (1949–1954)." *Social Compass* 3, nos. 5–6 (1955–1956) 261–71.
Elliott, John. *A Home for the Homeless: A Social-Scientific Criticism of 1 Peter, Its Situation and Strategy.* Minneapolis: Fortress, 1990.
Erni, John Nguyet. "Who Needs Strangers? Un-imagining Hong Kong Chineseness." *Chinese Journal of Communication* 5, no. 1 (2012) 78–87.
Farrer, James. "Cosmopolitanism as Virtue: Toward an Ethics of Global City Life." *Policy Innovations* (January 21, 2010). http://www.policyinnovations.org/ideas/commentary/data/000166.
Friese, Heidrun. "The Limits of Hospitality." *Paragraph* 32, no. 1 (2009) 51–68.
Fung, Victor Keung. "Opening a Floodgate to Refugees Would Be a Big Mistake." *China Daily* (HK Edition), December 7, 2012. http://www.chinadaily.com.cn/hkedition/2012-12/07/content_15993799.htm.
Gatrell, Peter. *Free World? The Campaign to Save the World's Refugees, 1956–1963.* Cambridge: Cambridge University Press, 2011.
Gentle, Nick. "Pets Better Served Than Refugees, Say Lawyers." *South China Morning Post,* December 5, 2004. http://www.scmp.com/article/480789/pets-better-served-refugees-say-lawyers.
Greer, Rowan. *Broken Lights and Mended Lives.* University Park: Pennsylvania State University Press, 1986.
Griffin, Jasper. "Introduction." In *The Oxford History of the Classical World*, edited by John Boardman et al., 1–13. Oxford: Oxford University Press, 1986.

Groody, Daniel. "Crossing the Divide: Foundations of a Theology of Migration and Refugees." *Theological Studies* 70, no. 3 (2009) 638–67.
Hallie, Philip. *Tales of Good and Evil, Help and Harm*. New York: HarperCollins, 1997.
Hambro, Edvard. *The Problem of Chinese Refugees in Hong Kong: Report Submitted to the United Nations High Commissioner for Refugees*. Leiden: Sijthoff, 1955.
Hannerz, Ulf. *Transnational Connections: Culture, People, Places*. London: Routledge, 1996.
Hansen, Peter. "Thanh loc—Hong Kong's Refugee Screening System." In *The Chinese/Vietnamese Diaspora: Revisiting the Boat People*, edited by Yuk-wah Chan, 85–98. London: Routledge, 2011.
Hawthorne, Steve, and Graham Kendrick, *Prayerwalking*. Lake Mary, FL: Charisma House, 1993.
Hayes, James. "Hong Kong: Tale of Two Cities." In *Hong Kong: The Interaction of Traditions and Life in the Towns*, edited by Marjorie Topley, 1–10. Hong Kong: Royal Asiatic Society, 1975.
Hobbs, T. R. "Hospitality in the First Testament and the 'Teleological Fallacy.'" *Journal for the Study of the Old Testament* 26, no. 1 (2001) 3–30.
Hocart, A. M. *The Life-Giving Myth and Other Essays*. London: Tavistock, 1969.
Homer. *The Odyssey*. Translated by Richmond Lattimore. New York: HarperCollins, 1967.
Hong Kong Catholic Church. *Hong Kong Catholic Church Directory 2015*. Hong Kong: Catholic Truth Society, December 2014.
Hong Kong Christian Council. *News and Views* (March 1979).
Hong Kong Christian Service. *Activities Report* (1979, 1980, 1981).
Hong Kong Christian Service. *Annual Report* (1982–83, 1983–84).
Hong Kong Church Renewal Movement. *Report on 2014 Hong Kong Church Survey*. Hong Kong: HKCRM, 2015.
Hong Kong Council of Social Service. *Centre for Social Impact Newsletter*, September 28, 2010.
Hong Kong Government. *Hong Kong Hansard: Reports of the Sittings of the Legislative Council of Hong Kong (1979–1980)*. Hong Kong: Hong Kong Government, 1979–1980.
Hong Kong SAR Government Central Policy Unit. Policy 21 Limited. "A Study on New Arrivals from Mainland China," January 2013. http://www.cpu.gov.hk/doc/sc/research_reports/A_study_on_new_arrivals_from_Mainland_China.pdf.
Hong Kong SAR Government Immigration Department. *Annual Report 2011*. http://www.immd.gov.hk/publications/a_report_2011/en/ch4/index.html.
Hong Kong SAR Government Information Services Department. *Hong Kong 2003*. http://www.yearbook.gov.hk/2003/eindex.html
———. *Hong Kong 2015*. http://www.yearbook.gov.hk/2015/en/.
Hong Kong SAR Government Security Bureau and Social Welfare Department, "Humanitarian Assistance for Torture Claimants, Asylum Seekers and Mandated Refugees in Hong Kong." LC Paper No. CB(2)1630/12–13(01), Information Briefing to Legco Panel on Welfare Services, July 2013. http://www.legco.gov.hk/yr12-13/english/panels/ws/papers/ws0722cb2-1630-1-e.pdf.
Hong Kong SAR Government Security Bureau et al. "Situation of Refugees, Asylum Seekers and Torture Claimants in Hong Kong." LC Paper No. CB(2)2747/05–06(01), Information Briefing to Legco Panel on Security and Panel on Welfare

Services, July 2006. http://www.legco.gov.hk/yr05-06/english/panels/ws/papers/sews0718cb2-2747-1e.pdf.

Hughes, Richard. *Borrowed Place, Borrowed Time: Hong Kong and Its Many Faces*. London: Deutsch, 1976.

Ignatieff, Michael. *The Needs of Strangers*. London: Hogarth, 1990.

Jacobsen, Douglas. "Hospitality and Holiness." *Prism* 22, no. 2 (2008) 51–58.

Jesuit Refugee Service. *Working with Urban Refugees: A Handbook*. Rome: JRS, 2013. https://www.jrs.net/assets/Publications/File/UrbanRefugeesBooklet1.pdf.

Jimenez, Cher S. "Abuse Me Please, Sir." *Asia Times Online*, November 18, 2011. http://atimes.com/atimes/Southeast_Asia/MK18Ae01.html.

Jipp, Joshua. *Divine Visitations and Hospitality to Strangers in Luke-Acts*. Leiden: Brill, 2013.

Johnson, Luke Timothy. *The Acts of the Apostles*. Collegeville, MN: Liturgical, 1992.

Karakayali, Nedim. "The Uses of the Stranger: Circulation, Arbitration, Secrecy and Dirt." *Sociological Theory* 24, no. 4 (2006) 312–30.

Kearney, Richard. "Guest or Enemy? Welcoming the Stranger." Australian Broadcasting Company (ABC) Religion and Ethics: Opinion, June 21, 2012. http://www.abc.net.au/religion/articles/2012/06/21/3529859.htm.

Kim, Heup Young. *Christ and the Tao*. Hong Kong: Christian Conference of Asia, 2003.

———. "Embracing and Embodying God's Hospitality Today in Asia." *CTC Bulletin* 28, no. 1 (2012) 1–13.

King, Ambrose. "The Transformation of Confucianism in the Post-Confucian Era: The Emergence of Rationalistic Traditionalism in Hong Kong." In *Confucian Traditions in East Asian Modernity*, edited by Tu Wei-ming, 265–76. Cambridge, MA: Harvard University Press, 1996.

Klassen, Ernest Eugene. "Exploring the Missional Potential of International Churches: A Case Study of Capital City Baptist Church, Mexico City." DMin diss., Asbury Theological Seminary, 2006.

Koenig, John. "Hospitality." In *The Anchor Bible Dictionary*, edited by David Freedman, 3:299–301. New York: Doubleday, 1992.

———. "Hospitality." In *The Encyclopedia of Religion*, edited by Mircea Eliade, 6:470–73. New York: Macmillan, 1987.

———. *New Testament Hospitality: Partnership with Strangers as Promise and Mission*. Philadelphia: Fortress, 1985.

Kowloon Union Church. *Annual Report 2012*. Hong Kong.

———. *Annual Report 2013*. Hong Kong.

Ku, Agnes. "Immigration Policies, Discourses, and the Politics of Local Belonging in Hong Kong (1950–1980)." *Modern China* 30, no. 3 (2004) 326–60.

Ku, Agnes S., and Ngai Pun, eds. *Remaking Citizenship in Hong Kong: Community, Nation and the Global City*. London: Routledge, 2004.

Kwok, Pui-lan. *Globalization, Gender, and Peacebuilding: The Future of Interfaith Dialogue*. New York: Paulist, 2012.

———. *Postcolonial Imagination and Feminist Theology*. Louisville: Westminster John Knox, 2005.

Kwong, Paul. *Identity in Community: Towards a Theological Agenda for the Hong Kong SAR*. Contactzone: Explorations in Intercultural Theology. Berlin: Lit Verlag, 2011.

Langmead, Ross. "Refugees as Guests and Hosts: Towards a Theology of Mission Amongst Refugees and Asylum Seekers." Paper presented at International Association for Mission Studies (IAMS) Conference, Toronto, Canada, August 2012. http://rosslangmead.50webs.com/rl/Downloads/Resources/RefugeesIAMSAug12FullPaper.pdf.

Lashley, Conrad, and Alison Morrison, eds. *In Search of Hospitality: Theoretical Perspectives and Debates*. Oxford: Butterworth-Heinemann, 2000.

Lau, D.C. "Introduction." In Confucius, *The Analects*. Translated by D.C. Lau, ix–liii. Hong Kong: Chinese University Press, 1992.

———. "Introduction." In *Mencius*. Translated by D. C. Lau, ix–xlviii. Hong Kong: Chinese University Press, 2003.

Lau, Siu-kai. *Society and Politics in Hong Kong*. Hong Kong: Chinese University Press, 1982.

Lau, Siu-kai, et al., eds. *New Frontiers of Social Indicators Research in Chinese Societies*. Hong Kong: Chinese University Hong Kong Institute of Asia-Pacific Studies, 1996.

Law, Kam-yee, and Kim-ming Lee. "The Myth of Multiculturalism in 'Asia's World City': Incomprehensive Policies for Ethnic Minorities in Hong Kong." *Journal of Asian Public Policy* 5, no. 1 (2012) 117–34.

———. "Socio-Political Embeddings of South Asian Ethnic Minorities' Economic Situations in Hong Kong." *Journal of Contemporary China* 22, no. 84 (2013) 984–1005.

Lee, Haiyan. *The Stranger and the Chinese Moral Imagination*. Stanford: Stanford University Press, 2014.

Lee, Leo Ou-fan. "Postscript: Hong Kong—A Reflective Overview." *Postcolonial Studies* 10, no. 4 (2007) 499–509.

Letellier, Robert Ignatius. *Day in Mamre, Night in Sodom: Abraham and Lot in Genesis 18 and 19*. Leiden: Brill, 1995.

Lethbridge, Henry. "Caste, Class and Race in Hong Kong Before the Japanese Occupation." In *Hong Kong: The Interaction of Traditions and Life in the Towns*, edited by Marjorie Topley, 42–64. Hong Kong: Royal Asiatic Society, 1975.

Leung, Beatrice and Shun-hing Chan. *Changing Church and State Relations in Hong Kong, 1950–2000*. Hong Kong: Hong Kong University Press, 2003.

Levinas, Emmanuel. *Totality and Infinity: An Essay on Exteriority*. Translated by Alphonso Lingis. Pittsburgh: Duquesne University Press, 1969.

Liverani, Mario. *Myth and Politics in Ancient Near Eastern Historiography*. London: Equinox, 2004.

Lo, Lung-kwong. "Taiwan, Hong Kong, Macau." In *Christianities in Asia*, edited by Peter C. Phan, 173–96. Malden, MA: Wiley-Blackwell, 2011.

Loescher, Gil. "The International Refugee Regime: Stretched to the Limit?," *Journal of International Affairs* 47, no. 2 (1994) 351–77.

Loescher, Gil and James Milner. "UNHRC and the Global Governance of Refugees." In *Global Migration Governance*, edited by Alexander Betts, 189–209. Oxford: Oxford University Press, 2011.

Louden, Bruce. *Homer's Odyssey and the Near East*. Cambridge: Cambridge University Press, 2011.

Luz, Ulrich. *Matthew 21–28: A Commentary*. Hermeneia. Translated by James Crouch. Minneapolis: Fortress, 2005.

Ma, Mary. "Ticking Time Bomb." *The Standard*, April 23, 2012. http://www.thestandard.com.hk/news_detail.asp?pp_cat=21&art_id=121754&sid=36148468&con_type=1&d_str=20120423&isSearch=1&sear_year=2012.

Malherbe, Abraham. *Social Aspects of Early Christianity*, 2nd ed. Philadelphia: Fortress, 1983.

Man, Joyce. "Refugees in Hong Kong See Little Improvement from New Screening System." *South China Morning Post*, February 16, 2015. http://www.scmp.com/news/hong-kong/article/1714243/refugees-hong-kong-see-little-improvement-new-screening-system.

Marfleet, Philip. "Understanding 'Sanctuary': Faith and Traditions of Asylum." *Journal of Refugee Studies* 24, no. 3 (2011) 440–55.

Mark, Chi-kwan. "The 'Problem of People': British Colonials, Cold War Powers, and the Chinese Refugees in Hong Kong, 1949–62." *Modern Asian Studies* 41, no. 6 (2007) 1145–81.

Marty, Martin. *When Faiths Collide*. Malden, MA: Blackwell, 2005.

Massignon, Louis. *L'hospitalité sacrée*. Paris: Nouvelle Cité, 1987.

Mathews, Gordon. *Ghetto at the Center of the World: Chungking Mansions, Hong Kong*. Chicago: University of Chicago Press, 2011.

Mathews, John Bell. "Hospitality and the New Testament Church: An Historical and Exegetical Study." ThD diss., Princeton Theological Seminary, 1964.

Matthews, Victor. "Hospitality and Hostility in Judges 4." *Biblical Theology Bulletin* 21, no. 1 (1991) 13–21.

Matthews, Victor, and Don Benjamin. *Social World of Ancient Israel, 1250–587 BCE*. Peabody, MA: Hendrickson, 1993.

Mauss, Marcel. *The Gift: The Form and Reason for Exchange in Archaic Societies* [1925]. Translated by W. D. Halls. London: Routledge, 1990.

McDonald, Alison. "Asylum Application and Christian Belief." London: Methodist Refugee Working Group, 2005. https://ctbi.org.uk/wp-content/uploads/2014/11/ctbi_asylum_applications_and_christian_witness_in_court.pdf.

McGavran, Donald. *The Bridges of God*. New York: Friendship, 1955.

———. *Understanding Church Growth*. 3rd ed. Grand Rapids: Eerdmans, 1990.

Mencius. *Mencius*. Translated by D. C. Lau. Hong Kong: Chinese University Press, 2003.

Michel, Thomas. "Where to Now? Ways Forward for Interreligious Dialogue: Images of Abraham as Models of Interreligious Encounter." *The Muslim World* 100, no. 4 (2010) 530–38.

Min, Anselm. *The Solidarity of Others in a Divided World*. New York: T. & T. Clark, 2004.

Neill, Stephen. *A History of Christian Missions*. Harmondsworth: Penguin, 1964.

Newman, Elizabeth. *Untamed Hospitality: Welcoming God and Other Strangers*. Grand Rapids: Brazos, 2007.

Nguyen, Paul. *My Adventure to the New World*. Portland, OR: River Breeze, 2014.

Nicols, John. "Hospitality among the Romans." In *The Oxford Handbook of Social Relations in the Roman World*, edited by Michael Peachin, 422–37. Oxford: Oxford University Press, 2011.

Nouwen, Henri. *Reaching Out: The Three Movements of the Spiritual Life*. Garden City, NY: Doubleday, 1975.

O'Connor, Paul. *Islam in Hong Kong: Muslims and Everyday Life in China's World City*. Hong Kong: Hong Kong University Press, 2012.

Oden, Amy, ed. *And You Welcomed Me: A Sourcebook on Hospitality in Early Christianity*. Nashville: Abingdon, 2001.
Ogletree, Thomas. *Hospitality to the Stranger: Dimensions of Moral Understanding*. Philadelphia: Fortress, 1985.
Palmer, Parker. *The Company of Strangers: Christians and the Renewal of America's Public Life*. New York: Crossroad, 1981.
Peachin, Michael, ed. *The Oxford Handbook of Social Relations in the Roman World*. Oxford: Oxford University Press, 2011.
Pederson, David. *Expatriate Ministry: Inside the Church of the Outsiders*. Seoul: Korean Center for World Missions, 1999.
Peristiany, J. G., and J. Pitt-Rivers, eds. *Honor and Grace in Anthropology*. Cambridge: Cambridge University Press, 1992.
Phan, Peter C., ed. *Christianities in Asia*. Malden, MA: Wiley-Blackwell, 2011.
Pickering, Sharon, and Julie Ham, eds. *The Routledge Handbook on Crime and International Migration*. New York: Routledge, 2015.
Pitt-Rivers, Julian. *The Fate of Shechem or The Politics of Sex*. Cambridge: Cambridge University Press, 1977.
———. "Postscript: The Place of Grace in Anthropology." In *Honor and Grace in Anthropology*, edited by J. G. Peristiany and J. Pitt-Rivers, 215–46. Cambridge: Cambridge University Press, 1992.
Plaut, W. Gunther. *Asylum: A Moral Dilemma*. Westport, CT: Praeger, 1995.
Pohl, Christine. *Making Room: Recovering Hospitality as a Christian Tradition*. Grand Rapids: Eerdmans, 1999.
Pun, Ngai, and Ka-ming Wu. "Lived Citizenship and Lower-class Chinese Migrant Women: A Global City without Its People." In *Remaking Citizenship in Hong Kong: Community, Nation and the Global City*, edited by Agnes S. Ku and Ngai Pun, 125–38. New York: Routledge, 2004.
Rabben, Linda. *Give Refuge to the Stranger: The Past, Present, and Future of Sanctuary*. Walnut Creek, CA: Left Coast, 2011.
Rain, Susan. "In Bangkok Detention, Refugee Learns of Christ." *Baptist Press*, July 20, 2012. http://www.bpnews.net/bpnews.asp?id=38311.
Ralston, Joshua. "Refugees and the Role of Religious Groups." Australian Broadcasting Company (ABC) Religion and Ethics, July 28, 2010. http://www.abc.net.au/religion/articles/2010/07/28/2966921.htm.
Reece, Steve. *The Stranger's Welcome: Oral Theory and the Aesthetics of the Homeric Hospitality Scene*. Ann Arbor: University of Michigan Press, 1993.
Reynolds, Thomas. "Toward a Wider Hospitality: Rethinking Love of Neighbour in Religions of the Book." *Irish Theological Quarterly* 75, no. 2 (2010) 175–87.
Ricoeur, Paul. *On Translation*. Translated by Eileen Brennan. London: Routledge, 2006.
Risse, Guenter. *Mending Bodies, Saving Souls: A History of Hospitals*. New York: Oxford University Press, 1999.
Ross, Cathy. "Creating Space: Hospitality as a Metaphor for Mission." *Anvil* 25, no. 3 (2008) 167–76.
Roukema, Riemer. "The Good Samaritan in Ancient Christianity." *Vigiliae Christianae* 58, no. 1 (2004) 56–74.
RTHK. "Asylum Seekers in Hong Kong." *The Pulse*, December 2, 2011. http://programme.rthk.org.hk/rthk/tv/programme.php?name=tv/thepulse&d=2011-12-02&p=2862&e=161545&m=episode.

Ruiz, Lester Edwin J. "Race, Power, and Migration: Reimagining *Graduate* Theological Education." In *Contemporary Issues of Migration and Theology*, edited by Elaine Padilla and Peter C. Phan, 211–31. Basingstoke, UK: Palgrave Macmillan, 2013.
Russell, Letty. *Church in the Round: Feminist Interpretation of the Church*. Louisville: Westminster John Knox, 1993.
———. *Just Hospitality: God's Welcome in a World of Difference*. Louisville: Westminster John Knox, 2009.
Sanders, E. P. *Judaism: Practice and Belief, 63BCE–66CE*. London: SCM, 1992.
Sautman, Barry. "Hong Kong as a Semi-Ethnocracy: 'Race,' Migration and Citizenship in a Globalized Region." In *Remaking Citizenship in Hong Kong: Community, Nation and the Global City*, edited by Agnes S. Ku and Ngai Pun, 115–38. New York: Routledge, 2004.
Schwartz, Susan. "Weighing the Cost of Boat People against the World's Woes." *South China Morning Post*, September 9, 2001. http://www.scmp.com/article/357169/weighing-cost-boat-people-against-worlds-woes.
Selwyn, Tom. "An Anthropology of Hospitality." In *In Search of Hospitality: Theoretical Perspectives and Debates*, edited by Conrad Lashley and Alison Morrison, 18–37. Oxford: Butterworth-Heinemann, 2000.
Sharma, Arvind, ed. *Our Religions: The Seven World Religions Introduced*. San Francisco: HarperSanFrancisco, 1993.
Simmel, Georg. "The Stranger." In *On Individuality and Social Forms*, edited by D. N. Levine, 143–49. Chicago: University of Chicago Press, 1971.
Sinn, Elizabeth. "Lessons in Openness: Creating a Space of Flow in Hong Kong." In *Hong Kong Mobile: Making a Global Population*, edited by Helen Siu and Agnes Ku, 13–43. Hong Kong: Hong Kong University Press, 2008.
Siu, Helen, and Agnes Ku, eds. *Hong Kong Mobile: Making a Global Population*. Hong Kong: Hong Kong University Press, 2008.
Smith, Carl T. *Chinese Christians: Élites, Middlemen, and the Church in Hong Kong*. Hong Kong: Oxford University Press, 1985.
———. *A Sense of History: Studies in the Social and Urban History of Hong Kong*. Hong Kong: Hong Kong Educational, 1995.
Snyder, Susanna. *Asylum-Seeking, Migration and Church*. Burlington, VT: Ashgate, 2012.
———. "The Dangers of 'Doing Our Duty': Reflections on Churches Engaging with People Seeking Asylum in the UK." *Theology* 110, no. 857 (2007) 351–60.
Society for Community Organization, et al. "Denial of Asylum Seekers' Rights," LC Paper No. CB(2)2747/05–06(03), Submission to Panel on Welfare Services and Panel on Security, July 2006. http://www.legco.gov.hk/yr05-06/english/panels/ws/papers/sews0718cb2-2747-3e.pdf.
Soden, Wolfram von. *The Ancient Orient: An Introduction to the Study of the Ancient Near East*. Translated by Donald Schley. Grand Rapids: Eerdmans, 1994.
Spencer, John. "Sojourner." In *The Anchor Bible Dictionary*, edited by David Freedman, 6:103–4. New York: Doubleday, 1992.
Stählin, Gustav. "xenos." In *Theological Dictionary of the New Testament*, edited by Gerhard Friedrich and translated by Geoffrey Bromiley, 5:1–36. Grand Rapids: Eerdmans, 1967.
Stark, Rodney. *The Rise of Christianity: A Sociologist Reconsiders History*. Princeton: Princeton University Press, 1996.

Stock, St. George. "Hospitality (Greek and Roman)." In *Encyclopedia of Religion and Ethics*, edited by James Hastings, 6:808–12. New York: Scribner, 1959.
Tang, Edmond. "Identity and Marginality—Christianity in East Asia." In *The Oxford Handbook of Christianity in Asia*, edited by Felix Wilfred, 80–97. New York: Oxford University Press USA, 2014.
Taylor, John. *Classics and the Bible: Hospitality and Recognition*. London: Duckworth, 2007.
Thangaraj, M. Thomas. "Embodying God's Hospitality in a Multi-Religious World." *CTC Bulletin* 28, no. 1 (2012) 14–25.
Thaut, Laura. "The Role of Faith in Christian Faith-Based Humanitarian Agencies: Constructing the Taxonomy." *Voluntas* 20 (2009) 319–50.
Topley, Marjorie, ed. *Hong Kong: The Interaction of Traditions and Life in the Towns*. Hong Kong: Royal Asiatic Society, 1975.
Troester, Rosalie Riegle, ed. *Voices from the Catholic Worker*. Philadelphia: Temple University Press, 1993.
Tsang, Phyllis. "Refugees Need Legal Framework, Says Advocate." *South China Morning Post*, December 27, 2008. http://www.scmp.com/article/665061/refugees-need-legal-framework-says-advocate.
Tsang, Steve. *A Modern History of Hong Kong*. Hong Kong: Hong Kong University Press, 2004.
Tsui, Yvonne. "Asylum Seekers Who Filed Torture Claims Get Damages for Time in Jail." *South China Morning Post*, March 4, 2009. http://www.scmp.com/article/671949/asylum-seekers-who-filed-torture-claims-get-damages-time-jail.
Tu, Wei-ming. "Confucianism." In *Our Religions: The Seven World Religions Introduced*, edited by Arvind Sharma, 139–227. San Francisco: HarperSanFrancisco, 1993.
———, ed. *Confucian Traditions in East Asian Modernity*. Cambridge, MA: Harvard University Press, 1996.
United Nations High Commissioner for Refugees. "1951 Convention Relating to the Status of Refugees." http://www.unhcr.org/1951-refugee-convention.html.
———. *The State of the World's Refugees 2000: Fifty Years of Humanitarian Action*. Geneva: UNHCR, 2000.
———. "UNCHR Calls for End to Detention of Asylum-Seekers and Refugees." Press Release, July 3, 2014. http://www.unhcr.org/news/press/2014/7/53b550239/unhcr-calls-end-detention-asylum-seekers-refugees.html.
Vanier, Jean. *Befriending the Stranger*. Grand Rapids: Eerdmans, 2005.
———. *Encountering 'the Other.'* Mahwah, NJ: Paulist, 2006.
Vecchio, Francesco. *Asylum Seeking and the Global City*. Abingdon, Oxon: Routledge, 2015.
Vecchio, Francesco, and Alison Gerard. "Surviving the Politics of Illegality." In *The Routledge Handbook on Crime and International Migration*, edited by Sharon Pickering and Julie Ham, 179–92. New York: Routledge, 2015.
Volf, Miroslav. *Exclusion and Embrace: A Theological Exploration of Identity, Otherness, and Reconciliation*. Nashville: Abingdon, 1996.
Walton, John. *Ancient Near Eastern Thought and the Old Testament*. Grand Rapids: Baker Academic, 2006.
Welsh, Frank. *A History of Hong Kong*. Rev. ed. London: HarperCollins, 1997.
Westermann, Claus. *Genesis 12–36: A Commentary*. Translated by John Scullion. Minneapolis: Augsburg, 1985.

Wilfred, Felix, ed. *The Oxford Handbook of Christianity in Asia*. New York: Oxford University Press USA, 2014.
Wilson, Erin. "Be Welcome: Religion, Hospitality and Statelessness in International Politics." In *Hospitality and World Politics*, edited by Gideon Baker, 145–70. Basingstoke, UK: Palgrave Macmillan, 2013.
———. "Much to Be Proud of, Much to Be Done: Faith-Based Organizations and the Politics of Asylum in Australia." *Journal of Refugee Studies* 24, no. 3 (2011) 548–64.
Wong, Thomas W. P. "The Ethos of the Hong Kong Chinese Revisited." In *New Frontiers of Social Indicators Research in Chinese Societies*, edited by Lau Siu-kai et al., 361–83. Hong Kong: Chinese University Hong Kong Institute of Asia-Pacific Studies, 1996.
Wong, Yiu-chung. "The Policies of the Hong Kong Government towards the Chinese Refugee Problem, 1945–1962." MPhil thesis, Hong Kong Baptist University, 2008.
Woodman, Sophia, ed. *Hong Kong's Social Movements: Forces from the Margins*. Hong Kong: July 1 Link and Hong Kong Women Christian Council, 1997.
World Council of Churches. "Religious Plurality and Christian Self-Understanding." February 14, 2006. http://www.oikoumene.org/en/resources/documents/assembly/2006-porto-alegre/3-preparatory-and-background-documents/religious-plurality-and-christian-self-understanding.
World Council of Churches, et al. "Christian Witness in a Multi-religious World." June 28, 2011. http://www.oikoumene.org/en/resources/documents/wcc-programmes/interreligious-dialogue-and-cooperation/christian-identity-in-pluralistic-societies/christian-witness-in-a-multi-religious-world.
Wrobleski, Jessica. *The Limits of Hospitality*. Collegeville, MN: Liturgical, 2012.
Yang, Kuo-shu. "Chinese Social Orientation: An Integrative Analysis." In *Chinese Societies and Mental Health*, edited by T. Y. Lin et al., 19–39. Hong Kong: Oxford University Press, 1995.
Ying, Fuk-tsang. "Mainland China." In *Christianities in Asia*, edited by Peter C. Phan, 149–70. Malden, MA: Wiley-Blackwell, 2011.
———. *Yuan ni de guo jianglin: zhanhou Xianggang "Jidujiao Xincun" de gean yanjiu* (Your Kingdom Come: Case Study of the "Christian Cottage Villages" in Postwar Hong Kong). Hong Kong: Alliance Bible Seminary, 2002.
Yong, Amos. *Hospitality and the Other: Pentecost, Christian Practices, and the Neighbor*. Maryknoll, NY: Orbis, 2008.
Yueh, Hu. "The Problem of the Hong Kong Refugees." *Asian Survey* 2, no. 1 (1962) 28–37.
Yuen, Mary. "Hong Kong Catholics' Recent Participation in Social Movements." In *Hong Kong's Social Movements: Forces from the Margins*, edited by Sophia Woodman, 117–32. Hong Kong: July 1 Link and Hong Kong Women Christian Council, 1997.

General Index

Abrahamic faith, 56–57, 57n34, 62
Abrahamic hospitality, 3, 5–8, 5n4, 22–24
acceptance in society, 128–29
African asylum seekers, 119
African time, 145–46
"African Voices" (church choir), 140
Agamben, Giorgio, 63n51
agencies of hospitality, 24–25, 38–40, 74–76, 83n30, 113n9, 132–35, 179–80
. See also specific agencies by name
A-generation (NGO), 145, 149, 170
Ager, Alastair, 80
Ager, Joey, 80
Akpinar, Snjezana, 57
Ali, A. Yusuf, 56–57
Allard, Silas Webster, 57
Allen, Julee, 162
almsgiving, 35
"already but not yet," 47
American Congregational Church, 100
Amnesty International, 135
Analects (Confucius), 90
ancient Near Eastern culture, 3–8
ancient roots of hospitality, 173–74
Anglican Cathedral of St. John the Evangelist, 101
Anglican Church, 100, 102, 102n56, 162, 163
anthropological perspectives, 11–14
Ariarajah, S. Wesley, 59
Arias, Mortimer, 54
Arshad, Muhammed, 135

Arterbury, Andrew, 36
Ashby, Ian, 167
Asia Times Online, 122
Asian feminist theologians, 61
Asian religions, 59–61
associations (*haburoth*), 25
asylum and asylum seekers
    agencies (*See* agencies of hospitality)
    ancient sanctuary cities, 74
    Christian community issues, 74–76, 178–81
    concerns of, 123–29
    evaluation of, 187–89
    expectations, 185–86
    Hong Kong (2000–2014), 119–21
    institutions (*See* institutions)
    international community and, 177–78
    migration studies, 71–72
    political issues, 77–78
    public opposition, 184–85
    recognition rate for claimants, 124, 185
    term usage, 71–72, 74
    theological reflections on, 62–66
    torture claimants, 122
    voices of, 129–32
    waiting periods, 123–24
    . See also refugees
Asylum Seeker Concern Group, 170
Australia, refugee program, 72, 82, 113
Australian Red Cross, 82

banquet hospitality, 31–32, 91
Baptist Mission, 100, 102, 118
Baptist Press, 79
bare life, 63–65, 63n51
Barnes, Peter, 132
Barnes & Daly Solicitors, 132
Basel Missionary Society, 100, 134
Baudry, Gervais, 164
Bauer, Art, 107
beggars, 9, 18
Benedictine-Buddhist monastic hospitality, 55
Benveniste, Émile, 11, 14–15, 51
Béthune, Pierre-Françoise de, 55
biblical interpretations, Jewish culture, 22–24
biblical view, of hospitality, 22–24, 26–37
Bill of Rights (Hong Kong), 121, 122, 136, 191
Blessed Ministry Community Church, 170
blessings, 22–23, 31–32
boundaries, 51–53, 56, 176–77
Brandner, Tobias, 104n63
Bretherton, Luke, 28, 31–32, 47–48, 63–65, 63n51
British Red Cross, 113
Browner, Jesse, 15
Buddhist and Buddhism, 55, 60, 88, 102, 115n16, 177

Canada, refugees in, 113, 126, 127
Candea, Matei, 19
Canossian Sisters, 101
capacity, limits and, 53
care for the stranger, 23–24
Caritas Medical Centre, 126
Caritas-Hong Kong, 113, 115, 116–17, 170–71
Carroll, John M., 96n35
Castles, Stephen, 73
Catholic church. *See* Roman Catholic Church
Catholic Diocesan Justice and Peace Commission, 169
Catholic Relief Service, 111

Catholic-Protestant joint action, 115–16, 117
CEDAR Fund, 135
center vs. margins, 48–51
centripetal mission, 54
Chan, Jacqueline, 166
Chan, Kwok-bun, 114
Chan, Wing-tsit, 90
Chan, Yuk-wah, 114–15
Chang, Joyce, 116–17
charity vs. spirituality, 45–46
Cheng, Shirley, 163–64
Cheung, Fernando, 135
Cheung Chau Church, 170
Cheung-Ang Siew Mei, 161, 162
China
    Communist takeover, 96n35, 103, 110
    refugees in Hong Kong (1945–1954), 110–12
    traditions in Hong Kong, 88–92
China Daily (newspaper), 128
Chow, Leslie, 145–46
Christ Church Cathedral, Oxford, England, 81
Christian Action, 115, 132–33, 134, 161–62, 189
Christian and Missionary Alliance Tai Wai Church, 170
Christian and Missionary Alliance, 102
Christian community issues, 178–81
Christian faith-based agencies, 83n30
Christian hospitality
    church history survey, 37–42
    evaluation of programs, 187–89
    in Hebrew culture, 22–24
    in Jewish culture, 24–26
    nature and meaning of, 173–77
    in the New Testament, 26–33
    in New Testament church, 33–37
    overview, 21
    recommendations, 189–91
    tensions in (*See* tensions in hospitality)

Christian identity, 78–82
Christian persecution, 34

Christian sanctuary, 74–76
Chrysostom, John, 40
Chung King Ministry, 168–69
Chungking Mansions, 133, 161, 163, 166, 168, 183
Church of Christ in China, 102, 102n56
Church of the New Testament, 21, 33–37
Church World Service, 111
churches
　China refugee response, 111–12
　as first responders, 181–82
　in Hong Kong, 100–103
　sanctuaries, 74–75
　support from, 190
　survey of, 37–42
　Vietnamese refugee response, 115–19
　. See also specific churches by name
Cicero, 10
City of Sanctuary movement (United Kingdom), 75
Civic Exchange, 135
cliens/patronus, 11
colonialism, 86–87, 92–95
Communist Revolution (1949), 96n35
Community and Family Services International, 113
Community Chest, 133
compassion fatigue, 183–84
Confucius and Confucianism, 60, 88–92, 102, 177
congregational meals, 37
Constantine, Emperor, 39, 74
contemporary period
　tensions in hospitality, 44
　theological contributions, 176–77
Convention Against Torture (CAT), 120, 185
conversion, religious, 61, 78–82, 112, 157–60
corporate worship, 46
cosmopolitanism, 95
Council for World Mission, 161
covenant, 26, 26n8, 27
covenantal nomism, 26
creating space, 45, 54–55

Crossroads International, 135

da Col, Giovanni, 19
Daly, Mark, 121, 132
danger, associated with hospitality, 4, 173–74
Derrida, Jacques, 18, 51–52, 62–63
Dhavale, Samuel, 168
Dhavale, Shlivya, 168
Diaspora Jews, 24–26
Didache rules, 38
divine presence in guests, 9–10, 174, 175–76
Dixon (story of asylum seeker), 131–32
domestic workers, 122–23, 123n33
Dominican Fathers, 101
Donders, R., 112
double law of hospitality, 52
"dual-track" protection system, 120

economic migrants, 77, 114
ecumenical unity, 38
educational opportunities, 126, 163, 188
Elliott, John, 34
England
　asylum seekers, 81–82
　church sanctuaries, 75
Erni, John Nguyet, 98–99
Eurasian community, 94n32
Evangelical Alliance, 81
Evangelical Community Church, 167
Evangelical Free Church, 102
Evangelical Lutheran Church in America, 107
evangelism vs. interfaith friendship
　Abrahamic faith, 56–57
　mission and, 54–55, 181
　sharing in sacred spaces, 55–56
　theology of religions, 58–62
evangelization, 155–56, 184
Exclusion and Embrace (Volf), 50–51
exclusivism, 25–26, 65
exiles *(parepidemois)*, 33–34
Expatriate Ministry: Inside the Church of the Outsiders (Pederson), 106
expectations, 185–86

208 *General Index*

faith vs. fear, 65–66
faithful hospitality, 62–63
false prophets, 38–39
family, Chinese center of identity, 89
fear vs. faith, 65–66
fellowship programs, 153–55, 163–64
feminist theologians, 61–62, 62n47
feminist theory, 50
fictive kin, 91
filial piety (*xiao*), 89
first responders, 181–82
first-century Jewish culture, 24–26
folklore elements, 7
forced migrants, 72
foreigner, 22
France, asylum seekers, 75
Franciscan missions, 101
Fred (story of asylum seeker), 130–31
free gifts, 12, 13, 19
friendship and public support, 190–91
Friese, Heidrun, 13
funding, refugee ministries, 82–83

Gandhi, 61
gendered entrapment, 123
ger (sojourner), 22–23, 22n1
gift exchange, 9, 11–14, 31–32
globalization, 95
God
   divine presence in strangers, 9–10
   hallowing His name, 27, 63–65, 175
   as host, 23
   strangers, divine presence in, 174, 175–76
Good Samaritan parable, 29–30, 59
Gospels. *See* New Testament
grace, 18–19
gratuity, 18
Greco-Roman hospitality, 3, 8–11
guest-host relationship, 26

haburoth (associations), 25
hallowing bare life, 63–65, 63n51
Hannah (story of asylum seeker), 130
Hannerz, Ulf, 95
hao ke (hospitality), 90
Harrell-Bond, Barbara, 125
Hashmi, Syed Kamran, 166

Hebrew culture and tradition, 22–24, 175
Hellenistic Jews, 25
Henry (story of asylum seeker), 158–59
Henry VIII, (king), 75
Hinduism, 61, 102, 177
historical survey of the church, 37–42
holiness vs. hospitality, 47–48
Holy Spirit, 58–59
Homer, 3, 8–9, 15
Homeric literature, 10
homogeneous principle, 106
Hong Kong
   asylum and asylum seekers, 109
   Bill of Rights, 121, 122, 136, 191
   Chinese refugees (1945–1954), 110–12
   Chinese traditions, 88–92
   church in, 100–103
   Communist takeover of China, 96n35, 103, 110
   Dogs and Cats Ordinance, 121
   ethnic groups, 94n32, 98–100
   first responders, 181–82
   government responsibility, 120–21, 124–25
   hospitality as mission, 104–5
   humane deterrence policy, 113–14
   humanitarian and charity endeavors, 102–3
   international congregations, 105–7
   Japanese occupation (1941–1945), 103
   languages, 105
   local culture, 95–100
   overview, 85
   port of first asylum policy, 115
   refugees from (2000–2014), 119–21
   retrocession to China, 102
   social justice advocacy, 103
   Special Administrative Region (HKSAR) of China, 85, 94
   strangers and, 86–88
   Torture Claim Assessment Division, 120
   Western colonialism impact, 92–95
Hong Kong Bar Association, 132

General Index

"Hong Kong belonger," 96, 97
Hong Kong Catholic Church, 102, 116, 117, 170–71
Hong Kong Christian Aid to Refugees, 115, 133
Hong Kong Christian Council, 102n57, 116, 117, 161, 170
Hong Kong Christian Institute (HKCI), 169–70
Hong Kong Christian Service, 115
Hong Kong Church Renewal Movement (HKCRM), 102n57
Hong Kong Council of Social Service, 155
Hong Kong Council of the Church of Christ in China (HKCCCC), 147
Hong Kong Justice Centre, 134
Hong Kong Women Christian Council, 170
hospes, 10–11, 14–15, 16, 51
hospitality
   agencies (*See* agencies of hospitality)
   ancient Near East, 4–8
   anthropological perspectives, 11–14
   Benedictine-Buddhist monastic hospitality, 55–56
   biblical view of hospitality, 21–37, 41
   blessings and, 22–23
   Chinese traditions, 90–91
   Christian issues, 177–78
   definitions for, 10, 14–15
   ecumenical unity and, 38
   faithful hospitality, 62–63
   Greco-Roman, 3, 8–11
   holiness vs., 47–48
   as Hong Kong mission, 104–5
   institutionalization of (*See* institutions)
   international issues, 177–78
   linguistic perspectives, 14–15
   mission and, 54–55
   partnerships, 35–36
   as shared duty, 40
   tensions (*See* tensions in hospitality)
   vocabulary of, 14–15
   . *See also* Christian hospitality
hospitality myth, 10n18
Hospitality to the Stranger (Ogletree), 49
hospitals, 39
hospitium, 10
host, surrender of, 52
hostels, 39
hostility, 14, 17
"hostipitality," 18, 51
hostis, 11, 14, 16, 51
human rights, 185
humane deterrence policy (Hong Kong), 113–14
humans, natural equality of, 90n16

Iliad (Homer), 8
immigration, in Hong Kong, 96–100, 96n35, 96n36
incarnational justice, 154
Indian community, 94n32
Indonesian domestic workers, 122–23, 123n32
in-kind assistance, 126
Inner City Ministries (ICM), 166–68
inns
   establishment of, 24, 25, 25n5
   in New Testament period, 35–36, 36n23
institutions. *See* agencies of hospitality
interfaith friendship vs. evangelism
   Abrahamic faith, 56–57
   mission and, 54–55, 181
   sharing in sacred spaces, 55–56
   theology of religions, 58–62
International Baptist Church of Hong Kong, 166, 167
International Committee of the Red Cross, 73
international community issues, 177–78
international congregations, in Hong Kong, 105–7
international refugee protection regime, 72
International Rescue Committee, 73

International Social Service (ISS), 113, 126, 151
International Social Service-Hong Kong Branch (ISS-HK), 122, 133, 151
interreligious hospitality, 55
Islam and Muslims, 56–57, 102, 123, 135, 156, 164
Islamic Centre, 135
isolation of the needy, 40

Jacobsen, Douglas, 47
Jesuit Refugee Service, 77
Jesus
  banquet hospitality, 31–32
  Good Samaritan parable, 29–30
  last judgment parable, 32–33
  ministry of, 28–29
  salvation through, 58
  teachings of, 29–33
Jewish culture
  Abrahamic faith, 56–57, 57n34, 62
  Abrahamic hospitality, 3, 5–8, 5n4, 22–24
  biblical interpretations, 22–24
  commercial hospitality, 25n5
  first-century, 24–26
  restrictions on hospitality, 25–26
John (story of asylum seeker), 131
John Paul II (pope), 117
Joseph, Victor, 166
Josephus, 26
Judaism, 102
Jupiter (god), 10
just hospitality, 50

Kamran, Pastor, 166
Karakayali, Nedim, 99
Karani, Philip, 124
Kearney, Richard, 17
Keitzer, Naro, 167
Kim, Heup Young, 60
King, Ambrose, 91–92
Koenig, John, 24, 25, 26, 36
Kowloon Mosque, 135
Kowloon Union Church
  background, 139

Hong Kong Chinese churches, 146–50
Hong Kong Chinese perspectives, 145–46
ministry background, 139–41
outreach, 169
peacemaking program, 141–45
social justice, 189
Ku, Agnes, 96
Kwok, Pui-lan, 61
Kwong, Angela, 148–49
Kwong, Paul, 101

La Salle Christian Brothers, 101
laity, contribution by, 40
Langmead, Ross, 76
language of hospitality, 62
L'Arche communities, 45
last judgment parable, 32–33
Latin literature, 10
Lau, Emily, 135
Lau, Siu-kai, 93–94
Law, Kam-yee, 86–87, 99–100
law of hospitality, 9, 15–17, 52
"The Law of Hospitality" (Pitt-Rivers), 15
Law Society of Hong Kong, 132
Lee, Kim-ming, 86–87, 99–100
Lee, Leo Ou-fan, 95
Lee, Ralph, 112
legal sector resources, 132, 134
Letellier, Robert Ignatius, 7
Lethbridge, Henry, 94n32
Leung Siu-chun, 148–50
Levinas, Emmanuel, 48–49, 62
li (ritual propriety), 90
limits
  capacity and, 53
  on hospitality, 51–53
limits, on hospitality, 56, 176–77
linguistic hospitality, 57
linguistic perspectives, 14–15
linguistic twin, 17, 174
Little Flock Church, 102
living expenses, 126
Livy (Titus Livius), 10
Lo, Lung-kwong, 103
local congregations, 179, 183

local culture, in Hong Kong, 95–100
London Missionary Society, 100, 139
Lord's Supper, 37
Louden, Bruce, 10, 32
Love and Peace Ministry, 166
love of strangers (*philoxenia*), 26–27
Lutheran Church, 102
Lutheran World Refugee Service, 111
Lutz, Hans, 134
Luz, Ulrich, 33n18

MacLehose, Murray, 97
Macpherson, John, 152–55, 166
Malherbe, Abraham, 36, 36n23
Maori culture, 12
Marfleet, Philip, 74
margins vs. center, 48–51
Mark, Chi-kwan, 96n36
marriage, as means to permanent residency, 129, 129n49
Mathews, Gordon, 119, 125–26, 127, 129
Mathews, John Bell, 14–15, 27, 34
Mathieson, Maggie, 139–41
Matthews, Victor, 6
Mauss, Marcel, 11–13
McGavran, Donald, 106
Médecins Sans Frontieres, 73, 135
Mediterranean hospitality. *See* Greco-Roman hospitality
Mencius, 88, 89
Meren, Alem, 167
Methodist Church
  Britain, 82
  Hong Kong, 102, 111, 112
Michael (story of asylum seeker), 157
Michel, Thomas, 57, 57n34
Middle Ages period, 40
migrants and migrant studies, 71–72, 77, 114, 178
Milan Mission Seminary (later PIME), 101
Min, Anselm, 50
Minh, Fr. (Roman Catholic priest), 118
ministry
  challenges, 182–86
  refugee models, 76–77

mission
  in Hong Kong, 100–103, 101n55
  hospitality and, 54–55
Mission 21, 134
model of protocol, 6
Mok, Betty, 171
monasteries, 39, 47
monotheism and monotheistic religions, 26, 56
Moore College (Australia), 163
multiculturalism, 86–87
multi-faith setting, 155–56
multi-religious belonging, 59–60
Muslims. *See* Islam and Muslims
mutual respect, 49
myth, 10n18

"Naked Backs" (rap music album), 131–32
National Catholic Welfare Conference (USA), 111
National Council of Churches USA, 107
Native American culture, 12
Near Eastern culture of antiquity, 3–8
Neill, Stephen, 101n55
Nethersole Fund, Council for World Mission, 161
New Testament
  Christian hospitality, 26–37, 175–76
  church of, 21, 33–37
Newman, Elizabeth, 46
Next Magazine, 128
Nguyen, Paul, 118–19
Njuabe, Roy, 143, 145, 147
non-discrimination, witnessing through, 39
non-reciprocity, 18
non-refoulement, 72–73
Nouwen, Henri, 45, 54, 177
"numinous reciprocity," 7

O'Connor, Paul, 123
Oden, Amy, 38
O'Donovan, Oliver, 47
Odyssey (Homer), 8, 10, 13, 15
Ogletree, Thomas, 48–49

Opium War, 101
organizations. *See* agencies of hospitality
Orthodox Christian churches, 102
Orume, Abraham, 143
the Other, 48–49, 95, 176
OXFAM, 73

Palestine, 24, 25
Palmer, Parker, 49
Pam Baker & Company, 132
parepidemois (exiles), 33–34
Paris Foreign Missions Society, 101
paroikos (resident alien), 33–34
Parsee community, 94n32
partnerships, in hospitality, 35–36
Pascal, Blaise, 47
patronage relationships, 11
peacemaking program, 141–45
Pederson, David, 106–7
Pentecostal Church, 102
People's Republic of China, 110–11, 114, 119–20
persecution
  biblical passages on, 170
  early Christians, 34, 35
  political refugees, 72, 78
  religious refugees, 41, 72, 80–82
personal responsibility, 40, 45
philanthropia, 26
Philo, 26
philos (dear friend), 9
philoxenia (love of strangers), 26–27
Pitt-Rivers, Julian
  on grace, 18–19
  hospitality study, 11
  law of hospitality, 15–17
planning, refugee ministries, 77–78
Plaut, W. Gunther, 76
Playback Theatre, 146
plurality of beliefs, 58–61
pneumatological theology, 58–59
Pohl, Christine, 33, 40, 41, 177
Policy 21 Limited, 97–98
political issues, asylum seekers, 77–78
poor
  alms for, 35
  solidarity with, 40

port of first asylum policy (Hong Kong), 115
Portuguese community, 94n32
potlatch, 12
Prakash (story of asylum seeker), 130
prayerwalking, 166, 166–67n33
Presbyterian/Congregational Church, 102
prison visitation, 166, 169, 188
Protestant reformers, 41
Protestant-Catholic joint action, 115–16, 117
public opposition, 184–85
public support, 190–91
Pun, Ngai, 100

Qur'an, 56

Rabben, Linda, 75
rabbinic literature, 24
Race Discrimination Ordinance (2008), 99
Radford, Martin, 167–68
Rajeevan (story of refugee), 79
rationalistic traditionalism, 92
Reaching Out (Nouwen), 45
Read, Tony, 151–52, 154, 155, 156, 160–61
reciprocity, 11–14, 16, 18–19
recognition rate for claimants, 124, 185
reconciliation, 51
Red Cross, 73, 82, 113
Reece, Steve, 8
Refugee Advice Unit, 134
refugee beggars, 126
Refugee Concern Network, 134, 185
Refugee Convention (1951), 72, 119, 120, 125, 128, 178, 191
Refugee Ministry Group, 134, 164
refugees
  agencies and organizations (*See* agencies of hospitality)
  Australia, refugee program, 72, 82
  Baptist Press, refugee story, 79
  Chinese in Hong Kong (1945–1954), 96n35, 110–12
  Christian community and, 178–81

General Index   213

Christian identity, 78–82
concerns of, 123–29
evaluation of, 187–89
funding, 82–83
Hong Kong (2000–2014), 119–21
international community and, 177–78
international refugee protection regime, 72
ministry models, 76–77
strategic planning, 77–78
term usage, 72
theological reflections on, 62–66
UNHCR (*See* United Nations High Commissioner for Refugees (UNHCR))
United Nations Human Rights Committee, 99
Vietnam (1975–2000), 113–19
voices of, 129–32
. See also asylum and asylum seekers
relational theology of the Way (Tao), 60
relationship building of trust, 146
religions, theology of, 58–62
"Religious Plurality and Christian Self-understanding" (WCC), 58
religious traditions of hospitality
ancient Near East, 4–8
anthropological perspectives, 11–14
Greco-Roman, 8–11
linguistic perspectives, 14–15
overview, 3
ren (humanity or benevolence), 88
Republic of China, 110–11, 110n2
Repulse Bay Baptist Church, 150
resident alien (*paroikos*), 33–34
respect, 49
Reynolds, Thomas, 56
Rhenish Missionary Society, 100
Ricoeur, Paul, 57
righteousness (*yi*), 90
ritual propriety (*li*), 90
Roman Catholic Church
   Caritas–Hong Kong, 113, 115, 116–17, 170–71

Catholic Diocese, 102n57
evaluation of programs, 188
in Hong Kong, 101
Hong Kong church, 116, 117
refugee conversion, 112
refugee experience, 118
sanctuary councils, 74–75
Ross, Cathy, 54–55
Russell, Letty, 49–50

Sabbath eve, 24
sacred spaces, sharing in, 55–56
St. Andrew's Church, 163–64, 166–67
St. James Settlement, 155
St. John the Baptist (Anglican church), 148–50
St. Luke's Orthodox Cathedral (Greek), 102n59
St. Paul de Chartres Sisters, 101
St. Thomas Coptic Orthodox Church, 102n59
St. Vincent de Paul Society, 101, 164
SS. Peter & Paul Church (Roman Catholic), 164–65
SS. Peter & Paul Parish (Russian Orthodox), 102n59
Salvation Army, 102
Samuel (story of asylum seeker), 157–58
Sanders, E. P., 25–26
Sautman, Barry, 99
Save the Children Fund, 113
secularization, 41
"Seeking Refuge" (website), 128, 128n48
the Self, 48–49, 176
Selwyn, Tom, 17–18
Semitic culture, 3
Semitic religions, 59
Seneca, 10
September 11, 2001 terrorist attacks, 56, 119
Sermon on the Mount, 61
"settled residence," 96
Seventh Congress of Asian Theologians (CATS VII), 60, 62n47, 177
Shamanism, 60
shared duty, 40

sharing in sacred spaces, 55–56
Shum Oi Church, 170
Sikhism, 102
Simmel, Georg, 99
Sino-Japanese War (1937), 96n35
Sino-Vietnamese War (1979), 113, 120
Siu, Minnie, 164, 165
Smith, Carl T., 103n61, 104
Snyder, Susanna, 65–66, 76–77
social justice, 62, 103, 150–51, 189
social welfare, 40
Society for Community Organization (SoCO), 121, 133
sojourner, 22
solidarity of others model, 50
solidarity with the poor, 40
South Asian asylum seekers, 119
space, creating, 45, 54–55
Special Administrative Region (HK-SAR) of China, 85, 94
spirit of hospitality, 52–53
spiritual segregation, 47
spirituality vs. charity, 45–46
S.S. Huey Fong, 117
Stählin, Gustav, 25
The Standard (newspaper), 128
Stephen (story of asylum seeker), 159–60
Stock, St. George, 11
strangers
　care for, 23–24
　divine presence in, 9–10, 174, 175–76
　Hong Kong context, 85–88
　undeserving strangers, 38–39
　welcoming of, 38
strategic planning, refugee ministries, 77–78
Student Christian Movement, 170
synagogues, 24

table fellowship, 28–29, 37
Taiping Rebellion (1851–1864), 96n35
Taiwan, 110–11
Tang, Edmond, 60
Taoism, 60, 88, 102, 177
"Taste of Grace" (cooking course), 168

Taylor, John, 9
"Telema—An Authentic African Musical," 153
tensions in hospitality
　ancient period, 17–18
　boundlessness vs. boundaries, 51–53, 56, 176–77
　center vs. margins, 48–51
　contemporary period, 44
　evangelism vs. interfaith friendship, 54–62
　fear vs. faith, 65–66
　hospitality vs. holiness, 47–48
　spirituality vs. charity, 45–46
terrorist attacks, September 11, 2001, 56, 119
Thangaraj, M. Thomas, 60–61
Thaut, Laura, 83n30
The Gift (Mauss), 11
theological contributions, 176–77
theology of religions, 58–62
theoxeny, 10, 32
They Sojourned in Our Land (Chang), 116
time, cultural difference in, 145–46
Torture Claim Assessment Division, Hong Kong, 120–21
torture claimants, 122, 125–26
Treaty of Nanking (1842), 100, 101
True Jesus Church, 102
trust, relationship building, 146
Tsang, Steve, 94
Tsing Yi Chuen Yuen Church, 147–48
Tsung Tsin Mission, 102, 161
Tu, Wei-ming, 91

Underground Railroad, 75
undeserving strangers, 38–39, 53
United Kingdom
　Christian conversion, asylum seekers and, 81
　church sanctuaries in England, 75
　City of Sanctuary movement, 75
　colonialism, 92–95
　employment for refugees, 127
　People's Republic of China, 110–11
　refugees for settlement, 113

United Nations Convention Against Torture (CAT), 120, 185
United Nations High Commissioner for Refugees (UNHCR)
  approach taken by, 116
  Beijing office, 119–20
  Caritas Medical Centre, 126–27
  Caritas-Hong Kong, 171
  Christian Action, 133, 189
  definitions, 72–73, 77
  funding, 82
  Hong Kong office, 119–20, 124–25
  limitations, 178
  recognition rate for claimants, 124, 185
  refugee reimbursement costs, 115
  refugee resettlement process, 113
  resettlement time, 182
United Nations Human Rights Committee, 99
United Nations, Republic of China and Taiwan position, 110–11
United States
  Chinese refugee situation, 110, 110n2
  terrorist attacks, September 11, 2001, 56, 119
  Underground Railroad, 75
  Vietnam refugees, 113
urban setting, Jewish hospitality in, 24

Vanier, Jean, 45–46
Vecchio, Francesco, 127–28, 129n49
Vietnam refugees (1975–2000), 113–19
Vietnamese-American, memories from, 118–19
Vine Church
  background, 150
  ministry background, 151–53
  multi-faith setting, 155–56
  social justice, 150–51, 166, 189
  weekly fellowships, 153–55
Vision First, 134
Vitalis N.M., 169
vocabulary of hospitality, 14–15
voices, of refugees and asylum seekers, 129–32, 157–60

"Voices of Peace" (church choir), 140
Volf, Miroslav, 50–51, 177
voluntary migrants, 72

waiting periods, 123–24
Walton, John, 8
welfare system, 122, 126
Wesleyan Methodists, 100
Western colonialism, in Hong Kong, 92–95
"Where is My Future?" (rap song), 131–32
Wilson, Erin, 62–63, 76, 77
wisdom teachers, 24–25
witness, through non-discrimination, 39
women, 50, 61–62, 62n47, 129, 129n49, 144–45
Wong, Davy, 169, 170
Wong, Phyllis, 141–45, 147, 148
Wong, Thomas, 90n16
Wong, Wai-cheong, 147–48
World Council of Churches (WCC), 58, 111
World Food Programme, 73
World Migration Day (2000), 117
World Refugee Day, 143, 153, 170
worship, 46, 176
Wrobleski, Jessica, 46, 52–53
Wu, John Baptist (Catholic bishop), 116
Wu, Ka-ming, 100

xenos (foreigner), 9, 9n13, 15
xiao (filial piety), 89

Yang, Kuo-shu, 89
Yenching College, 147
yi (righteousness), 90
Ying Fuk-tsang, 102n56, 111n4
Yong, Amos, 58–59
Youth With A Mission, 167
Yueh, Hu, 111

Zeus, 9, 36
zone of obligation, 6

Scripture Index

OLD TESTAMENT

Genesis
12	5
12:1–3	7
15:1–6	7
17:15–21	7
18	56, 174
18:1–16	3, 5, 7
21:1–7	7
24:1–49	22
43:16–34	23

Exodus
2:15–22	23
20:10	23
23:9	23
23:12	23

Leviticus
19:18	29
25:23	23

Numbers
35:6–34	74n6

Deuteronomy
4:41–43	74n6
5:14–15	23
6:5	29
26:5–11	23

Joshua
2	23
20:1–9	74n6

Ruth
1–4	65–66

1 Samuel
9:18–27	23

1 Kings
17:1–24	22

2 Kings
4:8–37	22

Ezra
3:3	65
4:4	65
9:1–4, 10–12	65
10:11	65

Nehemiah
13:3	65
13:23–27	65

Psalms
23:5–6	23

Proverbs
25:6–7	31

Isaiah
25:6–9	23
58:7	25

Joel
3:18	23

Amos
9:13–15	23

NEW TESTAMENT

Matthew
2	116–17, 170
6:9	63
7	160
9:9–13	28
10:40–42	29
14:13–21	28
25	30, 170, 178
25:31–46	29, 32–33
25:40	32
25:45	32
26:26–29	28
28	158

Mark
2:13–17	28
2:18–22	29
6:8–11	29
6:30–44	28
7:24–30	65
14:22–26	28

Luke
5:27–32	28
7:31–35	29
7:36–50	28
9:10–17	28
10:1–12	29
10:25–37	29–30
10:25	59
10:38–42	28
11:2–3	29
11:2	63
14:1–24	29, 31–32
14:1–14	29
14:12–14	31
14:15–24	29, 31
15:11–32	29
19:1–10	28
22:14–20	28
24:28–32	28

John
2:1–11	28
6:1–14	28
6:25–59	29
13:1–11	28
21:1–14	28

Acts
3:1–10	35
4:32	35
4:36–37	35–36
5:1–10	35
9:10	36
9:36	35
9:43—11:18	36
10:2	35

Romans
12:13	27, 36
15:7	37

1 Corinthians
11:17–34	37

1 Timothy
3:2	27

Hebrews
13:1–2	36
13:2	27

1 Peter
1:1	33
2:4–5	34
2:11	34
4:9	27, 36